TRAVELERS' TALES BOOKS

Country and Regional Guides
America, Australia, Brazil, Central America, Cuba, France, Greece,
India, Ireland, Italy, Japan, Mexico, Nepal, Spain, Thailand;
American Southwest, Grand Canyon, Hawai'i,
Hong Kong, Paris, San Francisco, Tuscany

Women's Travel
Her Fork in the Road, A Woman's Path, A Woman's
Passion for Travel, A Woman's World, Women in the Wild,
A Mother's World, Safety and Security for Women
Who Travel, Gutsy Women, Gutsy Mamas

Body & Soul
The Spiritual Gifts of Travel, The Road Within,
Love & Romance, Food, The Fearless Diner, The Adventure
of Food, The Ultimate Journey, Pilgrimage

Special Interest
Not So Funny When It Happened,
The Gift of Rivers, Shitting Pretty, Testosterone Planet,
Danger!, The Fearless Shopper, The Penny Pincher's
Passport to Luxury Travel, The Gift of Birds, Family Travel,
A Dog's World, There's No Toilet Paper on the Road Less Traveled,
The Gift of Travel, 365 Travel, Adventures in Wine

Footsteps
Kite Strings of the Southern Cross, The Sword of Heaven, Storm,
Take Me With You, Last Trout in Venice, The Way of the
Wanderer, One Year Off, The Fire Never Dies

Classics
The Royal Road to Romance, Unbeaten Tracks in Japan,
The Rivers Ran East, Coast to Coast, Trader Horn

Coast
to Coast

Janet + Stu!

Coast to Coast

A Journey Across 1950s America

Happy travelling — + editing!

Jan Morris

Jan Morris

TRAVELERS'

– TALES –

CLASSICS

2002

TRAVELERS' TALES

San Francisco

Travelers' Tales and Travelers' Tales Guides are trademarks of Travelers'
Tales, Inc., 330 Townsend Street, Suite 208, San Francisco, California 94107.
www.travelerstales.com

Cover Art Direction: Michele Wetherbee/doubleu-gee
Cover Design: Stefan Gutermuth/doubleu-gee
Interior Design: Claudia Smelser
Cover Photograph: © Getty Images/The Image Bank
Page Layout: Cynthia Lamb, using the fonts Minion and Mrs. Eaves

Distributed by: Publishers Group West, 1700 Fourth Street, Berkeley,
California 94710.

Library of Congress Cataloging-in-Publication Data
Morris, Jan, 1926-
    [As I saw the U.S.A.]
    Coast to coast : a journey across 1950s America / Jan Morris.
        p. cm.
    Originally published under title: As I saw the U.S.A. New York : Pantheon, 1956. With
new introd.
    ISBN 1-885211-79-1 (alk. paper)
    1. United States—Description and travel. 2. United States—Social life and
customs—1945-1970. 3. Morris, Jan, 1926—Journeys—United States. I. Title.

E169.02 .M648 2002
917.304`92—dc21   2002019638

Printed in the United States of America
10 9 8 7 6 5 4 3 2 1

CONTENTS

A NEW INTRODUCTION TO
COAST TO COAST

BY JAN MORRIS

FORTY-SIX years is not long in geological terms, but it is quite a chunk in the life of a nation, and it's the better part of an average human lifetime. Forty six years it is since I published this, my very first book: and if a great deal has happened to me since then, the passage of history has transformed its subject, the United States of America.

My own story is simple, if relatively unusual—I was James Morris when I wrote the book, but twelve years later completed a shift of sexual role and emerged with a new persona as Jan. But the changes in the circumstances of the United States have been infinitely more dramatic: I just went through a so-called change of sex, but since the 1950s America has experienced such triumphs and such traumas, such colossal challenges, such tragic and marvelous adventures, that it has virtually re-invented itself as a nation. It has sent its rockets to the moon! It has been humiliated in war! Since the time when I wrote this book it has grown so incomparably powerful, so unconscionably rich, so sure of itself that it has become in effect the only Great Power, equally admired, envied, resented, copied, and abhorred around the world.

It was not so in 1956, when I ended a year's traveling fellowship in the United States, and offered this book to my sponsors in lieu of the report I was obliged to present. I had come from a Britain that was still war-scarred, poverty-stricken, and disillusioned, and found an America bursting with bright optimism, generous, unpretentious, proud of its recent victories, basking in its universal popularity but still respectful of older nations. I did not know it then, and nor did America, but chance had brought me across the Atlantic at the very apex of American happiness. I doubt if there has ever been a society, in the history of the world, more attractive than this republic in the decade after the second world war.

Of course it had its downsides. Crime and corruption was rampant. Racism was ugly. Senator McCarthy was on the prowl. There were the first signs (or so I thought) of the social and economic arrogance that we now call globalization. But it was an innocent time for most people. Television was in its infancy then, the Big Mac had not been invented, drugs were hard to come by, and the same popular music had a simple appeal for almost everybody— "Chattanooga Choo-Choo" was the theme-tune, so to speak, of my introduction to America.

Can you wonder that *Coast to Coast* was written in enjoyment? That year's wandering in America, in the prime of my youth, through a country so buoyant with success and generosity, was one of the very best presents of my whole life. If the United States of America is not always so much fun today, is not always regarded around the world with the same grateful affection, I can still look back to my first journeys there, nearly half a century ago, as to a dream of young times, hopes, and friendships.

The book is a period piece now. Physically, my America of 1956 exists no longer, but never mind—its soul goes marching on.

INTRODUCTORY

Not many citizens of the United States, perhaps, realize the existence of a Standard American. The eggheads have been talking for a decade or more of the dire uniformity that is overcoming their country, the growing sameness of it all, the drugstore civilization, the Kleenex age. But it is possibly only the foreigner who has, so to speak, crystallized all these awful warnings into a living symbol—different in every way from the Mr. Citizen accepted as representative by most American cartoonists. From Glasgow to Benares everyone knows the Standard American, and his figure is summoned instantly to the foreign mind whenever the American Way is mentioned. He is alien to almost all our ways, whatever our patrimony; but we feel we know him well.

Like many another observer, I am not much enamored of this new ambassador, successor in reputation to the dashing clipper captains or grandiloquent tycoons of other generations: but fortunately my book is a record of a journey, through all the forty-eight contiguous states of America, in which I discovered to my pleasure that he is not yet, by any manner of means universally predominant in his homeland. The romance of America has always lain in its glorious profusion of elements, welded and transfused by a common environment, but each redolent in some small way of an older civilization, an inherited philosophy, or at least aspirations familiar to us all. In this old patchwork America, so free and expansive, we could all see ourselves reflected, and feel some small proprietary pride. "America, thou half-brother of the world" as Philip Bailey observed, "with something good and bad of every land."

One day, perhaps, some version of the new all-American society will have swamped that noble country, its old ideals will be warped or banished, and the Standard American, who admits no deviationists, will be supreme. But for the moment America is something of a patchwork still, and still related (if only distantly, or morganatically) to the rest of us elsewhere. You cannot escape the new Americanism as you travel through the United States, especially when you reach the Middle West; nor can you blind yourself to the dulling spread of uniformity. But there is still a splendid variety to the life of the Americans; much sprightly individualism and homely kindness; much brashness, violence, and hocus-pocus; and much of that bold personal initiative (the making of money apart) that we associate with the frontier and the plainsman. Such resilient reminders of a younger America are what my book chiefly describes.

During our travels my family and I wandered, with many sedentary intervals, through the five great regions of the Republic—the East, the South, the West, the Pacific Coast, and the Middle West—traveling generally by car, sometimes by train, ship, or aircraft, and covering in all nearly 70,000 miles. There is only one place to begin an American journey of this kind, however often it is described, however tempting it is to launch an account from Kansas City or San Diego: the gateway of America, and the most dazzling expression of its lingering diversity, is still the City of New York. "New York, is a wonderful town!" run the words of an exhilarating popular song; and brilliant indeed, if a trifle frosty, is the smile on the face of the tiger as the visitor is swirled and eddied into the miraculous streets of Manhattan.

PART ONE

THE EAST

New York, New York!

T ONE time or another I have approached some splendid places, most of them instinct with mystery or age: Venice on a misty post-war morning, silent and shrouded, like a surrendered knight-at-arms; Everest, the watchtower, on the theatrical frontiers of Nepal and Tibet; or Krak of the Crusaders, high and solitary in the mountains of Moab. All are celebrated in history or romance; but none lingers so tenaciously in my memory as the approach to the City of New York, the noblest of American symbols.

The approach from the sea is marvelous enough, but has become hackneyed from film and postcard. It is the road from inland that is exciting now, when Manhattan appears suddenly, a last outpost on the edge of the continent, and the charged atmosphere of the place spreads around it like ripples, and you enter it as you would plunge into a mountain stream in August. A splendid highway leads you there. It sweeps across the countryside masterfully, two white ribbons of concrete, aloof from the little villages and farms that lie beside it. You can enter in only at tollgates, and stop only at specified places (for a hamburger or a tankful of petrol), so the cars move in

3

an endless, unbroken, unswerving stream. They carry the savor of distant places: cars from Georgia, with blossoms wilting in the back seat, or diesel trucks bringing steel pipes from Indiana; big black Cadillacs from Washington, and sometimes a gaudy convertible (like a distant hint of jazz) from New Orleans or California.

Through the pleasant country they pass, the traffic thickening as the big city draws nearer, and into the grimy industrial regions on its periphery; past oil refineries spouting smoke and flame, ships in dock and aircraft on the tarmac, railway lines and incinerators and dismal urban marshes; until suddenly in the distance there stand the skyscrapers, shimmering in the sun, like monuments in a more antique land.

A little drunk from the sight, you drive breathlessly into the great tunnel beneath the Hudson River (turning on as you do so the radio on your dashboard; the Lincoln Tunnel has its own radio station for the benefit of cars passing through it, and it seems churlish not to use it). You must not drive faster than thirty-five miles an hour in the tunnel, nor slower than thirty, and there is an ominous-looking policeman halfway along in a little glass cabin; so that you progress like something on an assembly line, soullessly. (This impression of slug-like impassivity may be heightened if you happen to observe the construction work going on just outside the entrance. They are putting another tunnel under the river, and they are doing it simply by pushing a huge metal tube into the earth, inch-by-inch, month-by-month, with hundreds and hundreds of jacks. There is something blind and mindless about such a method.)

When you emerge into the daylight, though, there is a sort of daily renaissance, a flowering of the spirit. The cars and trucks and buses, no longer confined in channels, suddenly spring away in all directions with a burst of engines and a black cloud of exhausts. At once, instead of uniformity, there is a profusion of variety. There are policemen shouting and gesticulating irritably; men pushing racks of summer frocks; trains rumbling along railway lines; great liners blowing their sirens; dowdy dark-haired women with shopping bags, and men hurling imprecations out of taxi windows; shops with improbable Polish names, and huge racks of strange newspapers; bold colors and noises and indefinable smells; skinny cats and very old dustcarts; and bus drivers with patient, weary faces. Almost before you know it, the *mystique* of Manhattan is all around you.

There is a richness to the life of this extraordinary island that springs only partly from its immeasurable wealth. A lavish fusion of races contributes to it, and a spirit of hope and openheartedness that has survived from the days of free immigration. The Statue of Liberty, graphically described in one reference book as "a substantial figure of a lady," is dwarfed by the magnificence of the skyline, and from the deck of a ship it is easy to miss it. But in New York, more than anywhere else in America, there is still dignity to the lines carved upon it:

> Give me your tired, your poor,
> Your huddled masses yearning to breathe free,
> The wretched refuse of your teeming shore.

Here in the space of a few square miles all the races mingle, and the extremes of human nature clash. This is not the all-American city, but rather (as Lord Bryce remarked) a European city of no particular country; enlivened, sharpened, and intensified by the American ideal.

Everyone has read of the magical glitter of this place; but until you have been there it is difficult to conceive of a city so sparkling that at any time Mr. Fred Astaire might quite reasonably come dancing his urbane way down Fifth Avenue. It is a marvelously exuberant city, even when the bitter winds of the fall howl through its canyons. The taxi drivers talk long and fluently; not so well or so caustically as a Cockney cabman, but from a wider range of experience, for they may speak of a pogrom in old Russia, or of Ireland in its bad days, or speculate about the Naples their fathers came from. The waiters press you to eat more, you look thin. The girl in the drugstore asks so particularly sweetly if she may borrow the comic section of your newspaper. On the skating rink at Rockefeller Center there is always something pleasant to see: pretty girls showing off their pirouettes;

children staggering about in helpless paroxysms; an old eccentric sailing by with a look of profoundest contempt on his face; an elderly lady in tweeds excitedly arm-in-arm with an instructor.

Boundless vivacity and verve are the inspiration of Manhattan. In its midtown streets (away from slums and dingy suburbs) you are in a world of spirited movement and color. The new buildings are glass aeries, gay as cream cakes. One structure on Park Avenue has a garden for its ground floor and a slab of green glass for its superstructure. A bank on Fifth Avenue has creepers growing from its ceiling, and the passerby, looking through its huge plate-glass windows, can see the black round door of its strong room. Outside a nearby typewriter shop a real typewriter is mounted on a pedestal, for anyone to try. Once when I passed at two in the morning an old man with a ragged beard was typing with hectic concentration, as if he had just run down from his garret with an exciting new formula or a translation of the Knossos Plates.

The traffic swirls through New York like a rather slobby mixture running through a cake mold. There are fewer solid traffic jams than in London, but a more inexorable oozy progression of vehicles. Some seventy-five years ago an observer described New York traffic as being "everywhere close-spread, thick-tangled (yet no collision, no trouble) with masses of bright color, action, and tasty toilets." The description is not so far from the mark today, and the colors especially are still bright and agreeable. The women are not afraid of color in their clothes; the shop windows are gorgeous; the cars are painted vividly. From upstairs the streets of Manhattan are alive with shifting colors.

Sometimes, as you push your way through the brisk crowds, there will be a scream of sirens and a little procession of official cars will rush by, pushing the traffic out of its way, crashing the lights with complacent impunity, on its way to the Waldorf or the City Hall. The motorcycle police, hunched on the machines, look merciless (but are probably very kind to old ladies). The reception committee, in dark coats and Homburgs, is excessively official. And there in the recesses of the grandest car can be seen the distinguished visitor, opera singer, or diplomat or bronzed explorer, shamefully delighted at being able to ignore the traffic rules. I once rode in such a cavalcade, and found that the psychological effect can be disturbing. A mild little man sharing my car was soon hurling vicious abuse at the less agile of the pedestrians, and the wife of the distinguished visitor fainted.

There is a row of hansom cabs at the corner of Central Park, each with its coal heater (if it is winter), each tended by an elderly gentleman in a top hat, the horses a little thin, the wheels a little wobbly. Lovers find them convenient for bumpy dalliances in the park. If you wander down to the waterside on either side of the island you may stand in the shadow of an ocean liner, or watch a tug (with a high curved bridge, a nonchalant skipper, and an air of Yankee insolence) steaming under the black girders of Brooklyn Bridge. Outside Grand Central Station, through a grill beneath your feet, you may see the gleaming metal of a Chicago express down in the bowels; passengers on the smartest of these trains are ushered into them along deep red carpets. You could live permanently in Grand Central Station without ever seeing a train, for they are all secreted below in carpeted dungeons.

The stores of Manhattan bulge with the good things of the earth, with a splendor that outclasses those perfumed Oriental marts of fable. "Ask for anything you like," says the old waiter at the Waldorf-Astoria with pardonable bombast, "and if we haven't got it we'll send down the road for it." Furs in the windows shine with an icy distinction. Dresses are magnificent from Paris, or pleasantly easygoing in the American manner. There are shoes for every conceivable size; books for the most esoteric taste; pictures and treasures summoned from every age and every continent; foods of exotic delight; little dogs of unlikely breed; refrigerators already stocked with edibles; haughty Rolls-Royces; a myriad of toys; endless and enchanting fripperies; anything, indeed, that fancy can demand or money buy. It is a storehouse of legendary wonder. What a prize it would be for some looting army of barbarians, slashing their way through its silks and satins, ravishing its debutantes, gorging themselves in its superb French restaurants!

Yes so obvious and dramatic are the extremes of New York that you see many beggars about its streets. They stand diffidently on the pavements, decently dressed but coatless, asking civilly for help before they leave the bright lights and go home for the night to the hopeless squalid doss houses of the Bowery. They are ambassadors from another Manhattan: the countless gloomy streets where Negroes and Puerto Ricans, Poles and poor Italians live in unhappy neighborhoods, fighting their old battles and despising one another. In is an unpleasant thing to see the current crime register in a Harlem police station. Page succeeds page in terrible succession. Thronged with stabbings and rapes, robberies and assaults, acts of lunatic spite or repellent perversion. "Well," you say as casually as you can, a little shaken by this vast superfluity of Sunday journalism, "well, and how many weeks of crime do these pages represent?" The police sergeant smiles tolerantly. "That's today's register," he says.

You can taste a little of all this horror simply by driving through the dark back streets; or buying a drink in an East Side bar, surrounded by companions of advanced animal instincts, funneled from the slums of half a dozen countries. Or you can feel the tensions down at the dockside, where union clashes with union, docker with docker, with a frightening fervor. The dockers, speaking many languages, shuffle here and there like automatons. There is a feeling of cold incipient brutality; and if you make a habit of hanging around the docks you will never be surprised to read, as you often will, of bodies found in the water and bloody wharfside brawls.

These are the heirs to those millions of hopeful immigrants who crossed the Atlantic in the Victorian Age, fleeing from despotisms or famines, looking for an Eldorado. The poor European immigrant is a dominant figure of American history, and his spirit still haunts the squares and streets of the Battery, at the tip of Manhattan, and loiters around the landing-places where the ferry leaves for Staten Island. He is the true symbol of American liberalism, not today's brave professors and newspapermen; and it is typical paradox that though politics drove him from Europe, often enough, it was material ambition that made him an American. America is the land acquisitive, and few Americans abandon the search for wealth, or lose their admiration for those who find it.

So the unassimilated New Yorkers, the millions of un-Americans in the city however poor or desolate they seem, however disappointed in their dreams, still loyally respect the American ideal; the chance for every man to achieve opulence. Sometimes the sentiment has great pathos. An old man I met in a cheap coffee shop near the East River boasted gently, without arrogance, of the fabulous wealth of New York; for all the world as if its coffers were his, and all its luxuries, instead of a gray bed-sitting room and a coat with frayed sleeves. He said: "Why, the garbage thrown away in this city every morning—*every* morning—would feed the whole of Europe for a week." He said it without envy and with a genuine pride of possession, and a number of dusty demolition men sitting near by nodded their heads in proud and wondering agreement.

All the same, it is sometimes difficult to keep one's social conscience in order among the discrepancies of Manhattan; the gulf between rich and poor is so particularly poignant in this capital of opportunity. There is fun and vigor and stimulation in New York's symphony of capitalism—the blazing neon lights, the huge bright office blocks, the fine stores and friendly shop assistants; and yet there is something distasteful about a pleasuredrome so firmly based upon personal advantage. Everywhere there are nagging signs that the life of the place is inspired by a self-interest not scrupulously enlightened. "Learn to take care of others," says a poster urging women to become nurses, "and you will know how to take care of yourself." "The life you save may be your own," says a road safety advertisement. "Let us know if you can't keep this reservation," you are told on the railway ticket, "it may be required by a friend or a business associate of yours." Faced with such constant reminders, the foreign visitor begins to doubt the altruism even of his benefactors. Is the party really to give him pleasure, or is the host to gain some credit from it? The surprise present is very welcome, but what does its giver expect in return? Soon he is tempted to believe that any perversion of will or mind, any ideological wandering, any crankiness, any jingoism is preferable to so constant an obsession with the advancement of self.

But there, Manhattan is a haven for the ambitious, and you must not expect its bustling rivalries to be too saintly. Indeed, you may as well admit that the whole place is built on greed, in one degree or another; even the city churches, grotesquely Gothic or Anglican beyond belief, have their thrusting social aspirations. What is wonderful is that so much that is good and beautiful has sprung from such second-rate motives. There are palaces of great pictures in New York, and millions go each year to see them. Each week a whole page of *The New York Times* is filled with concert announcements. There are incomparable museums, a lively theater, great publishing houses, a famous university. The *Times* itself ("All the News That's Fit to Print") is a splendid civic ornament, sometimes mistaken, sometimes dull, but never bitter, cheap or malicious; at lunch in its palatial offices the following grace is said:

O Lord, the Giver of All Good,
In whose just Hands are all our Times,
We thank Thee for our daily Food
Gathered (as News) from many Climes.
Bless All of Us around this Board
And all beneath this ample Roof;
What we find fit to print, O Lord,
Is, after all, the Pudding's Proof.
May Those we welcome come again
And Those who stay be glad, Amen.

And the city itself, with its sharp edges and fiery colors, is a thing of beauty; especially seen from above, with Central Park startlingly green among the skyscrapers, with the tall towers of Wall Street hazy in the distance, with the two waterways blue and sunny and the long line of an Atlantic liner slipping away to sea. It is a majestic sight, with no Wordsworth at hand to honor it, only a man with a loudspeaker or a fifty-cent guidebook.

So leaving Manhattan is like retreating from a snow summit. When you drive back along the highway the very air seems to relax about you. The electric atmosphere softens, the noise stills, the colors blur and fade, the pressure eases, the traffic thins. Soon you are out of the city's spell. Only pausing to look behind, over the tenements and marshes, to see the lights of the skyscrapers riding the night.

ℭ **2.** ℭ

Country Style

VERY QUICKLY you can find yourself in the country. I lived for a time with my wife and children in a little anachronistic village called Cranbury, New Jersey, that was almost in sight of the great highway, and within easy commuting distance of Manhattan. Nobody goes there very much, for it is off the beaten track. There are no "scenic wonders" (as Americans insist on calling any natural phenomenon, from a geyser to a precipice), few historical associations, little business, and no bucolic freakishness. It is just a small market center, where farmers do their shopping and a few commuters to the city have established their homes. But it is notable all the same, because it has openly and successfully defied all those powerful influences of modern Americanism that are always pulsing and pushing just over the hill.

The place is at its best on a frosty evening in winter, when the stars are sharp and the white weatherboard houses of Main Street shine in the moonlight. On such nights the people of Cranbury often go skating on the village pond, to the accompaniment of music from loudspeakers mounted on the roof of the fire station. The lake is illuminated by the headlights of cars, but it is a pleasantly old-fashioned scene—a compound of Grandma Moses and the elder Brueghel. Most of the villagers are skating. There are farmers in check shirts and earmuffs, moving with unexpected grace. Girls waltz pointedly in pairs, wearing blue ski trousers and white jumpers. A man who looks like an insurance agent steers a ponderous course over the ice, his black hat still sedately on his head. Small children totter in desperate instability toward the bank, and boys with toboggans shoot about like rockets. Various men with a tendency toward authority stand in municipal attitudes on the perimeter.

Across the road in the fire station the fire engines stand vigilantly gleaming. The man on duty pokes his head out of an upstairs window for a chat with a friend below, and one or two of the more daring children sneak in, when they can, to climb into the driver's seat. The fire station is a center of activity in Cranbury, following an old American tradition. For many years all fire brigades were amateur and voluntary, and it became a basic duty of the rural American male to join the local brigade; firefighting became a social function, and the fire brigade acquired the status of a team or club. In Cranbury this system still prevails. The fire chief is the local garage man, and very proud he is of the smartness and alertness of the brigade. Often and again he has told me of its prowess, and once he gave a lecture on the subject to the Lions Club.

All around the lake stand the comfortable houses of Cranbury. They are mostly built of white weatherboard, in vaguely colonial style (those householders blessed with verandas have recently been tearing them down to heighten the eighteenth-century appearance). They are generally trim, clean, and newly painted, their smartness enhanced rather than spoiled by a few yellowing renegades with peeling paintwork. The nearest thing to a mansion is a hilarious Victorian structure on an eminence, bursting with urns and ornaments with a grand carriageway and multitudes of outhouses; the nearest thing to a slum is a little group of plain houses with cracked windows, where the Negro community lives. There is a row of unpretentious shops and a couple of drugstores; and an eighteenth-century inn where the turkey is excellent, and where Washington is alleged to have spent a night. There is also a small school of music, from which you may sometime hear, even on skating nights, the strains of thin and ill-disciplined melody.

It is a fairly well-heeled village, and there is a good deal of comfort in these white houses. Everyone has a refrigerator, of course, and most people have television; many also possess washing machines, dishwashers, gadgets for making waste matter swill away down the sink, cookers that time themselves and ring a bell when the meat is done, radios that wake you up with a cup of coffee, electric sewing machines, white telephones, and microphones to transmit the sounds of sleepless babies. Almost every family has its car (wrap-around windscreen, duomatic drive, "electric eye" dippers, ultra-vision glass) and the slimmest daughter handles it like a lorry driver. Almost every house has its central heating, and from time to time a truck arrives to pump oil through heavy pipes into the basement furnaces.

If you stand beside the lake and look to the west, you may see a constant scurrying stream of headlights. They mark our highway to Manhattan, a highway alive with energy and industry. Within a few miles that road will take you to the oil refineries of Elizabeth, acre upon acre of derricks and tanks and convoluted mechanism; to the new steel plants arising among Trenton, fed on iron from Venezuela; or to the immense industrial complex that surrounds Newark and Jersey City. If you are imaginative you can almost hear the crashing of hammers and the whirr of machinery; but the skaters are mercifully deaf to it.

Go a little way to the other side of the village and you may see the lights of Princeton, one of the great American centers of learning, a prime force in the development of American knowledge and culture. It is a historic place. In one of its old buildings Washington presided over the Continental Congress, after beating the British on a nearby battlefield. Later it was fashionable for Southern gentlemen to attend this university, and they would arrive there splendidly with their elegant clothes and fascinating accents, attended by personal slaves.

Many famous Americans have graduated from Princeton, and Woodrow Wilson was once its president.

But Europe and modernity, twin watchdogs, guard its campus. Its buildings are well-tuned echoes of Oxford, shady quadrangles and staircases and more than one Magdalen Tower. Its streets are full of little English cars (very deliberately English cars) and its young men wear hacking jackets by Brooks Brothers out of Leicestershire. One shop in town hangs prominently in its window a framed reproduction of the regimental colors of the British Army. The bookshops are well stocked with Penguin books. English comedies and Continental sophistication prosper in the cinemas. All this is far enough removed from the spirit of Cranbury (only a few miles down the road) but it is only half of Princeton; for there is no community in the United States that reflects more accurately the undeviating American passion for material progress. Princeton is a positive powerhouse of research. The Institute for Advanced Studies is here, with its memories of Professor Einstein. At Princeton Dr. Gallup and his minions arrange their polls and analyze their findings with a touching confidence. Here the United States Navy has a laboratory concerned with guided missiles, rocket projectiles, and the like. (These mundane if awful technicalities are helping to spoil the U.S. Navy as a profession. I once asked a lady whether her son, a conscript ensign in destroyers, intended to make the Navy his career. "Oh dear me no," she said in a voice that might have amused Nelson, "Oh dear me no, he's a young *New York intellectual!*")

But it all passes Cranbury by, this concentration of alien sympathies and advanced inquiry. The skaters are simple people still, with some of the qualities of the pioneers who founded Cranbury not so very long ago (in the 1780s there was nothing here but an Indian village in a forest clearing). The predominant influence in Cranbury is not Princeton or the industrial regions around the corner, but the Presbyterian church whose white steeple rises gracefully above the housetops. Religion in such a place as this is at once devotional, philanthropic, and social. On Sunday morning Main Street is crowded with the cars of the churchgoers, and the sidewalks (lined with trees) are full of people dressed very decidedly in their Sunday best. The children, in particular, shine with an unearthly hygiene, their hair slicked or curled, their faces pink with cold and soap, their hands considerably gloved. The boys wear bow ties and coats with fur collars, the girl's frilly party dresses.

You can hardly escape the advances of a lively American church of this kind. Almost before you have settled in your house you find yourself irrevocably committed to one activity or another. It may be the Stitch-and-Chatter group on Thursday, or the Helping Hand Club on Monday evenings. Perhaps there is a bazaar, or a discussion group, or a Bible study class, or even dinner at the minister's (good company and fine food, not even spoiled by a monopoly of blackberry wine). So friendly are these approaches, and so sincere, that you can scarcely object to them, even if you were brought up on scholarly canons, fan-vaulting, and Stanford in B Flat. For it is wrong to scoff indiscriminately at the American do-gooder, especially in these stable regions of the East. He is often unctuous, and sometimes asinine, but not usually a hypocrite. The group activities of such little American towns are generally hard on the side of the right and guided, all in all, by praiseworthy motives; and since they play an important part in the forming of national opinions, they should be taken seriously and given their due. By some involved delegation of ideas, rising through the gradations of public responsibility, a dam in Pakistan or a school in Iraq may depend upon the views on one of these imperceptible Stitch-and-Chatter gatherings; so only a fool would laugh at them.

Here in Cranbury they not only contribute to a healthy (if slightly priggish) climate of thought, but also perform works of active good. Each year bands of migrant workers, mostly Negroes, arrive in the district to help with the potato harvest. They are very poor, and often ruthlessly bullied by the Negro contractors who have engaged them and brought them from the South in lorries. They live in shacks and huts provided by the farmers, communing only with themselves, strangers to the country, like Israelites in Egypt. Every year the good people of Cranbury, through their various societies, take care of these unfortunates, arranging for the schooling of their children, providing meals and occasional outings. They care little about racial antipathies. Indeed, any distinction that I could detect between black and white in Cranbury was purely economic, the Negroes being mostly indigent and ill educated, for those Negroes resident in Cranbury migrated not long ago from the abyss of the South.

So life in Cranbury revolves around the church, the fire brigade, the drugstores; and the children. In a little town of this sort one can watch most closely the fabled American treatment of their young, and a very comfortable treatment it is. No soft Siamese, no quaint hamster, no irresistible Shetland has affection lavished on it quite so unstintingly as does the little American; no cosseted child of English fortune or Oriental splendor is more carefully cherished. "We love our children," say the road signs outside many American towns; rather as a Tibetan hamlet might announce its belief in rebirth, for indeed it goes without saying. There is a cloying sentimentality to this devotion that repels many Europeans, and indeed there is something sickly about the American inclination to think of children as being younger and more protectable than they are. Many an American child lives like a little gilded trinket in the bosom of its family, taking care to wrap up in innumerable warm woolies before venturing into the winter morning. Too often young Americans seem to lack the conventional spirit of adventure, of the Huckleberry Finn variety, and acquire an air (so overloaded are they with possessions, so warmly mothered through childhood) of blasé fragility.

And yet I used to find in Cranbury, where it is true these methods are not carried to extremes, that the little American often and again belies his reputation. Ghastly though he sometime appears (and the he, if anything, rather less ghastly than the she), he often turns out to be wonderfully good material. I remember the little boys of Cranbury, muffled to the ears, of course, in protective clothing, out in the snow with a shovel in their hands and a dollar in prospect, working hard and cheerfully (harder than their English equivalents) to clear the garden path. I remember with gratitude the girls who would come to our house, in between dates, to look after the baby with great care and competence. The truth is that American children develop national characteristics disconcertingly early. This is the land of opportunism, and the children realize it soon. The boys see no point in unnecessary hardship or risk, but are greedy for vicarious experience and useful knowledge, and will work well for fair reward. The girls seem to know before they leave the nursery that a good marriage must be their goal, and regulate their lives accordingly; so that to many an American girl of fourteen an English gym slip must seem a dreadful symbol of past barbarities, like child labor underground, or Scutari. Who can blame them? The first clause of a "program for education" produced by the National Education Association of America reads: "All youth needs to develop salable skills and those understandings and attitudes that make the worker an intelligent and productive participant in economic life." For the boy, this mouthful means a grasp of the methods of self-advancement; for the girl, a neat hand with a lipstick; and there are few to quote the Miltonic view, that "the end of Learning is to know God aright."

Anyway, the Cranbury children are but little corrupted by these philosophies, and are both friendly and well-mannered. On the frozen lake in the moonlight they look enchanting, but then so does almost everyone (though nobody could claim ethereal charm for the man in the black hat). These eastern country occasions offer some of the best of American life. In the eighteenth century Crèvecoeur posed the celebrated question: "What is he, the American, this new man?" His shade might well go to Cranbury for an answer, on a moonlit skating evening, and choose for itself a characteristic citizen. The elderly man leaning against the wall of the fire station, for example, chewing a harsh cigar and exchanging a few cryptic words with the fireman in the upstairs window. Such a man knows little of Europe and its values, but is quite willing to learn; dislikes and distrusts authority, but is ready to cooperate if nicely asked; can be a fearful bore, but tries to reach his conclusions fairly; enjoys watching the skating, but will be up early next morning; cares not two hoots for smart Princeton or dazzling New York; owns a fine car and a sound bank balance, but still approaches life with some humility. This was the new man of Crèvecoeur's century; now a hale survivor of the old America.

ᴄᴈ 3. ᴄ੭

Traditionalists

THERE ARE many such dogged Eastern traditionalists still. It is true that society along the Atlantic coast is more completely formed than it is in other regions of the country, and you can see one American mode of life more or less in its maturity; but it is wrong to imagine these old states as totally enshrouded in a pall of conformity. There is still a remarkable variety of independent communities, some anachronistic, some eccentric, some just stubborn in preferring unconventional forms and loyalties; from the Canadian lumbermen in Maine and Vermont to the Pennsylvania Dutch, with their quaint antique vernacular, their indelicate humor, and their irrepressible superstition.

The oddest of all these groups is perhaps the sect called the Amish, who live in Pennsylvania and have some distinctly unusual habits of thought and manner. You can often see them in the rolling farmlands of Lancaster County, their great stronghold, looking like figures from some almost forgotten Europe of the past, engulfed in traditions and dogma, but kindly and good-humored nonetheless. Most of the Amish came originally from Germany, and they are one of a number of intricately related sects subscribing to the Mennonite faith (almost as baffling as those innumerable persuasions, Jacobites, Gregorians, Syrian Catholics, Nestorians, Chaldeans, Armenian Catholics, which so entangle relationships in some parts of the Middle East).

The men, thanks partly to their costume, partly to their seraphical benignity of expression, often look like saintly patriarchs. Their hats are wide, black and stiff of brim, like the Vicar of Wakefield's. Their suits are black, too, and singularly plain and baggy. They have no buttons, only rough hooks and eyes, and their trousers have no flies, but open in the front in a wide flap. The Amish wear flourishing beards but no mustaches, and their hair is parted in the middle and smoothed down each side over the ears, not unlike an old-fashioned advertisement for hair cream.

As for the ladies, they are suggestive of the Salvation Army at the apogee of its Victorian propriety. Their dresses, coarse, black and heavy, reach almost down to their ankles, and their aprons are spiritually white, their black stockings are the ultimate antithesis of nylon, their shoes noticeably lack peep-toes or high heels; their cloaks are all-enveloping, their bonnets virtuous, their hair is parted in the center and plaited demurely round the back of the head to form that crowning token of respectability, a bun.

There is nothing doctrinaire or forbidding, however, about the small talk of Amish; they are most pleasant people to meet in the street, and speak readily enough of their beliefs and taboos. One elderly farmer I met in Harrisburg, Pennsylvania, willingly demonstrated to me the eccentricities of his dress. Why, I asked him, did the Amish use no buttons? It must be so tedious to rely, like babes-in-arms, upon tapes, hooks, eyes, and such elementary devices. He replied that first, the Amish did not approve of laborsaving devices in general, and the button certainly fell into that category. Secondly, they disapproved of the unnecessary killing of animals, and buttons were made of animal bones. Thirdly, he added (with only the suspicion of a twinkle in his eye), buttons were very useful to the Devil, when he "wanted something to hang things on."

The more conservative Amish certainly live up to their own

tenets. They wear no belts or neckties. Some forswear braces, some allow the use of one brace, so to speak, slung across the body like a bandolier, and imparting a graceful lopsided sag to the trousers. They ride around in high wooden buggies, pulled by handsome horses. The stricter Amish not only forbid cars, but even buggies with roofs, so that families must ride in all weathers totally exposed to the climate. (Some of the younger Amish, I was told, are simply not to be trusted with the family buggies; they are so inclined to speed.) Telephones, bicycles, central heating, musical instruments, carpets, even window curtains—among the Amish extremists all are banned as being "sinful pleasures of life." The orthodox Amish do not smoke, may read only sacred books, do not exert their right to vote, are conscientious objectors, and are never supposed to sleep outside their own houses. The simplicity of their life is fading a little, even under this rigid regime, but their society is still amazingly immune to the modern pressures that surround them. They are all still placid, content, and otherworldly, and show no signs of disappearing; and they are still objects of curiosity to their neighbors. A party of Amish recently paid a call on the United Nations headquarters in Manhattan; and the New York press, which has its choice of turbaned Pathans, Princes of Mecca, Nubians, and Eskimos, nevertheless devoted headlines and big pictures to the visit of those bewhiskered Pennsylvanians.

Not all the compact communities of the East are religious in origin; some are resistant or homogeneous because of the nature of their calling. The oystermen of Chesapeake Bay, for example, are individualistic still because their work required them to live among the coves and marshes of the Bay shore (a country full of haunting character) and to commune with the misty spirits of that waterway. I called on one such oysterman on the Maryland side of the Bay, off the main road, on one of the innumerable spits of land that project from the peninsula known as the Eastern Shore. There was snow on the ground, and the road struggled through scrubby dunes and harsh, sparse fields. Now and again we came across a gray lagoon, with its rushes bent by the wind and a sliver of ice around its banks.

The trees were thin and nasty; away over the marshes was the chilly line of the Bay.

Among all this desolation the oysterman lived, on the edge of the Bay, in a house with a shingle roof, painted a greenish yellow. When I reached this homestead across the snow I looked in through a window and saw an antique American interior. The house was built in the seventeenth century, and had a profusion of beams, niches, crannies, and fireplaces, and a flavor of smoke and old-fashioned food. Against this honorable background (as I peered through he window) the oysterman and his family moved with dignity. There was a woman of the house, plain and honest of face, like a Dutchwoman in a painting, in a blue woolen dress and carpet slippers; she was sitting in a worn wooden chair, saying something over her shoulder, and feeding a small baby. From time to time another child, a little older, propelled himself into my line of vision in an infant's chair mounted on wheels, which he maneuvered with some skill among the furniture and even up and down the steps and unevenesses which characterized the general surface of the floor. The householder, a youngish man in shirtsleeves, was doing something to his pipe with a penknife, half leaning, half sitting on a table. At one end of the room a wood fire blazed; and very soon I was warming my hands in front of it.

This man combined two trades. He farmed a few hard acres with the help of an elderly tractor, and he fished for oysters off the shore; from the window of his living room you could see the reedy creek, a melancholy inlet, where his boat was moored. The withered solitude of the place had affected him, and though he was obliging and kindly he seemed a remote and introspective person, living away there among the marshes; not so enigmatic as an oyster, perhaps, but akin in character to some sedgy water bird that stalks on spindly legs along the seashore. I complained to him, mildly, about the quality of the oysters of eastern America. They are cheap and available everywhere, in almost every coffee shop; but they are slobbery mollusks, unpleasant in appearance and unsubtle in taste, watery objects, commonly swamped (with reason) in tomato sauce. He agreed sadly that they were lacking in character. Even on the Pacific coast, where a few people were still breeding the small, delicate Puget Sound oyster, the huge Japanese variety (recently introduced into American waters, was flooding the market. "I guess that's the way with Americans," he remarked. "If it's big, it's gotta be good; and if it's only good, you gotta make it bigger."

⌘

Far up in the northern states, on the borders of Canada, live the French folk of Maine and Vermont, a sturdy racial minority. We stayed one night in a small town in Vermont, between Lake Champlain and the rich green country of the maple trees. It was a shabby little place, built on a crossroads, with a few murky drapers' shops, a tavern or two, a garage, and a general merchant's (where you could buy, so lavish is the American press, no fewer than thirteen daily newspapers). The best place to sleep seemed to be an inn with a wide veranda and slightly dirty windows. Its paint was flaking, its steps were cracked, and an aroma of hoary tobacco had lingered, down the generations, about its hall; but it looked warm, so in we went. We found ourselves at once in an atmosphere redolent not only of another people and time, but another continent.

French was the only language we could hear in the shadowy chambers of this hostelry. The manager was a small bony man with black, greased hair, who needed a shave but carried the unmistakable air of not intending to have one. He spoke to us in broken English that was barely understandable, and ushered us heavily upstairs. Nothing in this drab inn conformed with the American standard. On the landing there protruded from behind a calendar a gaudy picture of the Virgin, with some faded flowers pinned to it, and a scrap of palm frond, relic of some distant festival. Our room was large and unornamented, with monochromatic coverings. The bathroom was far away, and its broken door had to be fastened from inside with a piece of string. Several French magazines (damp because someone had been reading them in the bath, tattered because someone had been tearing out the dress patterns) lay forlornly on a wicker chair.

It was odd to find oneself so near in spirit to provincial Europe; for the predominantly English communities of the United States have long ago discarded their inheritance and developed mores of their own, so that you will search for long before you hear an echo of Moreton-in-the-March, or recapture the stolid phlegm of an English pub. From downstairs, in this old French enclave, we could hear somebody practicing the piano: an approximation of "Rustle of Spring," some Chopin played very slowly and with soulful emotion, a snatch of a pompous marching song. I went down to the bar for a glass of beer, and found it thronged with whole families of French people, talking cheerfully in a muffled intestinal patois. A very old man with a bush mustache, wearing a peaked cap, was playing shuffleboard with a pleasing swagger, followed everywhere by a couple of devoted urchins; and now and again from the darker recesses of the room he would arouse a murmur of admiration. The air was full of strong tobacco smoke, and there was a smell not of onions but of potato chips.

But even in such cultural islands the new Americanism sometimes intrudes. The escapist quality of that evening (which threatened to become nothing short of idyllic) was rudely shattered by an expression of changing philosophies. As I sat sipping my beer, watching the old shuffleboard man, and occasionally exchanging indecipherable witticisms with my neighbors, I became aware of activity outside the door of the bar. Shadowy shapes passed by, there was the clink of cutlery, the sound of furniture being moved, a growing murmur of voices; until suddenly into the barroom there burst the crash of an introductory chord on the piano, out of tune but immensely reverberant, and the heady opening lines, throatily delivered in male voice chorus, of "America, the Beautiful." The barroom stiffened. The barman looked virtuous. The urchins pulled up their socks. Even the shuffleboard king removed his eye from the board. This was a moment pregnant with emotion and significance, familiar to all Americans from one shoreline to the other, whether they speak in a European dialect or a Western drawl, the clipped pseudo-Oxford of Boston or the hideous distortions of Brooklyn: the Elks were beginning their weekly dinner.

To the south of Vermont, in New York State, I came across another cohesive society: a group of Shakers. In a pleasant country spot there stood a collection of brick buildings, grouped around a green, and among them moved a few middle-aged women dressed like Puritans, in rough gray dresses and aprons, severely devoid of make-up, their hair austere and their figures (like the Amish ladies') blameless of compulsion or pretense. These were members of "The American Shaker," a celibate religious community, named for the physical tremors that used to result from the ecstasies of their devotions. The order was imported from England in 1774, when a number of its adherents crossed the Atlantic under the leadership of the most famous of the Shakers, Mother Ann Lee of Manchester. The three basic principles of the Shaker faith are: Purity of Life, Confession of Sin, Consecration of Strength, Time, and Talent. Although both men and women can be Shakers, the order has a pronounced feminist bias (as Dickens discovered to his distaste when he visited a Shaker settlement in 1842). Among its declared beliefs are the Duality of the Deity, Father and Mother God; the Equality of the Sexes, and most startling, the Duality of the Christ Spirit, "as manifested by Jesus and Ann Lee." Such unorthodoxies led to the persecution of the sect in England, the imprisonment of Mother Lee, and the eventual *hegira* from Lancashire to New York State.

The Shaker women talked willingly, but with a virginal shyness. They told us that the Order was declining disastrously, chiefly because of a shortage of young recruits; young men who wanted to be Shakers were extremely rare (I had to agree that I had never met one with that precise ambition) and the positions designed to be held by men in the hierarchy of the Order were unhappily vacant; making the Shaker concept of sexual equality rather top-heavy in application. The Shaker statement of beliefs says that the community is to be perpetuated "by the admission of serious-minded persons, and the adoption of children." The serious-minded persons are mostly finding their vocations elsewhere, but the settlement we were visiting was in fact a children's home, where orphans were housed and educated. The women hoped that some of these boys and girls (whose carriage and behavior were decorous but cheerful) would subscribe as adults to the Shaker faith. The Shakers have always been famous for handicrafts, and there was a small gift shop in one building of the orphanage. It sold well-worked aprons, and dresses, in gay colors; books about the Shakers, with some forbidding portraits of eminent adherents of the past; and greeting cards made by the children, consisting of postage stamps put together to form pictures. It was all very clean, wholesome, and pleasant, with an air of tempered monasticism; so scrupulously tempered, indeed, that I suspect in fifty years' time there will be no more Shakers (this being an age and a country addicted to extremes of sin and sanctity).

But the most attractive and memorable of all the individualistic characters of the East is the American Yankee, what is left of him, descended, as often as not, from good old English families, a living reminder of the first brave settlers; with a reputation, resolutely upheld, of taciturn boldness and financial discretion. He is of distinctive appearance—very tall and upright, long-limbed and big-chinned, with fair hair and blue eyes. One or two distinguished New England families perpetuate these characteristics almost to the point of caricature; so that some of the Saltonstalls, for example, might stand as personifications of the Yankee tradition. The Yankees have always been famous as sailors, as masters of clippers and whalers, and the memory of their seagoing heyday is still alive everywhere in maritime New England.

Their real shrine, though, is the bridge at Concord, Massachusetts, where in 1775 a handful of Yankee Minutemen fought the first real battle of the Revolutionary War. It is a beautiful and moving place. The Concord River flows between meadows, and a lane lined with tall trees runs down to the bridge across it. All around, just in sight between the foliage, are handsome old colonial houses, with tall chimneys and shutters. To anyone who has seen the process of British withdrawal from some imperial responsibility or another, the little action that occurred at this spot is easy to envisage—the redcoats, withdrawing across the bridge, pulling up planks after them under the guidance of some stoic and disinterested sergeant; the eager Minutemen gathering behind the bushes on the other side ("Bloody wogs! Wot wouldn't I give for a cup of char!"); the first tentative shots (Isaac Davis of Acton was the first to die); and the fusillade. Often and again, in distant and disagreeable dependencies, such a first fusillade has led eventually to a convulsion and a reluctant withdrawal, the last ceremonies on the quayside, the troopships sailing gallantly elsewhere, and the establishment of yet another Independence, Emancipation, or Evacuation Day.

"The Minutemen did not pursue their advantage at first," we are told, "but crossed the river and waited behind the Jones house until the British company returned from the Barrett farm and the whole body started to return to Boston. At Meriam's Corner, however, reinforcements started a running attack from behind houses and stone walls, and soon the British were in a disorderly rout." Citizens of Concord watched the engagement from chinks in their shuttered windows. It was a lively little skirmish, which must have been (if it is not irreverent to say so) lots of fun for its participants.

An American engaged me in conversation while I stood at the Concord Bridge, and was amused to find that I was English. "Don't take it to heart," he said, "they were all Englishmen anyway." In this mellow spirit we looked together at the celebrated statue of the Yankee Minuteman, standing nobly beside his plow with his gun in his hand, in an open-necked shirt. Below him is the famous inscription: "Here once the embattled farmers stood, and fired the shot heard round the world." As an expression of the times there are some better lines on a monument at Lexington, a few miles away, which begin: "The Die was Cast!!! The Contest was Long, Bloody and Affecting." In 1875 James Russell Lowell was asked to write some lines for the common gravestones of the British soldiers killed in the fighting at Concord. How noble an opportunity for generosity, for soothing old squabbles and ending recriminations! But the American can still be unpredictable, and the pangs of creation brought forth:

> They came three thousand miles and died,
> To keep the past upon its throne.
> Unheard beyond the ocean tide
> Their English mother made her moan.

So there they lie, those poor profane soldiers, half of 'em liars and half of 'em thieves, commemorated in stone by four lines of lumpish verse, libeled in print by impertinent talk of disorderly routs, dominated by that priggish Minuteman and his air of unspeakable virtue, like an eighteenth-century Zionist defending his kibbutz.

Nevertheless they must have been a splendid people, the original Yankees; and the remaining specimens are splendid still. I met one at Gloucester, Massachusetts, who admirably looked and sounded the part. Gloucester is a famous fishing port, whose ships sail to the Newfoundland Banks, the Arctic, and many another far-flung fishing ground. I once saw a Gloucester boat tied up at Key West, the tropical port at the southern extremity of Florida. Not long ago the Gloucester boats were graceful two-masted schooners, such as Kipling described in *Captains Courageous*; now they are all diesel craft, and not a single schooner remains at work.

My Yankee was a watchman at a boatyard overlooking the gray shambles of the harbor. I had been told that one of the marine railways in Gloucester (used for hauling ships on to slipways) was powered by an engine originally installed in the monitor *Merrimac*, the celebrated Civil War ironclad; and, more from sentiment than from any passionate interest in marine engines, I made a tour of the yards to find it. It was Saturday afternoon, and this particular yard was deserted except for the watchman, a tall and sinewy man, who was standing at the end of the pier looking fixedly at the water. His body was somehow wreathed in languorous coils, as if all his limbs were double-jointed, and his hat was tilted to the back of his head. "I jest don't know," he murmured as I approached him, "I jest don't know if I can make it. It's a terrible, fearsome thing to ask a man to do!" It was his first week in the job, and he was finding it inexpressibly tedious. "It's a terrible imposition! There ain't no work, and there ain't no play, and that's the truth. When I was fishing we used to spend 300 days of the year at sea, and really at sea, that was, in the old sailing days. Now? I take a boat across the harbor there each morning to fetch the papers, and that's all! That's the day's work! And I ask you, what's in the papers when you get 'em? Nothing but women and gory murders! And they call this living!"

His views on the Gloucester fishing fleet were mournful, as befits a man who has seen such changes. None of the old-style American skippers were left, he said; most of the fishermen now were Portuguese or Italians, and you could "walk a mile in this town and see nobody but Dagos." They were a different breed, said he, from the classic skippers. "My father now, he was a schooner skipper, and he was a well-read man (like me). He brought us up on the encyclopedia, and he read all the magazines and the reviews and such. These Italians, all they read is the comic strips. *And that's all they're fit for!*"

We went inside to look at some engines. He had never heard of any *Merrimac* connection, and he was consumed with disbelief. One of these engines, he happened to know, had been working at the yard for a hundred years or more; but he asked you, how could a thing like that drive a ship? It wasn't the right way up. I could see that for myself, couldn't I? He had never heard such poppycock, coming there bothering him on a Saturday afternoon, as if he hadn't anything better to do than answer tomfool questions.

But ah! Gloucester in the old days, when the graceful sailing ships would slide in and out behind the breakwater. Often schooners would be lost at sea, and many families would be in mourning (between 1830 and 1951 nearly 5,000 Gloucester fishermen were drowned); but it was a proud place in those days, it had self-respect, you see. It was a real port, then. Now it was all artists and tourists and such. He remembered very well when Josh Slocum's boat (the one he sailed round the world) was tied up at that very quay. And Dr.

Cook's boat was there for a long time, being repaired. "Dr. Cook?" I queried. "The one who claimed to have got to the North Pole when he hadn't done anything of the sort?" "The same," my crusty friend replied, "and I know he was an imposter, and I know they put him in jail for forging checks, and I know all about him, so you needn't say. I'll tell you this, and you can believe me *if* you want to: he was a real gentleman to talk to."

A good man, the old-fashioned Yankee, who keeps his sturdy independence in good repair (Dagos, diesels, and such-like not-with-standing).

ငာ 4. ၯ

On Violence

IOLENCE is an ever-present element in American life, even in these Eastern states. We were once traveling through New York State, not far from the Shaker colony, when warning arrived of an impending hurricane. It had battled its way up from the South Atlantic and raged along the beaches of the Carolinas, before swinging inland toward the Great Lakes. The newspapers and the radio kept us informed of its detailed movements, and I resolved to experience its fury not snug in a warm bed, nor safe in a shuttered tavern, but on the banks of the Niagara Falls. I drove there accordingly, and stood in the dark beside the cataract while the storm passed by.

The night was very black and the rain teemed down in a wall of wet. I stood in a little park overlooking the American Falls, huddled in a raincoat, desperately holding a flapping umbrella. I was alone, and all around me the trees were swaying and hissing. Sometimes my feet squelched into the drenched turf, and the mud oozed horribly over the tops of my shoes. The wind was howling, but occasionally through its din I could hear the sounds of hammering and clattering; the townspeople's were barricading their windows and securing their doors. Now and then a branch would fall, with a harsh tearing noise, somewhere in the surrounding woods. It was desolate, damp, and awfully depressing.

In front of me, though, there was a very different scene. Swept by the great wind, swollen by floods, the Niagara River rushed down its narrow and crag-strewn channel, all white and foaming, passing with the perpetual roar only a few feet from my watching place. The water was moving with dizzy speed, dragging tree trunks and branches and tumbling boulders, shining like phosphorescence in the darkness, between wooded banks and stubborn little islands, until with an indescribable crash it leaped over the precipice of the falls, to rebound in a vaporish cloud of spray. Niagara is a sort of show nowadays, like a freak or a circus turn, and the falls were bathed in light from powerful searchlights; so that while the plunging water was brilliantly white, the void beyond was black, only relieved by a few blurred lights from the Canadian shore. I have never seen anything so bursting with elemental power as the Niagara Falls; they are the most satisfying of the great American wonders; and they are probably at their most tremendous on a rainy night in winter, with a hurricane passing by.

Violence is the very essence of Niagara. It is not the beauty of the falls that makes them so fascinating, but their unyielding ferocity. Year after year, night and day, the water hurls itself over these cliffs, only stilled for a few weeks in a decade when the severity of winter freezes it. There is a frenzy about the flying spray, and (however sweetly suburban they make the surrounding parks) a heartless sweep to the flow of the river. Whirlpools and dangerous sluices abound in the channel, and in the winter the ice is sometimes 100 feet thick. Even the history of Niagara is bloody, associated not only with barrels, tightropes, suicides, and honeymoons, but with wars and Indians too. (Once, during the War of 1812, some American soldiers were playing cards at an inn near Niagara. "What are trumps?" one of them asked, and was startled to hear an unmistakably British voice answer him through the window. "Gentlemen," it said nastily, "bayonets are trumps"; whereupon a platoon of rough

English troopers burst into the room and bayoneted all present, pinning the innkeeper ignominiously to the wall of his own taproom.) Only a short time before I stood on the edge of Niagara, there had been a titanic landslide on the American shore; in one morning 750,000 tons of rock and masonry broke away from the bank and fell into the river, with what one can only imagine to have been an almighty splash.

The whole American life is tempered by the threats or presence of such overwhelming natural excesses. Hurricanes and floods, droughts and storms and heat waves are disconcertingly common; and in almost every state there are turbulences of scenery, grotesque formations or things of feverishly exaggerated size. You must be prepared for savage vagaries of climate when you are traveling in America. When I set off on one journey to the extreme South I was pursued by a series of vicious rainstorms, the water beating down so thickly and endlessly that the puddles came splashing up between the floorboards, and the moisture seeped in between the cracks of the dashboard, until the whole car was dank, and I was shivering with the chill, and the cases fastened to the roof were pulpy from the rain. In a matter of hours I was in the swampy country of the Everglades; so hot now that the sweat was pouring through my shirt; so thirsty that from time to time I stopped and ate a whole pineapple like an ice cream; plagued by myriads of mosquitoes.

Earthquakes of a minor degree of awfulness are not uncommon. My wife and I were once sitting at a drive-in cinema (where one watches the film from the seat of one's car) when we felt a sudden curious vibration. The car began to shake and sway ominously on its springs, and, wondering for a moment if by some oddity of spontaneous combustion the engine had started itself, I jumped out to investigate, I found that the whole ground was ticking over, so to speak, but a cheerful voice from the next car said: "Don't worry, it's only an earthquake?"; and thus comforted I sat down again, wondering over what range of amateur seismography these mild shudders would extend. (The earthquake swallowed a farmhouse, not so far away, but hardly achieved a headline in the local press.)

We arrived in the wake of a hurricane at Vicksburg, Mississippi, a thousand miles to the southwest. When we reached that modest town, perched on a bluff above the Mississippi, we found it disfigured by great mounds of rubble, like a bombed city. Whole blocks of rickety houses had been torn down, and steep streets on the side of the hill were closed with barricades. More than forty people had been killed by the hurricane. It had come swirling suddenly up the river from the south, slashed its way through the town, and blown itself out on an uninhabited island across the Mississippi. There had been no warning. Many women were caught shopping, and a number of children attending a matinee were trapped in a cinema. All over the town roofs were damaged and windows blown in, but the people took it stoically. Well they might, for during the Civil War Vicksburg was besieged for forty-seven days by General Grant's forces and the population lived in caves, eating mule meat and rats and printing newspapers on the back of wallpaper. A survivor, whose children may well be living in Vicksburg now, told Mark Twain of those unhappy troglodytes: "Hunger and misery and sickness and fright and sorrow, and I don't know what, all got so loaded into them that none of them were rightly their old selves after the siege." But this same man's summing-up of the experience may well illustrate the surprising American resilience to disaster. He said: "It got to be Sunday all the time."

In the East one becomes accustomed to reasonable standards of public efficiency; to test this American resilience one must have a comparison to judge it by. I found an opportunity at the town of Eagle Pass in Texas (also with Civil War memories, for there the last unsurrendered Confederate force threw its flag melodramatically into the Rio Grande). I reached the place at a time when the river had overflowed its banks, demolishing the bridge that connects the United States with Mexico, destroying large numbers of adobe houses on both sides, and swamping both Eagle Pass and Piedras Negras, in Mexico. I first flew across the river by helicopter to see how the Mexicans were retorting to the catastrophe. The scene was chaotic. Crowds of homeless townspeople had gathered on the bleak hills above the town and were sheltering in little raggedy tents or erections of sticks and blankets. They had little food and practically no medical supplies. In the town, the Army was in dubious control. Platoons of dirty soldiers, unshaven and armed to the teeth, patrolled its watery streets, and gaudily embellished officers held court. In the emergency hospital there were no beds; the injured lay on school desks placed side by side. There was a general air of hopeless flurry, and my most vivid memory of the place is of three small dogs seen from the returning helicopter, trapped on the roof of the flooded house, alone among a waste of mud, rushing to and fro in an agony of fear and hunger.

It was enlightening to return to Eagle Pass, for there (although the physical conditions were much the same) all was calm and orderly. The streets were piled high with mud, left by the subsiding waters, blocking alleys and gateways, seeping into shops, like a soggy blanket. Through this mess the Americans moved with relaxed determination. Machines were sucking the mud away through pipes, and men and women were clearing the buildings by dogged hard work. Where the pavements were free of muck, the storekeepers had brought their stock outside to wash it down. As in Piedras Negras, the military was in control; but the National Guard, a genial force, looked like a collection of benevolent farmers in mild fancy dress. Doctors were active inoculating people against typhoid; helicopters and private aircraft were taking off frequently with supplies for the Mexicans; the local newspaper was humming; the hotel regretted that the water might be a bit funny, but offered beer instead. There had never been a flood like this before, in all the recorded history of the Rio Grande; but fierce strokes of fortune are in the blood of Americans, and they accept them (whether in Texas or in Delaware) without much fuss.

It is doubtless partly because of this tigerish environment, and partly because of historical circumstance, that a strain of violence emboldens the American character. The clash of arms and forceful opinion sounds through so much of American history, for the nation was built on revolution and on the bold movement to the West. The fearful Civil War, in which one out of every four participants was killed, was so recent and so near at hand that people still relive its battles and inherit its perilous prejudices. There were Indian wars within the memory of living men. Britain has lived by exerting the strength of her arms in foreign countries and distant seas; but American history has been made chiefly at home, with bloody skirmishes and flags, brawls and evictions and arson. Scarcely a great American city has not been, at one time or another, denigrated by dreadful fires. It is only thirty years since prohibition was greeted across the country with a wave of unbelievable brutal and conscienceless crime.

So in America, and not least in the East, you are never far from brutality; it is part of the stimulation of the country that the old arguments of force are still, so often, tacitly valid. It is not only that crimes of violence are still so common, that feuds and acts of cruel revenge are recorded in the papers almost every day; the whole national conception of self-advancement and perpetual competition presupposes an attitude of no-holds-barred. Most Americans are accustomed to violence. Elderly ladies will drive their cars undaunted through the ghastly shoving turmoil of city traffic, readier to push than to be pushed, on the frantic highways leading into the great metropolises they demand no courtesies if they stall or take the wrong turn, but simply barge back into the race again, brazenly. Indeed, Americans enjoy violence more than most people. I remember a moment in a big stockyard when, pressed to inspect the slaughtering process, I had turned away sickened at the sight; only to see a pretty young mother in a white hat holding up her child for a better view. Extortion and corruption is a commonplace (at least by hearsay) to most Americans. Mild shopkeepers in the industrial cities of the East will admit without excitement that they pay protection money to gangsters or crooked policemen. In New York recently it was announced that no less than one quarter of the city's mobile police force had been involved in a system of organized bribery.

You can sense this underlying savagery, restrained, of course, but present, at many gatherings of respectable business people; ambitious; anywhere in American where you feel the slogan of philosophy to be: "If you don't want to get on, move over, bud, and make way for a guy who does!"

ఌ **5.** ☊

Clean Steel

HIS is the undeniable motto of Pittsburgh, the steel city, which stands at the point where the Allegheny and the Monongahela Rivers join to form the Ohio; and yet it is one of the most agreeably exciting places in America. I had always thought of Pittsburgh as the smokiest, dirtiest, least enlightened of American cities, a metropolis of industry built upon coal, enmeshed by railway lines, and shrouded in gloom. It has always been famous as a vast and unrelenting machine of production and a magnet to workers of many nationalities. I drove over the Pennsylvania hills to Pittsburgh with a sense of virtuous foreboding, dreading its purposeful grime, but morally secure in the knowledge that it was a place I ought to see.

But, astonishingly, things had changed there. We entered the city along a magnificent dual highway, broad and sweeping, embellished with crossovers and tunnels and elaborate signs; along the banks of the muddy Monongahela, across a cantilever bridge, and into the famous Golden Triangle—the small business center of great wealth that is the heart of Pittsburgh. We gazed around us incredulously. Far from being smoky, the atmosphere was of a translucent brilliance. Wherever we looked there seemed to be bright new office blocks and growing gardens, and the whole place was bustling cheerily, like Manhattan. On the river towboats chugged by with the washing fluttering. A new building in the center of the district was sheathed entirely in aluminum; there was a gay new hotel, with flowers in the lobby windows; and a friendly Negro carrying a statuette of a baseball player (he had just been awarded it for a good season's play) directed us to our destination. It can be a dreary business, arriving at an American city, weary from the traffic, dazed with the noise, and confronted by tired and apathetic informants; but Pittsburgh gave us an invigorating welcome.

This was a sign of the times; for the city is undergoing a deliberate, self-imposed transformation. There is a movement among its citizens to change its entire aspect and personality, banishing ugliness and tiredness, substituting color, pleasure, and better health. To jaded English ears this plan may sound a little on the winsome side, but the campaign is conducted ruthlessly, as befits the place. The Chamber of Commerce says characteristically: "For years Pittsburghers said to themselves about their city, 'It may not be a good place to live, but it's a good place to make money.' You can still make your money in Pittsburgh, but now you can live the good life here, too." This is not all brag, and the story of the changes is a remarkable one; for coercion, legislation, and strict planning were all necessary in a place profoundly dedicated to the principles of capitalism.

To begin with, the Pittsburghers ridded themselves of smoke, with the advice of scientists of the Mellon Institute. (You cannot escape the Mellon steel family in Pittsburgh, and if you are wise you will not make too much fun of its ubiquity.) Ten years ago life in Pittsburgh was almost unbearable. The smoke was appalling, tainting everything, so that there was little relish in living. Throughout the states it was known as "The Smoky City," and when its name was mentioned people would screw up their faces in distaste. The smoke came not only from a myriad of factories and foundries, but from houses with coal fires, trains with steam locomotives, steam tugs, and countless varied smoky machines. Almost all has now been eliminated. Fuels that made much smoke were banned by law, first in the city of Pittsburgh, then in the surrounding districts. There was naturally strong opposition. Some of the most vociferous came from laundry operators, who foresaw a serious drop in business, and sometimes insisted on maintaining their own small belching chimneys, partly as a protest of principle, partly because (presumably) even a little laundry chimney dirties a few shirts. The railroads, after a show of reluctance, agreed to convert their trains almost entirely to diesel; to their secret delight, I am told, for they had wanted to make the change for years but had been prevented because the custom of coal producers was so important to them. Stern penalties were imposed upon those who violated the smoke laws, and remarkably soon the place began to look up.

Indeed, some of the effects of the reforms were miraculous. Pittsburgh now gets 60 percent more sunshine than it used to, and 60 percent less dust and soot falls on the city. It is warmer, too, for the old horrible pall sometimes reduced the temperature by as much as ten degrees. The Chamber of Commerce claims that despite the forlorn rearguard actions of the laundrymen, Pittsburghers have saved themselves an annual forty-one dollars per head in laundry bills. The city's air is now sharp and clean; it is queer, like examining a half-cleaned picture, to look about you now in Pittsburgh and see, defacing old buildings, degrading trees, clinging to crevices and corners, blackening bridges and staling factories, engriming all the shores of the Ohio River, the dingy sediment left behind by the smoke.

Their first battle won, the reformers turned to the rivers. Pittsburgh has always lived under the threat of floods. Year after year, when the rivers rose, the low-lying parts of the city were inundated. Because of this menace, people hesitated to bring new industries to Pittsburgh; and because houses were rotted and damaged by the water, the health of the community was affected. To put an end to all this a committee of businessmen, industrialists, and politicians resolved to create a series of controlling dams. Eight of them have been built, and the city is now said to be all but free of serious floods. This is the kind of claim which will almost certainly be followed, within a year or two, by a flood of unparalleled dimensions; but on paper, at least, the system can lop ten feet off the crest of any future inundation. The dams stand away from the city, in country backwaters and among quiet hills, high on the tributary rivers that feed the Allegheny and the Monongahela, and they have good American country names—Tionesta, Mahoning, Tygart and Conemaugh, Loyalhanna and Crooked Creek.

Next, Pittsburgh rejuvenated its communications. Its engineers built a great highway into the city from the west; it is twenty-seven miles long, and is so loaded with every kind of improvement and safety device that its cost would probably provide a complete road system for (say) Bhutan. They built another road to connect Pittsburgh with the Pennsylvania Turnpike, one of the great highways of the world, which starts near Philadelphia and crosses the entire state. This mighty thoroughfare thus becomes a direct approach to Pittsburgh from New York and the east. They built a new airport west of the city, with what Pittsburghers like to describe as "the world's largest, most modern, most beautiful, and most functional terminal building." Functional it undoubtedly is, for besides places for airplanes to land it has its own hotel, a cinema, a nightclub, beauty shops, restaurants, cafeterias, and a hundred other essentials to efficient airline operation. Six airlines run services through it. (Pittsburgh is also served by no fewer than seven railways, enough to daunt the most zealous of Socialist doctrinaires; and its river services handle more freight annually then either the Suez or the Panama Canal.)

Next, with smoke cleared, floods minimized, and access made easy, the reformers changed the face of the city. Huge areas of slums and ruinous business buildings were demolished. At the tip of the Golden Triangle, where the three rivers meet, a park was laid out; to complete it, a couple of big river bridges are to be demolished and rebuilt, for they are rather in the way at the moment. Nearby, in an area that used to be gray and unwholesome, a series of skyscrapers was begun, rather in the style of Rockefeller Center in Manhattan.

They are surrounded and interspersed by green areas, with trees and fountains; and though they are architecturally uninspired, they look clean and honest, neither of which commendation (I am assured) could always be applied to the old Pittsburgh. In the center of the business district some more arresting structures have been built. One, forty-one stories high, is coated with stainless steel, and is starkly and powerfully beautiful. Another is faced entirely in aluminum, a circumstance which may be connected with the fact that it is the headquarters of the Aluminum Company of America. On one side of it is a tall glasshouse, five stories high, forming a lobby; trees grow inside this massive conservatory, and a variety of shrubbery, and old retainers, watering the plants look as if they might easily tip their hats and tell us we must not miss the monkey-puzzle tree, down there by the Richmond Gate, past the tearooms. Just around the corner no fewer than twenty-one separate properties have been bought and pulled down to make way for a little park among the skyscrapers. It has trees, an ornamental fountain, and statuary, and underneath it is a garage for 900 cars. (The unwearying publicists, in a moment of lyricism, describe it as "a green oasis for pavement-weary Pittsburghers.") Farther uptown the planners propose more grandiose improvements. In a former slum district they are going to build a mammoth "civic and cultural center." It will have an arena-auditorium, with a retractable circular roof, an exhibition hall, a concert hall, and a theater; and around its perimeter will be tall blocks of flats looking like thin slices of hard cheese.

But all these are simply material improvements. The creators of this new Pittsburgh are determined to achieve a psychological revolution too. They want to instill a new civic pride into Pittsburghers, starting with the children; and in this, alas! in their excesses of local patriotism, they sometimes display an unhappy boastfulness. The American is always at his most arrogant when he is talking of local achievements (and at his silliest, too; a man in Philadelphia once pointed out a bridge to me with the proud if unlikely claim: "In 1928 that bridge here was the second largest single-span bridge in the western hemisphere—*of its kind!*") The educators of Pittsburgh seem to be cherishing a generation dedicated to this kind of pompous and sententious complacency. I saw some booklets produced for Pittsburgh children positively bursting with incentives to jingoism. Sometimes Miss Willard (an imaginary schoolmistress) takes her charges to the summit of a neighboring hill and discusses the city lying at their feet, paying tribute to the work of the committee of "outstanding leaders" which is making Pittsburgh bigger, better, more beautiful, richer, grander, and holier than anywhere else on the face of the earth. Once she foists on the children a list of twenty industrial activities, of indescribable tedium, in which the sheer bigness of Pittsburgh is unexcelled. Sometimes an odious child called Sandra intervenes with such remarks as: "And don't forget that all these projects will make Pittsburgh a more beautiful and convenient place in which to live!" This is not a phenomenon peculiar to Pittsburgh. The parochial pride of Americans is intrusive everywhere; it does little to help the spread of uniformity, as its advocates claim, but merely transforms (often enough) the pathetic into the irritating.

Anyway, Pittsburgh is not a cultural desert, forced to rely for its prestige upon the biannual production of ball bearings. It has a fine symphony orchestra, good libraries, a magnificent medical center, and many pioneer research institutions. The Mellon Institute has played a brilliant part in the development of American industry, and the design of its classical palace is so infused with intellectual symbolism (even the lift doors have their significances) that in future centuries the seers may well abandon the Pyramid of Cheops, and base their unhinged prognostications upon its measurements and hidden meanings. There is a famous university in Pittsburgh, housed in a skyscraper, and called disconcertingly "The Cathedral of Learning." There are six art institutes, three theaters, four daily papers, and four television stations. The Salk vaccine was discovered there. The climate of thought is lively and invigorating, and sometimes distinguished; remarkable to consider, when we remember that 200 years ago Pittsburgh was simply a river fort, visited only by soldiers, trappers, and adventurers, with scarcely a book and hardly a breath of symbolism among the lot of them.

So I recommend Pittsburgh, the old Smoky City, to all despondent city dwellers; to the fatalistic, the irresolute, and distrusters of change; to young men looking for causes; and above all to Londoners, who have suffered so long from fog, smoke, dirt, and traffic, and who deserve a sunnier, more spacious future (as Sandra would say).

༄ 6. ༄

A Corner of the World

ONLY 400 miles to the east of Pittsburgh (a trifling distance by American standards) lies the island of Nantucket, the old seat of the whaling kings, and a place of diametrically opposing temperament. "See what a real corner of the world it occupies," wrote Melville in *Moby Dick*. "How it stands there, away off shore, more lonely than the Eddystone lighthouse." Nantucket is still a little spiritual kingdom of its own. It is as spare and windswept as ever, far out at sea, its light the first reminder to Atlantic liners that they are in American waters.

To get there we took passage in an elderly ferry steamer sailing out of New Bedford, on the Massachusetts mainland, and spent a long few hours sipping coffee from cardboard cups in the saloon, and watching the line of Cape Cod and Martha's Vineyard slip by outside. All manner of odd objects are conveyed on this old steamship, crated firmly or veiled in canvas. Cows are slung aboard, and cars, and gallons of milk. If you are traveling in winter, there is a throng of people in heavy coats and mufflers, returning to the island; all knowing one another, and stopping each other in passageways, and swapping gossip on deck. In the corner of the big saloon the manager of the Pacific Bank may be deep in serious conversation with a prosperous burgher, and passersby will step carefully, knowing that big money is being discussed. A few commercial travelers gather heartily at the coffee bar to discuss the market for dishcloths or blotting paper. Rugged native islanders, scarcely dressed by Dior, examine with detailed interest the strangers in gossamer shoes and New York hats. The Nantucketers, islanders by temper as by environment, talk of people from the mainland as "visitors from America."

The ship arrives, after about five hours' steaming, in the harbor of the town of Nantucket, perhaps the most perfectly preserved eighteenth-century town in the whole of America. From this elegant little port, in the late eighteenth and early nineteenth centuries, the world's greatest whaling fleets sailed for the Antarctic. Their crews were familiar with half the world. Often they would water in the Pacific islands, or visit the China coast, or even sail to London for stores and equipment. (Many a Nantucket attic contains faded daguerreotypes of Fijian chiefs or magnificent mandarins.) Immense fortunes were made by these expeditions, and a number of families, enriched and intermingled, achieved a local hegemony; remaining, to this day, among the social arbiters of Nantucket affairs. Few socially conscious Nantucket households are unable to claim relationship with one or another of these families, and their mansions still dominate Main Street. Most of them are of handsome white clapboard. There of the finest are of red brick, splendid Georgian town houses. With white classical ornamentation and rich front doors. These three houses, identical and adjacent, once all belonged to a single family; so that within a few hundred yards there were three separate, teeming colonies of Starbucks. There is another fine red Georgian building in the cobbled main square of the town. It is the Pacific Club, once the haunt of the whaling captains, who sat and drank and played cribbage in its low-ceilinged rooms between their prodigious voyages to the other side of the earth. It was once the office of a ship owner, and on its lintel are inscribed the names of his vessels, *Independence* and *Hiawatha*—two of the ships involved in the Boston Tea Party. They still play cribbage at the Pacific Club, and among the company there is one man—only one—who remembers going a-whaling.

I have a cousin living on Nantucket, a widowed lady whose house was built at the end of the seventeenth century in the original Nantucket settlement to the west. Early in the 1800s the villagers moved to the site of the present town, where there was better water and a more satisfactory harbor, and my cousin's house was moved with them. It is a pretty cottage faced with shingles, with old-fashioned open fireplaces and glass panes in the doors of the rooms (the original Nantucketers were Quakers, and these little internal windows were designed to play the part of chastity belts: my cousin covers them with chintz curtains). She is keenly interested in things genealogical, and seems to be related to most of the Nantucket worthies. On the walls of her drawing room two family trees hang. One, an orthodox up-and-down tree, concerns her English family, and ends with my mother. The other is a characteristic Nantucket tree, semicircular instead of vertical, so that lateral descent may be traced, intricate quirks of relationship, avuncular connections, and obscure cousinships. From this lady I learned a good deal of the curiously inbred and introspective quality of Nantucket, an aloofness that must baffle and irritate the many tourists who visit the place in summer.

Women dominate the life of Nantucket (perhaps they always have, since the days when most men of virility and character were away with the whaling fleets). The most famous native of Nantucket was a woman. She was Maria Mitchell, the astronomer (closely related, I need hardly say, to my cousin), the daughter of a Quaker bank cashier, who studied astronomy under her father's tuition, discovered a comet, and became world-famous as one of the first women to practice her profession with distinction. Honors were showered upon her, she is portrayed in the Hall of Fame at New York University, she became Professor of Astronomy at Vassar, and died an unmarried celebrity.

The memory of this remarkable person strongly pervades the intellectual life of Nantucket, for in her memory there was founded a

Maria Mitchell Association. It has an excellent little scientific library and an observatory, and is run chiefly by women. For many years now it has maintained a resident astronomer, and the present occupant of the office is another distinguished woman, Miss Margaret Harwood. Though she is near the age of retirement, she is a gay and schoolgirlish sort of person, who shoves her felt hat anyhow on the back of her head, and will talk into the small hours if the opportunity arises. She lives in her charming little house next door to the observatory, exchanging data with men of science all over the world, attending the great international astronomical conferences, observing her especial portion of the heavens from Nantucket.

She is not the only prominent professional woman in the place. I was told that the leading lawyer was a woman, and so was one of the most successful real estate brokers. The only hotel open all the year was owned and managed by two sisters; one of the two papers was edited by a woman; and the new airport (this must surely be unique) was managed by a woman. Everywhere in Nantucket women seemed to be in the ascendant, and I shall always associate the island with the conversation of intelligent women, just as one thinks of London in terms of taxis and good suits.

My cousin took me for a trip around the island. We were driven by an elderly man with a passionate interest in matters of descent and relationship, so between them my two guides seemed qualified to answer any conceivable query on Nantucket that was sufficiently compounded on the insular and the heraldic. They took me first to a lonely house on the moors, a few miles from the town, to show me some heather. Heather is not indigenous to the United States, and in most parts is regarded as a sort of mystical fancy of legend, like the phoenix or the Holy Grail. In Nantucket, however, some time during the last century, some heather plants arrived from Britain by accident with a consignment of fir trees, and in a sheltered corner of the island they took root and spread moderately. Their presence was discovered months afterwards, and kept a secret. It became a distinct social asset to know where the heather grew, and a club took existence around the knowledge. To this day the location of the wild heather is not know to many, but at this solitary house on the uplands various species had been cultivated, and grew wanly, not with the splendid flourish of heather at home, but with a hangdog, apologetic air, as if they were doing the best they could, but were homesick for Scotland. The house was shuttered, for the occupants lived there only in the summer; it looked cold and inhospitable, and a few slates from the roof had been blown off by the mighty winds that sweep in from the ocean.

Later my guides pointed out to me a moorland ridge beyond which, they said, was "the hidden forest." Nantucket is an almost treeless island, a lump of land rising bare-backed from the sea; but it appears that at this place there is a sizable wood. Again the islanders have done their best to keep it secret, so that its isolation will not be disturbed by droves of tourists in the summer. No road reaches the trees, and they are well hidden down in the hollow, generally allowing Nantucket people to be alone there when they wish to commune with their spirits of seclusion. Poor souls, they are annually offended by the influx of holiday visitors, larger each year. The previous summer's batch had been grosser than ever; it evidently came from the worst quarters of Philadelphia (where the Nantucket authorities had inadvertently bought advertising space in a peculiarly unsuitable newspaper). "All they did last summer," one dignified lady complained, "was stand about at the corners of streets, *talking*." It seemed a harmless sort of tripperism, but was doubtless galling to the energetic islanders.

Nantucket is, of course, almost part and parcel of the ocean; as much in league with the waters as Venice, its very buildings seasoned with tar and the salt winds. There is a fine museum commemorating its whaling days. It is full of bits of ships and jaws of whales; the great deck ovens which they used to reduce the whale blubber to oil; pictures of whalers and sea tragedies (almost an entire whaling fleet was once lost in the ice); gee-gaws from distant countries; family trees and logbooks and harpoon spears. There is a fascinating account kept by the wife of a whaling skipper of the arrival of her first child, born at sea at some improbable and uncomfortable latitude;

the crew seemed to have treated her very delicately. There are programs of entertainments mounted by the crews of ships at sea—the first act of *Othello* was staged by one whaler with particular success. A letter from a skipper, in wirelike handwriting, describes a Christmas celebration, when four Nantucket ships met by arrangement in far southern waters, and had an agreeable time. There are cases devoted to scrimshaw, which many consider to be the only important indigenous folk art, Indian handicraft excepted, to have come out of America. Scrimshaw is the practice of carving bone and ivory, especially whales' teeth, into intricate patterns and objects. The museum has innumerable pretty specimens, from walking sticks with knobby heads to dainty needle cases and birdcages. A favorite product was the ornamented busk used to support the front of a nineteenth-century corset. One of these is inscribed with the lines:

> Accept, dear girl, this busk from me;
> Carved by my humble hand.
> I took it from a Sparm Whale's Jaw,
> One thousand miles from land!
> In many a gale
> Has been the Whale
> In which this bone did rest.
> His time is past
> His bone at last
> Must now support thy brest.

I wanted to buy a model of a clipper ship, and asked my guides if they knew of any for sale on the island. They replied that, oddly enough, there lived on Nantucket a maker of ship models generally considered to be the best in America, if not in the world; and they directed me to his home. His name is Charles Sayle, and he lives in a small house near the harbor. In the great days of Nantucket that lowlying area of the town was not much in demand among the wealthier sea captains. Lately it has acquired favor, and there are a number of colorful small houses near the waterfront, Mr. Sayle's is distinctive because in his garden there is an enormous iron anchor, rescued from a mud-bank and carried there by a group of toiling friends. He is a former Gloucester fisherman, like the Yankee watchman, who sailed for many years in schooners and knows much about seamanship. He has a big black bushy beard, and wears sweaters and boots. His workshop is a jumble of half-finished ship models, plans, books, pictures, and tools, and he sits on a high stool working with minute implements on infinitesimal pieces of material. When I visited him he was making a model of a fishing boat, four or five inches long, but several other uncompleted models were near at hand. One was a magnificent clipper ship, mastless yet, but already full of grace. He works on a ship when he feels inclined. Sometimes his mood directs him toward a little dory, sometimes to a majestic ocean vessel; and he builds them much as a shipyard builds a real ship. He works from shipbuilders' plans and from published details of sailing ships (he found especially valuable some publications of the Maritime Museum at Greenwich), and he reckons that one of his models takes him as long to build as the original ship took at the shipyard. His prices are high, for much work goes into his exquisitely finished models; for a full-rigged clipper he charges about $1,500. In any case, he is booked up for months in advance, with orders from many parts of America and several places abroad. Mr. Sayle uses a wide variety of woods. The little model whales which he carves as household ornaments have all been made from supplies of ebony retrieved from the wreck of a ship off the island. The waters of Nantucket are treacherous, and there have been countless wrecks; those near the shore have mostly been emptied of their cargoes, but there are sure to be many farther out to sea that contain undiscovered treasures.

There used to be a little railway on Nantucket (its rolling stock ended their days in the war, I believe, helping to serve the American Army at the port of Bordeaux). We followed the course of its track to the eastern extremity of the island, and stood on the shore to look out over the Atlantic. It is a proud boast of the Nantucketers that there is no land between Siasconset, on their eastern coast, and the distant shore of Spain. Indeed, my guides seemed quite moved by the fact, as we stood looking out to sea; partly, perhaps, because of the perpetual golden glitter of Spain, so magical to consider in unfriendly climates; and partly because no native of Nantucket seems able to look upon the sea without emotion. It plays so intimate a part in all their lives. The bank manager, if you chance to see him on the returning steamer, seems perfectly at home among the rigging as he discusses stock yields and bank-reserve requirements; and even the astronomer told me quite casually of the evening when a hurricane, storming in from the ocean, ripped the dome off her observatory.

It is an assured and contented little island, Nantucket, well insulated against the conflicts and squabbles of the mainland. It was our last halt during our travels in the East, and the transition was abrupt indeed from its honest marine placidity to the perfumed grumbles of the South.

PART TWO

THE SOUTH

☙ 7. ❧

Adam Called It Paradise

OU MAY well hate the South, but you can never accuse it of dull uniformity, for it is a pungent entity of its own. It is not simply a region; it is an amalgam of sensations, memories, prejudices, and emotions; a place of symbols, where excesses of nostalgia can be prompted by the cadence of a voice or a glimpse of a crumbling mansion. Two races only dominate the southern states—the Anglo-Saxon and the Negro. The white people, already homogeneous, were fused into a new unity by the Civil War, a disaster and a humiliation which has bound them in resentful clannishness ever since. The Negroes, freed by the conflict, their reputation perverted by the subsequent horrors of Reconstruction, remained without cause of loyalty or pride, knowing no other home, but despised and distrusted everywhere; it is their presence, and the blind passions engendered by it, that gives the South both its sense of separation, and its overpowering atmosphere of rottenness and menace.

The poorer Anglo-Saxons contribute to this feeling by a shameless virulence of thought and speech; the more educated by a subtle unpleasantness that inspires their attitudes not only toward racial questions, but in anything (so insidious are the complexes of defeat) that affects themselves or their status. But it is, of course, when the Negro question arises that the underlying malice seeps most ominously to the surface. I was in Atlanta, a great southern manufacturing city, the day after the Supreme Court in Washington decreed that racial segregation in schools was illegal. For Southerners, this was the greatest internal issue of the post-war years. The abolition of separate schools for Negroes and whites would be the beginning (they felt) of federal measures against segregation in general, enforced by Washington without regard to the rights of individual states, and without knowledge of the intricate psychological structure of the South. For months the decision of the Court had been awaited, and every Tuesday (the day on which the Court announces its decisions) newspaper editors stood by expectantly for the big news. Dreadful consequences were threatened by the South if the Court decided against segregation. Several states gave warning that they might abolish public schools altogether, and rely on a private system where Jim Crowism would be legal by any standards. There were rumors that the Ku Klux Klan would be on the march again, that there would be lynchings and bloody race riots.

When the decision was announced, all the simmering discontent of the Southerners boiled over; though, mercifully, chiefly only in bitter words. I spent the day in Atlanta listening to angry men and women. The abuse they used was at once so theatrical and so repetitive that I could scarcely believe it had not been plucked wholesale from some common phrasebook of prejudice. I joined a conversation, in a coffee shop, with the manager of the place and a man who told me that he was a senior officer of the police. They spent some minutes reminiscing about race riots of the past, talking comfortably of "niggers" bashed and beaten in the streets; and of one especially, hounded by the mob, who had thrown himself into the doorway of that very coffee shop, only to be pushed back onto the pavement. "The only place for a nigger," said the manager with finality, "is at the back door, with his hat in his hand."

Other, gentler Atlantans, as horrified as anyone by these expressions of brutality, advocated other ways of sustaining white supremacy. Drugged by the sentimentality of the Old South, they would say, like sanctimonious jailers: "Leave the matter to us. We understand the Negroes, and they understand and respect us. After all, we've lived together for a long time. We know them through and through, and believe me, their minds are different from ours. Leave it all to us. *The South takes care of its own.*" If I were a Southern Negro, I would prefer the loudmouthed to the soft-spoken; for it is those who subscribe to the legend of the South, to its traditions of heritage and Southern gallantry, who will probably fight longest to keep the Negro down. The poor white, who talks so horribly, has grown up a Nigger-hater because he was for long in economic competition with the Negroes, sharing with them the poor fruits of a poverty-stricken land; but the South is booming now, with new industries arising everywhere, and the *raison d'être* of his bias is fading. It is the Southern gentleman, all string ties and gracious living, who is likely to perpetuate the agony. The average Dixie politician, at least where segregation is concerned, has passed far beyond independent judgment, so feverishly does he represent his electorate. A friend of mine was interviewing a celebrated Southern Governor when news arrived that two Negroes had been caught gambling in the state capitol. The Governor paused only a moment before issuing an edict that fitted admirably with the medieval arrogance of his nature. "Throw them into the chain gang!" he said. (Road gangs of convicts are a common sight in the South; but the chains he added by dramatic or gubernatorial license.)

The nature of the country itself contributes to the oppressive quality of the South. It is, generally speaking, a wide, dry, dusty, spiritless country; sometimes hauntingly beautiful, but usually melancholy; lacking robustness, good cheer, freshness, animation; a singularly un-Dickensian country. As you drive through South Carolina (for example) on a summer day, the endless cotton fields engulf you. Here and there are shabby villages, dusty and derelict, with patched wooden buildings and rusting advertisements, and with a few dispirited people, white and black, gathered outside the stores. Outside the unpainted houses of the poor whites there are often decrepit cars, and washing machines stand white among the cluttered objects on the verandas. Sometimes there is a little white church with a crooked steeple. There are frequent swamps, dark and mildewy, with gloomy trees standing in the water. The plantation mansions are sometimes magnificent, but often in depressingly bad repair.

I called at one such house for a talk with its owner and found it no more than a sad echo of a munificent past. Three generations ago the Parker plantation included some 10,000 acres, and was one of the great estates of the region. Now it is whittled down to about 150 acres, of cotton, tobacco, sweet potatoes, and corn. The drive up to the house is a narrow one between pine trees, unpaved; a cloud of dust rose up behind us as we drove along it. Near the road there were a couple of small wooden shacks, one of them inhabited, for there was a string of washing outside it, the other filled to the eaves with straw; and far at the end of the drive stood the big house, crumbling, classical, reminding me of Pharaoh's Palace at Petra, seen through the crevice of the *sik*. It had a wide and splendid porch, with four pillars. Mrs. Parker thought that only Washington or Thomas Jefferson could really do justice to it, but I felt myself better qualified to sit there when I noticed that its broad steps were rickety, that the frame of its front door was sagging, and that high in its roof there was a dormant wasp nest. Inside the house was agreeably untidy; in the hall, which ran clean through the building front to back, there was an elderly harmonium, with a large hymn-book propped on its music stand.

The planter, fresh from a tussle with his tractor, had greasy hands and wore a toupee and an open-necked shirt. But like most Southern gentlemen he had a talent for hospitality, and soon we were sitting on the balustrade of the porch, sipping long cool drinks and looking out through the pines. He told me that he ran the plantation almost single-handed, with only one full-time employee (paid two and a half dollars a day, plus a free house). His children go to the local public school and his wife does the housework. The five cabins on the estate are let to Negro families whose men work elsewhere, sometimes giving part-time help on the plantation; and "The Street," the double row of uniform cottages where the slaves used to live, is empty and tumbledown.

While we were talking on the porch a great cloud of dust approached us from the drive, and there emerged in stately motion two large mules. They were pulling a kind of sledge, a cross between a bobsled and Cleopatra's barge, and sitting on it, very old and wrinkled, very dignified, was a Negro in a straw hat. Round the corner he came in imperial state, the mules panting, the sledge creaking, the dust billowing all round us; and as he passed the porch he raised his hat by its crown and called: "G'd evening, boss, sir; g'd evening, Missus Parker." "Good evening, Uncle Henry," they replied.

Uncle Henry well illustrates the sad contradictions of the Southern mind. He is an old retainer of the Parkers who lives almost entirely upon their kindness. He is given a house and a few acres, firewood and storage space, and a loan when he needs one. The planter would not see him in distress for the world. He humors the old man's whims, never complaining at waste nor demanding recompense; enjoying watching Uncle Henry sail by on his sledge, kicking up the dust all over the porch. He likes exchanging greetings and accepting respect. He is sincere and generous in his charity. But to suggest that Mr. Parker might invite Uncle Henry into the house, or even shake hands with him, would be more than an impertinence; it might, such is the sudden intensity of passion in the warm South, be construed as a deliberate insult. Uncle Henry will always have a home, but, after all, the race must be preserved.

So there is a tinge of cruelty even to Southern kindliness; but the legend of crinolines, sweet accents, and scented summer evenings is not altogether a myth. I found myself wallowing, no less, in the fabled charm of the South during a hot summer stay at Oxford, Mississippi. This is a market and university town made famous by William Faulkner, who is a native of the place; and it is bursting with the combination of sordidness and heavy beauty that is the fascination of the South. The town is built around a central square and in the middle of it all is the courthouse, center of justice and administration, solid and ornate, aflutter with notice boards. Under the shade of the trees that surround this building the people of Oxford laze the hours away. There are innumerable old men whose chins are prickly with white stubble, wearing wide hats, chewing tobacco, spitting, and determinedly lounging. Little knots of Negroes gather separately, like boys from another form, who are not privileged to undo the second button of their jacket, or walk on the grass in Great Quad. Farmers, negligently sitting on parapets and leaning against walls, offer vegetables and fruits for sale. Little boys run up and down the steps, and through the courthouse, from one brown swing door to the other. Outside the hotel a few idle guests are reclining in chairs, smoking; a gaggle of plump women is doing its shopping in the square. On the first floor verandas of the buildings (their style reminiscent sometimes of the Wild West, sometimes of New Orleans, sometimes of the shuttered balconies of Baghdad) lawyers and realtors, in shirtsleeves, are exchanging business advice. The streets are dirty and dusty, and there is a tobacco-stained, beer-ringed ashtray atmosphere to the scene.

All around the square, though, are streets of lovely old houses; white and creeper-clad, with graceful porches and refreshing gardens; shaded by old trees in secluded corners, with tactful Negroes working in the gardens, and fountains watering the lawns. At dusk in summer these streets are suffused with an aromatic charm. The air is heavy and warm, and laden with the scent of roses and honeysuckle. Children scamper among the gardens, in and out of narrow lanes. Sometimes there is the sound of laughter from inside a house, or the raised voice of a scolding Negro mammy. A languid content lies thickly over the town, and down in the square the old men loll silently. I can smell Oxford, Mississippi, now, 4,000 miles away—a smell compact of flowers and dust and old buildings—and still feel the lazy seduction of its manner.

Indeed, the South is full of pleasant encounters. The poor white, a shambling, ill-jointed, colorless, ungainly figure of a man, gives the region an air of ignorant meanness; but even he has his agreeable side, and when the mountaineers go square dancing they make a gay company. I remember an evening of square dancing in the streets of Chattanooga, Tennessee, in the Middle South. The roads were closed to traffic, and a hillbilly band played from the back of a truck. In the dim lights of the street lamps the dancers looked like sinewy leprechauns in check shirts and flounced skirts, prancing with an infectious abandon. They danced till late at night, and then piled into their disjointed trucks to drive back to shambling villages and isolated poor broken farmhouses, with mules and water wells, or to dirty wooden cabins hidden away in the hills.

In another kind, I recall with affection the crusty bachelor who lives alone at the mansion of Longwood, outside Natchez, Mississippi. Natchez, once a lawless river port, famous for thieves and gamblers and horse traders, has acquired an excessive Southern fragility because of its many well-preserved old houses (old, that is, by the standards of the inland South; they are mostly early nineteenth century, and, despite the hushed pride of the local ladies, are furnished much as our grandmothers' houses were furnished in England). The regional myth is thus powerful here. Racial animosities are especially bitter, and many people (seeing themselves, perhaps, as present-day O'Haras) proclaim a pride in poverty. Longwood is the oddest of the mansions of Natchez. It was begun shortly before the Civil War, a wild architectural extravaganza, octagonal, topped with a dome, surrounded by balconies. Northern workmen were brought in to work on it, but soon after the war began they were withdrawn; they dropped their tools and left. Leaving the house unfinished; and unfinished it remains, with their hammers and wheelbarrows and paint pots still lying about, with ladders propped against walls, and scaffolding still in place, exactly as they left it. It stands in a wooded garden, a grotesque monument of "steamboat Gothic," its glassless windows gaping, on its porch a dusty and disintegrating barouche.

Only the ground floor of Longwood is inhabitable, and in it there lives a Mr. John Price, white-haired and near-sighted, who is always ready to show visitors around, only excusing himself when they want to climb up the workmen's ladders and see the upper floors. Mr. Price lives alone, attended by an elderly Negro woman who inhabits an outhouse (specifically the *garçonnière*, where the intending proprietor of Longwood proposed to house his sons, in the old French manner). He once gave us an admirable lunch. This was a feat, for he seems normally to live entirely upon marshmallows and fig rolls, and his servant is no great cook. However, a jolly cousin of his (very active in the ladies' activities of Natchez) came in to do the cooking, and the results were capital. Mr. Price had no tablecloth handy, but a sheet on the table served just as well; and we ate Southern fried chicken, in enormous quantities, and blancmange and cheese; finishing with either fig rolls or marshmallow, I forget which. I dare say that in the minds of these delightful Southerners there were latent prejudices that would have horrified me; but they never protruded. Instead, as we ate, the room was filled with good things of the South; much laughter, and pungent conversation; audacious gossip; talk of steamboats, and gamblers and country balls; the smell of well-cooked food; and charm of a rather fey kind (inherited, surely, from the early Scots-Irish laboring immigrants rather than the little band of English aristocrats with which every Southerner likes to claim kinship).

As for the country Negroes, they seem identical still with those pictured in old prints of the slave-owning times; still toiling half-naked in the fields, still addicted to color and gaudy ornaments, still full of song, still ignorant and unorganized; a people of bondage, infinitely pitiful. They look like well-trained domestic animals as they board the buses, confined to the back seats, sitting blankly by the windows with their parcels on their laps; and often, when the drink is in them, they develop an animal ferocity. Few of them appear to think deeply about their social status, but they reflect it often enough in a sad apathy. I talked once with a Negro farmer in Alabama, and asked him if things were getting any better for the colored people. "Things ain't gettin' no better, suh," he said, "and things ain't gettin' no worse. They jess stay the same. Things can't ever get no better for the colored people, not so long as we stay down here." He was not so badly off, though. He owned his few acres of land, and lived in his own house. He had two mules. But he seemed incapable of ambition or aspiration, and his two sons had left him, and gone off to Chicago in an old car, to work out their salvation among its slums and rubbish. Another farmer I met seemed to think I was representing some political group, perhaps the Communist party, which has been active in the South. "We can't change things down here by ourselves," he said, and added with an unpleasantly suggestive leer: "Not by ourselves, that is, not without people to help us." He was surrounded by a swarm of children as he spoke; poor little creatures, they were very scabrous pickaninnies, and badly needed some soap behind the ears.

The Southern Negro still retains his traditional gaiety, all the same, whether expressed in riotous jazz in the New Orleans bar, or in the flashing smile of a train conductor. My wife and I once took a middle-aged Negro woman to the zoo at Jackson, Mississippi; she viewed every animal with hand-clapping delight, as pleased with the elephant as she was with the alligator, eating a messy ice cream as she wandered, in a blue floral dress and a hat with a feather in it. Another old Negro woman, encountered on the edge of a swamp in Louisiana, was fishing in the oozy water with a long home-cut rod. She had already caught a few fish, and they were floundering in the shallows tied up in a net. She told me she had been dropped there that morning from the train, which passed nearby; her husband worked on the railroads, and in the evening, when the train came back again, it would slow down past the swamp and allow her to scramble aboard a freight car with her rod and her net of fish, clutching her enormous floppy straw hat. She asked me to drive a little way down the road and fetch some Coca-Cola. I bought her four bottles, and she seemed well satisfied; the last I saw of her, she was standing on the boggy bank with the rod in one hand and a bottle raised to her lips with the other; a portly, statuesque figure against a gloomy background of cypress trees.

For me, the temper of the deep South is best exemplified by the city of Memphis, on the Mississippi River. It is a sprawling place with a business district of assertive skyscrapers and a fine promenade along the river; and it is alive with the familiar associations of the South. Here W. C. Handy wrote the Memphis Blues. He is honored by a shabby little park in the Negro district. All around it the black people move with loose-limbed grace, through dirty streets full of pawnbrokers and rooming houses and cheap clothing stores, with pictures of Negro actresses in their windows. Cotton, the master crop of the Old South, rules Memphis still. Here are the offices of the great cotton brokers, and you can see bales of the stuff lying outside their doors. One of the big hotels is called the King Cotton. There is violent racial feeling in Memphis, and much political chicanrey; when I was there E. H. Crump, most famous of the "bosses," was still in power, a funny old man with a wizened face and a wide-brimmed hat, who liked going to football matches; at election time one was offered a list of candidates "approved by Mr. Crump."

There was a battle of Memphis in the Civil War, and a naval engagement on the river, watched by huge crowds lining the banks. You can hardly escape the river there, for it bounds the business section, and there are always towboats passing by and hooters sounding; "river rats," shanty men, and the like live along its banks (until recently there was one slovenly shack dweller who had an Oxford degree and talked, in his cloaca, in an impeccable English accent). Memphis has its share of Southern high spirits, too; the Cotton Carnival, held annually in May, is the least inhibited of American festivals. In the lobby of one of the hotels five ducks live comfortably in an ornamental fountain; each evening they waddle in file into a passenger lift and are taken up to the roof for the night.

Memphis is heavy with prejudice and poverty, but buoyant with a primitive gusto. For many people in several states it represents the lights and the music, excitement, opportunity, grace, culture, fun; they marvel at its flashing signs, its cool riverside parks, its hint of elegance and friendly charm; and indeed, seen at night across the dismal dust of the cotton fields, or from the steps of some miserable one-roomed hovel, it seems to very embodiment of the fabled Southern flavor.

Dey den made Dixie trim and nice,
And Adam called it "Paradise."
Look away! look away! look away! Dixie land!

↻ 8. ↺

The Rebel Yell

HAT a wonderful country it would be were it not for schism and defeat! It has so omnivorous a capacity for enjoyment; so many beauties of manner and design; such haunting memories (not all of them bogus) of gallantries and delicacies. Charleston sums up this tragedy of the South. It is a lovely city, warm and graceful; but over it hangs a pall of obsession, distorting thoughts, and perverting motives, turning almost every conversation into a rude clash of prejudices. The mind of educated Charleston is dominated first by the endless conceits of pedigree; secondly (and more horribly) by the task of maintaining total white supremacy. Just as there is no snob quite like a Charleston snob, so no shiftless cracker from the Tennessee hills has more hate and bilious spleen in his system than the well-bred ladies who live in Charleston's mansions. "Death on the Atlantic," they used to call the city; and, though the economic basis for the insult has disintegrated, there is still the sick aroma of a mausoleum about its virulence.

Charleston is a colonial seaport, marvelously preserved, with its predominant flavor of seamen and pirates enriched by overtones of aristocratic society. The fabled Southern gentleman of old, of distinguished European lineage, was a rare bird, and many a Southerner who speaks of the ancestral place in England may have been persuaded, over the generations, into mendacity. Charleston is one place, however, where English gentlemen settlers flourished. They filled it with delicate ironwork and high-walled gardens, narrow streets and handsome doorways, steeples, shutters, and tall brick chimneys. Its houses, cool and reserved, are related to the plantation houses of the West Indies. They are often built at right angles to the road, facing a shady garden, and each story has its own pillared balcony (called a *piazza* in Charleston). This arrangement gives them an enchanted air of mingled mystery and invitation, as if unnamed delights are to be found behind the high brick walls of the garden or among the shadows of the *piazza*. Charleston is full of such innuendoes. It is a place of narrow lanes, with swinging lights and crumbling corners; of old taverns where sailors do their drinking; of shutters, dark squares, and squeaky staircases. The climate of Charleston is semitropical, and everywhere there are palm trees and bougainvillea and flaring Southern flowers. In the balmy summer evenings people move about the streets with unhurried calm, or sip cool drinks from frosted glasses in their shaded balconies, or stroll through their gardens chatting.

The nostalgic past still colors the streets of this wonderful old city. There is the slave market, Gothically turreted, with the buildings where the slaves were housed during their days in the hands of the brokers. (Most of the South Carolina planters refused to engage in the slave trade, says one of the Charleston guidebooks virtuously; but "no doubt there were merchants in Charleston who did.") At the City Market the Negroes, in straw hats, gaudy skirts, and headscarves, still congregate each day to sell avocados, fish, and vegetables. If you stand and listen to them you may hear snatches of the strange language. The Gullah Negroes, from the islands south of Charleston, have a language of their own, described by some etymologists as the worst English in the world, and containing both antique English and African elements. Their children are still given such barbaric names as Bambula, Ishi, Asigbe, and Momo, and their speech is a baffling jumble of contorted sounds. The Gullahs are strong, rawboned people, most amiable and courteous. Isolated for centuries on their little sea islands, they have developed a distinctive culture, with strange music and folk tales, and a firm independence of outlook.

There is a house in Charleston, a modest place with gables, where Blackbeard the pirate is said to have made his headquarters; once he lay off Charleston for nearly a week, and captured eight ships coming in and out of the harbor. Many famous pirates were hanged in Charleston in those brave eighteenth-century days, their execution processions headed by a man carrying a silver oar, their bodies buried in a shoal offshore, just above the low-water mark. A fine old theater is still active, and adjoining it is the Planter's Hotel, where planter's punch was allegedly invented. Not far outside the town, hidden in a little clump of trees, is a tiny chapel, for all the world like an English country church, left behind from the days of English hegemony. It has the arms of the Stuarts inside it, and the tombs of many an English worthy, and the smell of hassocks and prayer books; an old Negro woman with an itching palm is its caretaker, living in a small house beyond the churchyard (all gray headstones and flowery inscriptions) and once a year they hold a service there, attended by some churchgoers of habit, and many Charlestonians anxious to reassert their connections with the English nobility.

For these claims of ancient pedigree are dear, indeed, to the hearts of Charleston. This city once had its own orders of nobility, the grades of chivalry being barons, caciques, and landgraves; an exotic device instituted by the original Lords Proprietors on the advice of John Locke. But the resulting social partitions seem to have largely dissolved, and snobbery in Charleston concerns itself with still more distant honors; with English dukedoms and baronies, even sometimes with royalty itself. The Southern myth, of course, demands lengthy lineage no less than polished manners (though not a few planters will admit that their life, even in the spacious days, was a good deal nearer the soil than the propagators of legend will allow). Your hostess at dinner in Charleston, you may be sure, will soon be telling you of the moated castle in which her ancestors lived and died, of the battles they fought for the English crown, of the glories of feudalism and heraldry, some substantial echo of which they brought with them when they came to America. Do not laugh at her pretensions. It was partly the conviction of unshakable universal gentlemanliness, of unquestionable social superiority, which enabled the South to fight with such scornful brilliance in the Civil War; and it is the concomitant of this settled belief, the associated chivalry (involving honor and flourishing generosity and the flower of Southern womanhood) that still gives the South its pungent charm.

Soon enough, in any case, the conversation will move away from genealogy (unimpeachable beginnings having been emphatically established). Wherever you are in the South, and however you struggle to prevent the approaching clatter of prejudices, sooner or later the talk turns to the problem of the Negro; and nowhere more readily or more virulently than in Charleston. I was new to the game when I was there and I found the attitude of my hosts profoundly disconcerting. Their basic postulant was, of course, that the white man was intrinsically superior to the black; that his position of authority and organizing privilege must be maintained; and that there must therefore be strict barriers between the races, to be enforced by measures of total segregation. But upon this plank they erected a monstrous structure of logic and fantasy, of perversions and half-truths and distorted conclusions; drawing upon wildly disparate sources for their illustrations; plunging into arguments Christian and pagan, personal and political, ethnical, historical, biological, Mendelian, Darwinian, Hitlerian.

"It's no good trying to help the nigrahs," they will say. "They're incapable of progress. Anyway, they want segregation themselves, just as much as we do; they've been brought up with it, haven't they?"

"Politically conscious nigrahs? There are a few, and the fewer the better. They're exceptions, anyway, you can't quote them. They may suffer, certainly, but we can't help that; they're only a minority, and they've themselves to blame."

"Don't you realize that the whites will soon be outnumbered in the South? We have to preserve ourselves—there's a morality in self-preservation. Anyway, the nigrahs can never run the place—they're congenitally incapable of it. They've never produced a single genius."

"Class counts, you know. Do you think it's a coincidence that Churchill's descended from dukes? (My own forebears were associated with the Marlboroughs, you know. Did I tell you?) They're scarcely human, the nigrahs, you don't realize. Anyway, we always looked after them; in the old days they were like members of the family. I loved my old mammy dearly. You people don't realize how kindly the Old South treated its slaves."

"Obviously we can't mix socially with the nigrahs. It's common sense. How would you feel if you lived here, with nigrahs everywhere, and more of them every year, and soon we'll be outnumbered? I put it to you: *How would you feel if your daughter married a nigrah?*"

This last is the operative question, the culmination of every such perilous discussion (the whole conversation, of course, is informed with a rumbling danger, so that you feel, as you parry and counter, as if you are tampering with explosives, or walking a loose tightrope). It is asked, perhaps, a little more often by women than by men; for though the ideal of unblemished Southern womanhood, the quintessence of purity, was established by the Southern male, nevertheless it is undeniable that a large proportion of Southern Negroes have white blood in them; and for this we may blame the gallant Southern gentlemen (if we feel inclined to blame anybody) rather than his delicate wife, hampered by convention as by crinoline. Perhaps, indeed, the womanhood cult was established by Southerners as a deliberate penance, or camouflage, for their lascivious tendencies. It was certainly more than a casual expression of temperament. "Woman!!!" began the toast at a Southern dinner to celebrate the centenary of Georgia. "The center and circumference, diameter and periphery, sine, tangent and secant of all our affections!"

Alas! However much you sympathize with some tenets of the Southern argument, before the evening is over you feel the tightrope loosening more, and the powder keg growing ominously warm. Your Charleston hosts are unlikely to be abusive, however strongly they disagree with you; indeed, to the end they will ply you wholeheartedly with food and drink, and intersperse their diatribes with witty asides, and conduct differences with an easy humor; but gradually there will creep into their talk the suspicion of insult, so subtle that at first you will not notice it; an insidious *basso profundo* that will sound clearer when you recall the conversation the next morning. The Southerner is a master of the acrid inference, believing in the theory that a gentleman is never unintentionally rude. If your dress is a little crumpled, your hostess, some time during the evening, will be heard enumerating the delights of England: "Oh hunting, my dear, and green fields, and lovely old houses, and really good tea, and the simply immaculate turnout of English gentlewomen! How it's managed I just don't know!" If your origins are suspect, there will be an innuendo, no more, about the universal stamp of the *bourgeois*. If you happen to live in Nashville, Tennessee, it will be faintly intimated that most of the gathering has never heard of the place. If you are a Yankee from anywhere, you may hear, buried away in a heap of calculated comment, the faint, sharp, bitter echo of the Southern rebel yell.

I am sure that as the Negro slowly advances to equality, and as the memories of the war recede, the South will lose its festering stratum of resentment; the gaiety of its spirit, inherited from frontiersmen, and Negroes will eventually triumph, encouraged by new prosperity; the raucous clamors of snobbery will mellow, and become no more than that faintly eccentric interest in family trees and place names common among elderly Englishmen; and Charleston will one day enjoy the tranquility of spirit it deserves, unharassed by complexes and prejudices. But when I was there the old South was still struggling in defeat, desperately aware of the world's opinion, clinging to old mores and ways of thought, resentful of criticism, testy and paranoically rigid of view. It is pitiful that a country so full of delight should be so racked and tainted by disease.

∾ **9.** ∾

Jerks and Serpents

HE MOST primitive white people in all America, infinitely nearer the trees than any rural ancient in England, are the mountaineers of Kentucky and Tennessee, a peasantry of the hills which has never totally accepted authority, and which manages to remain a shuttered society tucked away in remote country corners. These folk still consider taxation a wicked alien imposition, distill their own moonshine whisky in defiance of local prohibition laws, and sometimes speak an archaic Scots-Elizabethan dialect; their raggedy children run barefoot about their cabins on the hillsides, and often and again there comes news that one horny mountaineer has disintegrated another with a blast from his shotgun. When I was staying in Lookout Mountain, on the border between Georgia and Tennessee, I saw a good deal of these people, for many of them live quite close to a luxurious suburb that has been built on top of the mountain; and you could scarcely escape experiencing, in one way or another, the extraordinarily earthy force of their religion, a force that pervades the whole of the South, but is to be found in its most curious forms among these simple and conservative countrymen.

One evening my wife and I were driving down a road on the out-skirts of Chattanooga when we saw, pitched beside the pavement, a dirty marquee; from it there came strains of music, played on a tinny piano and a guitar, with accompanying desultory snatches of women's voices. We stopped at once and went inside. At the end of the tent, on stage, so to speak, a very fat woman was lying on the ground quivering and shaking, sometimes tremulously, like a jelly, sometimes with sharp stabs of impulsive movement. Her dress was pulled up above her fleshy knees, sweat was on her forehead, a black hat was lying crumpled beside her, and she was breathing noisily. Two other women, wearing expressions of fanatical intensity, were supporting her head, and standing above them, waving his arms like a Paganini, prancing here and there crazily, now and then pushing back his streaming hair with dirty-nailed fingers, was a young man holding a guitar. In the background a little black girl, aged about ten, was banging a hymn tune on an upright piano, and a small group of Negro women, respectably dressed, looking a trifle bored, and some-times pausing to exchange gossip or look out of the tent flap, was halfheartedly singing some unlikely words.

The Lord is my brethern, my brethern is he;
Alone in the storm of the rage of the sea
I'll never go hungry or know poverty
So long as the good Lord is marching with me.
Marching with me! Marching with thee!
So long as the good Lord is marching with me!

Occasionally the young man would strum a few chords on his guitar and join in, his voice rasping and penetrative, and soon the prostrate woman, with heavings and convulsions and agonized writhing, tried to gasp a few words herself, rather as the dying man at the end of one of Poe's more terrifying stories wheezed a last phrase before dissolving into pulp. The two attendant women were galvanized. Seizing the patient (if that is the right word) by the front of her dress, they yanked her into a sitting position, and hissed urgent instructions into her ear. She was still jerking incessantly, sometimes falling sideways, to be pushed upright again, sometimes caught in mid-air as she fell backwards. "Take Him in! Take Him in! Oh Jesus! The glory of it! Rolling, rolling, rolling! Glory, glory, glory! Jesus, Jesus! Take Him in, oh! glory Jesus! Rolling, rolling, rolling!" Round and round danced the demoniac guitarist. On and on went the hymn, balefully; clang, clang sounded the old piano. The woman on the floor threw her body, as if in some hellish trance, into even more violent convulsions. "Take Him in! oh, rolling, rolling, rolling! Glory!"

There were rows of chairs in the body of the tent, and a few people were sitting in them silently, not together, but dotted about in the shadows. In front of me a middle-aged man was supporting a woman who was still jerking spasmodically from some earlier experience. A mother, gazing blankly and open mouthed at the spectacle, had with her two children, a small girl who sat on her chair sucking her thumb, and a boy who had reached that stage of squirming sordidness peculiar to children nearing exhaustion. A stout, sensible-looking man near the entrance to the tent told me that we were witnessing a session of Holy Rollers, a sect (he thought, he was not sure) affiliated to the Church of God. This strange church is indigenous to the South. It began as a group of fundamentalists who broke away from the existing nonconformist churches because they were losing the uninhibited emotionalism of the frontier times, and becoming more formal in their modes of worship. In Tennessee there are innumerable such dissident sects, calling themselves Pentecostal Churches, or Holiness Chapels, or a host of other grandiose titles; but the chief ones banded together to become the Church of God. It flourished, and achieved (relatively speaking) some intellectual maturity, founding a theological college at Cleveland, Tennessee. Though it had no ordained clergy, and believed in some odd manifestations of the Divine purpose, it acquired a status of local dignity. But alas! there were differences within the hierarchy, and before long there was a sprout of little, disagreeing Churches of God: the Church of God (Tomlinson); the (Original) Church of God, and the Church of God With Signs Following After.

The one whose ceremonies we were watching expounded the sacred significance of "the jerks"—the convulsions, voluntary and induced, which racked the woman on the floor. She evidently suffered from some disease, and believed that if the spirit entered into her (manifesting itself in jumps, jerks, falling, rolling, the wringing of hands and gibberish) it would be cured. "And they were all filled with the Holy Ghost," says the Acts of the Apostles of the day of Pentecost, "and began to speak with other tongues, as the Spirit gave them utterance." The followers of "the old religion," as these strange cults are familiarly called, believe that some of their number have acquired the understanding of unknown languages; and sure enough, as the hours passed, there crept into the insistent cries of the attendant women some words without meaning. Soon it was pouring out in floods from their mouths, a wild flow of words, like Romany or Lear; and occasionally even the patient herself, jerking and jumping, managed to croak from her constricted throat a few totally unintelligible syllables. ("These men are full of new wine," said the mocking doubters of Jerusalem.) When we left the marquee she was still unhealed. The guitarist still whirled about her; the piano still tinnily clanged; the choristers, their great brown and white eyes rolling around the tent, still whined their listless hymn; the little boy still crawled slimily over the chairs, on and off his mother's lap; and the poor convulsed patient, all her draperies loose by now, was still urged to "let Him in, sister! Glory, glory, roll it, roll it!" by the demon women at her side.

Some of the mountain religions are even more strikingly close to the grass roots of Christianity. I remember standing in the garden of a gentle Southerner who has built his house on the sheer side of Lookout Mountain, where it runs away down to Georgia and Alabama. We were waiting for the sun to set, for he has a theory that if you look at Jupiter backwards, through a mirror, you can see her moons with the naked eye. The view was splendid. Below us, in the valley, the high road ran southward to Atlanta; beyond it rose another range of hills, and another, wooded and kindly, with a little clearing here and there and a white farmhouse, or a cabin with its smallholding; and to our left the great rib of Lookout Mountain stretched into the distance. We stood on the precipitous edge of the garden, hoping to see a fox or a badger in the woods below, and my host said: "Ah have lived in this region all mah life, but ah can never accustom myself to the idea that some of mah neighbors are snake-worshippers."

He was exaggerating a little, I learned on pressing inquiries (a gift for stretching the facts being one of the more endearing Southern failings), but not too much. Not very far away, at the hamlet of Grasshopper, Tennessee, there had originated a sect which based its beliefs upon the last verses of the Gospel according to Saint Mark: "And these signs shall follow them that believe: In my name shall they cast out devils; they shall speak with new tongues; they shall take up serpents; and if they drink any deadly thing, it shall not hurt them; they shall lay hands on the sick, and they shall recover." Believing these words to be an injunction as well as a prophecy, members of the Church of God With Signs Following After make practice of handling rattlesnakes during their services. Often they are bitten, sometimes fatally, but though the custom is now illegal in Tennessee it persists widely and more or less openly. Now and again there is a news item about a particularly severe case of biting; occasionally some faded holy man appears in court; but in general it is tacitly accepted as "something that happens on the mountain." I was directed to a church, secluded among the woods, where I was told I could see this thing (the element of the circus about it, I must admit, drawing me more magnetically than any theological implications); but the place was deserted when I reached it, and a farmer sitting on the porch of a nearby shack only murmured incoherently when I asked him for advice. Such esoteric rites, though, were never far away from life on Lookout Mountain; I remember one elderly carpenter, himself an elder or preacher, prophet or evangelist, I forget which, remarking to me quite casually as he did some sandpapering: "I was brought up with the jerks, and the talking with tongues, but I don't hold with the serpents."

Even the more orthodox worshippers of the Bible Belt sometimes express their devotion strangely. I spent an Easter Day in the region of Chattanooga, and wandered about during its sunny morning observing the celebrations. For many weeks people had been preparing for Easter in one way or another. The garages were full of cars being washed (for it is a matter of social prestige to drive a shining car to Easter Communion). The shops were full of excited women; the telephones were always engaged, it being a season of invitations; from every Bunny, the American secular symbol of the festival.

Noisy evangelism dominated the radio programs, but there was still time for a few such songs as "I was riding to Chapel on Easter Morning…when I saw the cutest Easter parade." When I visited the cable office to send a telegram, I was nicely asked if I would care to send an Easter Bunnygram instead; several suitable messages were suggested, a typical one being: "The Easter Bunny is on his way—So be a good little boy (girl) every day." The city of Chattanooga was alive with activity from earliest morning. At sunrise there was a mass evangelical meeting, attended by a brigade of clerics, the Governor of Tennessee, and trumpeters who greeted the sunrise with a fanfare. By mid-morning the streets were thronged with churchgoers of many denominations. Bright convertibles hurried through the sunshine, father driving in a gray suite with a carnation buttonhole, mother clutching her picture hat, Sis in a very flouncy party dress, Junior being scolded for leaning out of the car. Negro families were as bright as peacocks in smiles and fripperies, and innumerable small boys of some unidentified youth group marched about the place in white ducks and blue tunics. Sitting in a car outside the courthouse I saw a young Negro, looking extremely worried, listening to a threatening sermon (all hellfire and penitence) on the radio. Almost everybody seemed to be going to church; leaving only a few faithless, in grubby shirts or flowered housecoats, reading the Sunday papers on the porches of their homes.

I drove out of the town toward the Georgia border, and before long stopped at a small white wooden Baptist church on a ridge. It was a sunny day, and the door of the church was open. Outside a few boys were playing about in the dust with sticks; through the door I glimpsed a pastiche of open-necked shirts and headscarves, baggy trousers, and garish cotton frocks from country stores. A very slow and tuneless hymn was being sung. A few members of the congregation stirred as I put my head diffidently around the doorpost; I caught the eye of a red-haired girl of a sluggish aspect, still mouthing the words of the hymn as she stared, but so unaccountably enthralled by my arrival that the voice faded from her throat. She nudged her husband, who whispered to an old man holding a large hymn book to the level of his eyes, who turned around with a great clattering of feet and wheezing; and presently a space was cleared for me on a bench near the back of the church. The congregation was constantly in motion. There were many young mothers with children, and whenever a baby began to cry it was carried out of the church; so that before long, out in the sunny road, there were numbers of women strolling up and down, dressed in their fineries, crooning to their babies. Now and again a couple of men went out for a breath of fresh air, or some latecomer pushed his way in with heavily whispered greetings and some muted badinage. The church was hot and airless.

The order of service was complicated. A number of elderly men with grave faces took it in turn to read lessons or deliver impassioned impromptu sermons. They were called to these duties by a man who was evidently the pastor; he was fat and perspiring, dressed in a gray double-breasted suit with a garish tie, and holding perpetually under his arm a book which, by its binding and deportment, could only be of utter sanctity. He stood expansively in the middle of a raised platform at the end of the church, ushering elder after elder to the rostrum with reverent gestures. Sometimes he made an appeal for some worthy cause ("Can you sit and see, brethren and sisters, sit and see these little ones suffer? Think again, my friends think again, dear brethren, and deliver unto us some trifle, some poor offering, some widow's mite for the Society for the Protection of Orphans of the Storm.") Sometimes he threatened those who did not regularly attend church, and on these occasions I sometimes thought the dread fire of his eye landed directly on me. "There may be some among you, my friends, I make no accusations, I say unto no one 'Thou art fit for hell-fire,' but I say again, brethren, there may be among you, here among us today, here in this sacred edifice, among these hearts lifted unto the Lord, some sinner, some poor wicked sinner, who does not come each Sabbath Day unto this edifice to offer praise and thanksgiving with us. If there be such, my friends, I say unto him, 'Brother, the sun doth not shine so hotly— nor the winds blow so cruelly—nor the ice freeze so cold—as the everlasting torments which thou art storing up for thyself in the everlasting awful halls of perpetual damnation!'"

Hymn followed hymn, and gradually I sensed among the worshippers a growing intensity of devotion. An old bespectacled farmer stood alone at the rostrum to sing an unaccompanied hymn, and during the performance some of the massed elders began to interrupt him with mournful shouts of "Amen, amen! Glory be! Amen!" These interpolations grew more frequent during the succeeding hymns, and soon the whole congregation (barring a few totally insensible yokels) seemed gripped by some undefined passion, and stood singing the hymns with a strange tenseness. Four young men with a banjo sang a long Easter hymn, *molto adagio*, and during this the elders fostered in themselves a regular frenzy of devotion. From all corners of the room there now came deep-throated "Amens!" with supplication, ejaculations, cries of joy and despair and awful imprecations. "Oh yes, Lord! That's right, Lord! Jesus, Jesus! Ah glory be to the Lord! Yes! Oh, oh, save us, glory be! O Lord save us miserable sinners! Oh, the hell-fire! Must we be condemned, Lord! Oh, no, glory be! The hell-fire! Glory be! Save us, save us! They shall be cast into the darkness of the pit! Hallelujah! Hallelujah, hallelujah, hallelujah, glory, glory, glory, glory be!!! Amen! Yes, Lord, glory be, amen, miserable sinners!"

By now the scene was one of general confusion. Everywhere men were raising their arms to the heavens, or clutching at their hair with both hands. Around me people were swaying from side to side, muttering snatches of prayer, or suddenly bursting into ear splitting yells of "Glory!! Glory be!!!" The pastor strode between the ranks of his flock, the book still under his arm, alternately denouncing and beseeching its members. "Oh, you poor miserable brethren, poor suffering sheep, repent, repent! My friends, come with me and repent! Come to the altar! The fires of everlasting perpetual hell will be upon you forever and ever! The flames of the inferno will lick you, my brethren! Oh, you sinners, you wicked children of sin, it is not to late. No! Come to the altar! Will you come, my friends? Will you come? Ah, salvation! Come, my friends, miserable sinners!" At the end of the church the quartet was now singing a syncopated hymn, to the strumming accompaniment of the banjo. Now and then, through the babel, I could hear some of its words:

I'd rather be a beggar and live
In a shack beside the road
Than lay up treasure without
Arranging for a future abode.

The minister shouted harder and more furiously, and eventually one or two elderly men, shaking with emotion, staggered out of their benches and threw themselves on the floor. Others followed, and soon from all parts of the church groups of quivering worshippers were moving toward the front, to hurl themselves out of my sight beyond the benches. The pastor swirled around them, shrieking commands and entreaties; the tears were streaming down his cheeks. A number of women were sobbing helplessly, and large numbers of children were screaming, and the strident cries of the elders filled the church.

At once deafened and bewitched, I left the building in a kind of blasted trance, and stood for a moment on the steps. A small boy who had been kicking stones about the road approached me with the information that, according to his mother, the pastor was a genuine saint; that he lived in the mountains and drove twenty miles to the church every Sunday; and that his grandfather was a full-blooded Cherokee Indian. I thanked him, and drove away down the country road, pursued by the raucous cacophony from the church; the faint earnest voices of the singers, the thump-thump of the tireless piano, and an occasional penetrating "Hallelujah, Lord! Glory, glory be!!"

In every hamlet and prosperous suburb, as I traveled back to Chattanooga through the sunshine, the churchgoers were on the move again, home to a handsome lunch. Whether, they had echoed the cool formality of an English cathedral, or had screamed their declamations to the Almighty, they went home contented, each in his way. And perhaps nearest to the soul of the South were those determined *yogis*, hidden away in mountain cabins, who had spent their Easter morning among the serpents.

ᗞ 10. ᗜ

The Mississippi

ERVENCY of race and religion has molded the nature of the South; but scarcely less pervasive has been the influence of the Mississippi, in many ways a secret and eccentric river. It is slow, sticky and yellow ("running liquid mud" is how Dickens described it); but also huge and overbearing, powerful in character, aged, laden with memories, sometimes sleepy and placid, sometimes menacing, always rolling and changing its course, full of strange currents and drifts, twisting and tortuous, unpredictable, remote yet always familiar, awful but lovable; like some tough old wayward warrior, sprawling across half a room with a glass of brandy in his hand. The Mississippi and its minion streams drain half a continent, from the Rockies to Pennsylvania and the Gulf of Mexico, and all this water pours down to New Orleans in an endless ooze. The best way to appreciate the grandeur of the process is to stand on the point at Cairo, Illinois, where the Ohio River joins the Mississippi, and to watch the waters from these two masterful rivers combine; the one stream from Kentucky and the mills of Pittsburgh, the other down from the north, from the dairylands of Wisconsin and Minnesota. Or, in an isolated spot in the squalid outskirts of St. Louis, you can watch the muddy waters of the Missouri come in. (There is an allegorical representation of the scene outside the St. Louis railway station, all nudity and dolphins, entitled *The Meeting of the Waters*; but it is strangely difficult to penetrate to the confluence itself.) A score of great rivers contributes to the Mississippi; the Illinois and the Tennessee, the Yazoo, the Arkansas and the North Platte, the Cumberland, the Allegheny and the White River; and their combined water, carrying countless tons of mud, sweeps down the valley to join the Gulf of Mexico near a humid, swampy, mosquito-ridden, desolate Louisiana village called Venice. The lower river lays its own bed, and is constantly changing its course, finding shorter or easier routes to follow, building up bars, banks, and islands, now overrunning its shores with terrible floods, now shifting its way and leaving some perfectly respectable old river town high and dry, an impoverished dowager.

So the places along the banks of the lower Mississippi, where the waywardness of the river is most dangerous, crouch warily beneath high levees. People have been building these protective walls since the Mississippi Valley was first settled (De Soto, in 1542, encountered a Mississippi flood). Sometimes, if you drive along the edge of the river, you will see a rotting, crumbling bank of soil, covered in grass, decidedly archaeological in character, that was built by the French pioneers in the 1700s. But everywhere there are modern levees, too, stout and well constructed, with a dirt track running along the top of them.

You can taste the arid, fascinating flavor of the Mississippi valley by driving along these tracks in the heat of a summer morning. Below on one side of the levee there is likely to be a tumbled mass of foliage, and beyond it, through the trees, you may catch a glimpse of the wide river. On the other side is the immense flat cotton country, stretching away into the distance where the colors blur. There in interminable mathematical rows stand the cotton plants, and sometimes you may see Negroes working in the fields, men and women, with big hats and bright clothes. Here and there, in ordered patterns, are the little shacks they live in, and sometimes away in the distance, surrounded by groves of trees, is the comfortable old house of a plantation owner. The checkerboard of the land is dotted with clouds of dust, marking the passage of a car along unpaved roads. Sometimes the levee track will take you past a river town, with some white frame houses, a dusty main street, and a church or two. There will be a general store (perhaps run by a cotton company) thronged with cheerful Negroes, all smiles and gaudy colors; and an old ship's outfitters, built to supply the Mississippi packets, open fronted, crammed with pans and stoves and hammers, with an old white man smoking his pipe on its broad steps, and a couple of Negro children playing hide and seek around its counters. The scenery varies little from southern Missouri, in the north, to Louisiana in the south; but the binding factor, the thing that makes this country rich, and brought it into being, and causes the little towns to squat so cautiously behind their levees, is the presence of the river; at once life-giving and destructive.

I was flown over the lower Mississippi in a small amphibious aircraft, to see the tremendous engineering problems the river offers, and how the American Army is tackling them. The first difficulty is the Mississippi's perpetual tendency to change its course. From the air it looks like a great brown twisting serpent, so erratic in its route that often a bend in the river nearly forms a circle. Often and again the Mississippi water, finding itself following a wildly circuitous course, decides to do without one of these great horseshoe bends and instead slices a shorter way across the neck of it. Such new channels are called "cutoffs" and a chart of the lower Mississippi is positively littered with them—between 1722 and 1928 twenty-two natural cutoffs occurred. Because of them, several old river ports are now not on the river at all. (One of them, Greenville, left a mile or two from the river by such a movement, has gone to the extent of cutting an artificial channel so that barges can come up to the town.) The old, semicircular river courses sometimes dry up, but sometimes remain as lakes, and very pleasant they can be, if a little muddy, to a traveler hot and tired from the dusty road. In one of them, at Lake Providence, Louisiana, I once saw a tame monkey being taken for a swim; he was a graceless but indomitable diver.

This maddening tendency to wander is now giving the engineers particular cause for worry. In our airplane we flew to a spot not far south of Natchez where a short channel connects the Mississippi with the Atchafalaya River. Through this channel an ever-increasing amount of Mississippi water is flowing into the Atchafalaya, and then running southwards to meet the Gulf of Mexico at a small fishing port called Morgan City. Every year more water goes this way, instead of following the Mississippi proper, and the engineers estimate that unless something is done about it soon, by 1975 or so, the Atchafalaya will be the main stream, and the great port of New Orleans will be on the way to extinction. They are understandably perturbed, and want to build a dam and various other works to prevent the water going the wrong way; but the funds have to come from Congress, and it is difficult to convince a politician that before very long the map of the United States is likely to change itself.

This direction of the stream is a chief preoccupation of the engineers, because if the water flows in a relatively deep and narrow channel it is less likely to spread itself in disastrous floods. Sometimes they create artificial cutoffs, for this reason, and they are always active in dredging the channel and building up the protective embankments. Over the years these levees have been repeatedly heightened, but luckily there is no truth in a popular belief that the bed of the Mississippi is always rising, and the level of the water rises as often as the level of the embankments; however much of the Mississippi wants to wander, the level of its bed remains the same. (It is interesting, though, that the first Federal levees, built in 1882, were only nine feet high, whereas the ones they build today are more than thirty feet high.)

Such protective measures are now designed to take care of the maximum flood believed possible. This is estimated at a flow of 2,450,000 cubic feet per second at Cairo, where the lower Mississippi might be said to begin. Under the existing control plan this water is to be confined by the levees and drawn off into unimportant areas by artificial means. From the aircraft, with the river meandering below us, we could see exactly how this would be done if ever so disastrous a flood occurred. First, 600,000 cubic feet would flow away through the old river, into the useless land in the Louisiana swamps, and eventually down the Atchafalaya. Then, by means of an immense concrete aqueduct, the Morganza Floodway, another 600,000 would also be diverted that way. Finally, embankments would be blown up north of New Orleans, and another 250,000 would rush away across the fields through a prepared channel into Lake Pontchartrain, and thence into the sea; leaving only a harmless 1,250,000 cubic feet to flow down the normal route to Venice and the Gulf.

It sounds simple enough, and from the air it looks simple, but the control of floods on the Mississippi is really one of the greatest of all engineering problems. Not only the main stream, but all the contributory rivers have to be restrained, and there are scores of dams and reservoirs and smaller floodways. To study the effect of the entire scheme, the engineers have built a gigantic model of the whole Mississippi basin to meticulous scale. It is on a site of 800 acres near Jackson, Mississippi, and it portrays the main stream and all its lower tributaries with scrupulous accuracy. Water is pumped down the model channel at a rate of about 1,000 gallons a minute, and its flow at various points is measured by immensely complicated little instruments. They are necessarily complex, for whereas the horizontal scale of the model is 1 to 2,000, the vertical scale is 1 to 100, and the resultant mathematical problems are distinctly above the Higher Certificate level. Any part of the model can be worked alone; that is to say, you can have a flood on the Red River, if you want it, without having one on the Yazoo. This wonderful device has already proved its value. In 1952 there was a big flood on the Missouri River. When the crest of the flood reached Pierre, South Dakota, the engineers introduced a similar crest on the model. They could soon see more or less what was going to happen farther downstream—that a levee would break there, or a revetment must be strengthened somewhere else—and were able to warn the people on the spot in good time. The first excavations for this model were made by German prisoners during the war. The purpose of the work was not explained to them, and at first some of them (led by a distinguished Afrika Korps general) refused to do it on the grounds that it was helping the American war effort. Told that they were beginning a big model of the Mississippi River, they went to work suspiciously, still half convinced that it was all some nuclear or stratospheric subterfuge; but, like the hand that rounded Peter's dome, they built better than they knew.

Besides preventing damage, all this work has done a great deal to help navigation on the river. Almost anywhere on its lower reaches the Mississippi is lined with a narrow wilderness. There are thick trees, with their roots in the water, and tall grasses, jumping insects, the cries of improbable birds, an occasional deer, mosquitoes, brambles, and sometimes a turtle sunning itself on the mud. It is a lonely little jumble, but if you manage to push your way through it, and emerge on the bank of the river itself, you are unlikely to preserve your solitude for long; before an hour is past you will almost certainly hear the distant pounding of engines, and see the long line of a Mississippi tow creeping downstream. The river had become a tremendous industrial artery, and there is a ceaseless flow of traffic on it, winter and summer. Few Americans know how important the Mississippi is to them, for they have been brought up to believe that river traffic was killed by roads and railways, and they think of the Mississippi instinctively in nostalgic terms of stern-wheelers, gamblers, ornate steamboat captains, Huckleberry Finns, and log rafts. It is true that passenger traffic is all but dead (despite many brave attempts to revive it) and there are probably fewer craft on the river than there were in the brassy days—in 1849 there were more than 1,000 packet boats on the Mississippi; but the tonnage carried is immeasurably greater than ever before. There are a few stern-wheelers on the river still, things of dignity, with black funnels belching smoke, and white upperworks, and great paddles churning up the muddy water; but most Mississippi boats are now steam or diesel screw-driven craft, very trim and sturdy, and they push (not pull) enormous loads of modern barges anywhere from Pittsburgh to Texas. These are the boats you will see go by from your vantage point among the brambles. They are powerful and well ended, generally spruce, with company crests emblazoned proudly on their funnels, and radar screens and wireless masts on their superstructures. Sometimes they push a miscellaneous collection of barges, lashed together shapelessly, piled high with coal or yellow sulphur; sometimes a line of "integrated" barges, made to fit each other, and generally containing oil. Occasionally you may see a triple-decker barge, looking rather like a waffle, carrying cars downstream from Detroit.

Sometimes the towboats move mammoth loads, in weight as in length. It is common for a string of barges to be as long as the *Queen Elizabeth*, and such a tow often carries 6,500,000 gallons of oil. The heaviest tow recorded was pushed by a mighty stern-wheeler, the steamboat *Sprague*, which now lies in honored retirement at Vicksburg, a beloved and familiar personality. On her big day she moved sixty barges, with a deck area of six-and-a-half acres; in them there were 67,307 tons of coal.

All this traffic moves in an unceasing stream from the industrial regions southwards, and from the southern oilfields up to the Middle West. Pittsburgh, on the upper Ohio, is an important river port, and is St. Paul, more than 2,000 miles from the Gulf of Mexico. There is river traffic on the Missouri, the Tennessee, the Allegheny, the Cumberland, and many other famous tributary rivers, and some barges go by canal eastward into Florida, or westward into Texas. A towboat can be 1,000 miles from its home port, and as isolated as any Atlantic liner; for the boats sail inexorably, day and night, never putting in at the river towns they pass, nor picking up passengers at stages nor stopping for wood as the old packets used to, nor delivering the mail to riverside plantations. From the banks of the Mississippi they seem totally cut off from life along its shores, as if they were part of the river, and cognizant of all its moods and manners.

ꙮ 11. ꙮ

Pilot's Progress

ECAUSE I wanted to learn more about these boats, pounding by so head-in-air, I stood alone one hot summer Southern evening at a landing stage on the banks of the Mississippi. I had arranged a passage on the towboat *White Gold*, and the landing stage had been arranged as a rendezvous, where a motorboat from the tow would pick me up. The stage was on a subsidiary channel of the Mississippi, and in the distance I could see the occasional light of a craft on the river proper. Behind me, on a bluff, the town of Vicksburg was all asleep, and usually there were only the noises of shunting trains and mosquitoes. Once a tug came close past me on the channel, its engines thudding; there were a few dim lights on its bridge, and a couple of shadowy figures, and I could hear muffled and desultory voices. Presently, away over the bluffs, I saw the repeated flash of a searchlight, and heard the distant beat of diesels; and soon my motorboat arrived out of the darkness, with a cloud of spray. Two jolly deckhands heaved my luggage aboard, there was a roar of motors, and we were away, scudding down to the river, with the man at the wheel shouting at me: "Cap'n says sorry we're late, we got held up at Natchez, he reckons we'll make it up between here and Greenville."

The Mississippi at night is the very quintessence of blackness. The tangled jungle banks are all black, and so is the water, and only occasionally could we see looming past the motorboat a floating trunk or a mass of jumbled branches. We kept our eyes on the flashing searchlight, though, and soon made out the long dark line of the barges. The *White Gold* was bound for Chicago from Louisiana, with a cargo of oil, and she had an integrated tow of five barges. As she approached, we swung around in a great arc to run alongside her. The motorboat's engines were cut off, a hoist lifted us out of the water, and a moment later we stood on one of the barges, still sweeping through the water, with the sound of slapping waves, and the lights of the towboat's pilothouse far astern. Such clandestine embarkations are often arranged, for crewmen who have to go ashore for emergencies, and join the tow again later on its voyage; or for the rare stranger who manages, despite the death of the passenger packets, to contrive a Mississippi passage.

There is (as I had suspected) a quality of supreme remoteness about the life aboard a Mississippi towboat. Hour after hour, day after day the silent banks slip by, with scarcely a sign of life on them; and you feel entirely separate from affairs behind the levees. Gradually the river encloses you, and when you pass a river town you examine it as you might a picture show, or a toy town, or something in a museum. There is something hypnotic about such an experience. From the glass windows of the pilothouse the yellow oozy water seems to stretch away endlessly. The sun is scorching and the sky cloudless, so that the decks of the barges shimmer, and the bare backs of the deckhands shine. Only rarely do you glimpse an old merchant town through a gap in the levee; a long hot main street, a few Negroes lounging on the pavement, a mule and buggy kicking up the dust. Sometimes, down by the water there is a crooked shanty boat, swarming with children, with a suntanned old philosopher idling his days away on its balcony. More often there is nothing at all but the merciless sun, the river, and the dark and desolate wooded banks.

In the pilothouse, though, there is always an underlying sense of tension, for navigating a Mississippi boat is still one of the most exacting tasks in the world. The master and pilot of the *White Gold* was Captain Robert Shelton. He was twenty-seven, and characteristic of the modern breed of Mississippi pilots. The modern towboat does not have a wheel, but instead a light touch on a polished metal bar steers the tow; and there Shelton would sit, one hand on this lever, his feet on a ledge in front of him, talking easily of anything from Tennessee Williams to French politics, sipping coffee brought at very frequent intervals by a willing deckhand, but always with a keen eye on the river and its banks. The Mississippi pilot still has to know more than any man has the right to know (as Mark Twain put it). Every foot of river and bank must be familiar to him, and he must recognize it in an instant. It is constantly altering, never looking the same twice, and he must notice any change instinctively and summon at once the necessary reflexes. He must know the name of every light on the riverbank, anywhere from New Orleans to Pittsburgh. He must know where to find slack water in the treacherous currents, where to sail in midstream and where to hug the banks (festooned with wild tree trunks). He must foresee a thousand and one perilous tricks of the river. He is utterly responsible for the towboat and its valuable cargo, night and day, often half a continent and several weeks from home. The good pilot is handsomely paid, and he is never unemployed; if he leaves one company, within a day or two there will be others bidding for his services. The days of the old gaudy steamboat pilots are over, and Shelton (whose grandfather was one of them) sometimes regrets those times of silk hats, diamond pins, embroidered waistcoats, and kid gloves; but the Mississippi pilot is a man of stature still.

It is queer to spend a morning in a towboat's pilothouse, for though you feel very much alone with the waters, to the pilot every moment brings some familiar landmark into view. Here we come up to Opossum Chute, where Joe Daniels ran his tow on a sand bar.

There's the light on Sarah Island, above Poverty Point. See that channel there? That's Bunch's Cutoff, where the river used to run up to Pilcher's Point Landing. There's the 575-mile mark. Over that bluff's where a town called Napoleon used to be, a big town in Mark Twain's time, 30,000 people or more, but it died when the river changed and made this cutoff. (*More coffee, Joe!*) Sometimes a tow will pass in the opposite direction, and the pilot is almost sure to know it. There well be an exchange of blasts on the sirens, and a deckhand will wave lethargically. Sometimes there will be a call on the radio, from another world: "Bob? Bob, you'd oblige me by calling on Ted Harris, when you get to Chicago, and tell him we fixed what he wanted, like he asked. O.K.? How's everything?" Or a friendly engineer's boat may call up with some advice (you can probably see its upperworks over the levee at the next bend, and the voice on the radio comes very loud and clear): "Keep way inshore past Salem Bar, cap'n. We've been moving the buoys there. Real hot, ain't it?"

Sometimes the towboat captain gives a hand to a friend in trouble. Very early one morning, as we moved upstream, we overtook a big steamboat struggling with a heavy load. It was a difficult bend in the river, where the current ran especially strongly, and the towboat was making slow progress. Shelton recognized it at once, and knew its pilot, and very gingerly we approached to help. The *White Gold*'s barges were 800 feet long, the other towboat's more than 1,000; and these two huge strings of barges, each as long as an Atlantic liner, had to be joined in midstream, without pausing, in a place wrecked by eddies and cross-currents, so that the towboats could combine their energies. When I climbed up to the pilothouse (bleary-eyed and unshaven, for it was only just dawn) I found it charged with a routine excitement. The steersman, a sort of apprentice pilot, stood tensely in a corner. Shelton was cool and poised at his twin tillers. Far down on the barges two deckhands waited with hawsers. From the portholes of the other boat a few sleepy heads emerged, one of them in curlers (for many Mississippi boats carry women cooks, laundresses, and stewardesses). Slowly, slowly, the tows approached each other, and the two pilots exchanged glances through their windows, and the porthole heads craned a little farther, and the deckhands gathered their ropes for the throw; until with a scarcely perceptible bump the barges touched, the hawsers were cast, and the two tows became one. Shelton handed the tillers to his steersman, and the rest of us sauntered across to the other tow for a gossip and a taste of someone else's coffee.

Sometimes during our voyage Shelton passed the tillers to me. It is a disconcerting experience to handle a Mississippi tow for the first time. The atmosphere of the pilothouse is at once placid and nerve-racking, for it has the silence of an operating theater, only broken by the quiet click-click of the tillers, and a few murmured remarks from any off-duty deckhand who has chosen to come and sit on the high leather bench at the back. You are instructed to keep the head of the tow on such-and-such a sandbank, or such-and-such a tree; but soon, in the hot haze of the river, one bank merges with another, and the shape of the tree changes, and the horizon becomes blurred and featureless. When you touch your tillers gently, you find that the whole immense tow swings suddenly and alarmingly, so that for a moment you are afraid the barges will be swept broadside on to the current, and carried away helplessly in the opposite direction. "Keep her well inshore," says the pilot indulgently, and if you are timid about it he will tell you again, and again, and again, until the barges are barely escaping the roots of trees, and the gloomy overhanging foliage is brushing the upper works of the towboat. The Mississippi pilot pursues his profession with great dash and élan. The emergencies are generally slow—a gradual swinging with the current, so that the leading barge hits the pillar of a bridge, or an inch-by-inch movement toward collision; but the dangers are very real. (Sometimes, indeed, the perils are less leisurely; in flood time a tow may have to be maneuvered downstream, through all the intricate, shifting, treacherous difficulties of the river, at fifteen or twenty miles an hour.)

For the deckhands, life on a towboat seems invitingly tranquil. During the long days on the river there is really very little to do, and they spend much of their time keeping the boat spick and span, painting its upperworks and polishing its brass. Often and again they saunter back to the galley for a cup of the coffee that is constantly on the boil. Or, leaning against the sternrail in the sunshine, they watch the frothy churning of the screw (they call it the "wheel," so strong is the Mississippi tradition) and swap mildly vulgar anecdotes. They need have no worry about currents and shore lights. Some of them have no idea where they are, measuring their progress only in terms of days out of port. There are unpredictable handicaps, of course—not long ago sixteen men were drowned when a towboat hit an Ohio bridge, and one of the *White Gold*'s barges has a buckled front because of an oil explosion; but in general the deckhand lives an easy life, enjoyably.

His quarters, if the towboat is modern, are excellent, with comfortable bunks and shower baths, and his food is comparable with that in one of the less penurious London clubs. On the *White Gold*, master, mate, chief engineer, and all sat together at a high counter and were served by a Filipino cook with a dry sense of humor; and the choice of the dishes was enviable. Mississippi River food has always been good. Here is the dinner menu on board the steam packet *Monarch*, sailing between Cincinnati and New Orleans, on 31 March 1861.

BILL OF FARE

Steamer Monarch, Cincinnati, Memphis
and New Orleans
Union Line Passenger Packet

———

J.A. Williamson, Master   A.D. Armstrong, Clerk

Soup
Green Turtle   Oyster à la Plessey

Fish
Barbecued Red à la Maitre Décate
Trout à la Vertpré

Roast

Beef   Pork   Pig   Mutton
Turkey   Chuck Veal   Chicken

Hot Entrees

Scallop of Chicken with Mushrooms and Green Corn
Vol au Vent of Oysters à la Buchmer
Tendons of Veal a la Dumpling and Green Peas
Fillets of Fowl with Truffle Supreme Sauce
Curbancedes of Mutton Garnished with New Potatoes
Vegetables of the Season

Cold Dishes

Potted Fowl and Tongue Ornamented with Jelly
Boned Turkey, Champagne Jelly
Cream of Apple Jelly

Boiled

Mutton   Country Ham   Corned Beef
Turkey   Tongue   Chicken

Condiments

Radishes   Oyster   Catsup   Green Onions
Spanish Olives   Worcestershire Sauce
John Bull Sauce
Lettuce   Chow Chow   French Mustard
Raw Tomatoes   Chives   Horseradish
Cucumbers
Shrimp Paste   Cold Slaw   Celery
Pickles   Pickled Onions

Game

Pâté Chaud of Pigeon à la Chausseur
Teal Duck Braised à la Madeira

Pastry and Deserts
(Pies)
Apple   Whortleberry   Peach   Cherry
Gooseberry and Mince
(Tarts)
Apple and Gooseberry
(Puffs)
Chocolate
(Miscellaneous)
Cabinet Pudding   Custard Sauce   Lemon Ice Cream
Russian Cream   Apple Tarts with Quince
Macaroons
Jelly Pie   Ornaments   Boiled Custard
Apple Meringue
Naples Biscuit   Boston Cream Cake
Orange Jelly
Almonds   Cheese   Cake
Cocoanut Cream

Cakes
Pound   Fruit   Jelly   Sponge   Plum   Cloud

Confectionery
Candy Kisses   Golden Molasses
Cocoanut Drops   Cream Figs
French Kisses   Lemon Drops   Gum Drops

Nuts and Fruits
Raisins   Almonds   Prunes   Brazil Nuts   Pecans
Peanuts   Filberts   English Walnuts   Pineapple
Oranges   Bananas   Figs   Apples   Dates
Coffee

D.H. Kendalle, Steward

("Cold Slaw," among the condiments, is the most interesting entry here. It is a salad of grated cabbage, and it was introduced to America by the Dutch of New Amsterdam. They called it *koolsla*— *kool*, cabbage, *sla*, salad—which became in English "cole-slaw"; but simple Americans, to this day, insist on further Anglicizing it as Mr. Kendalle did on board the *Monarch*.)

Such memories of the grand old days of the river color the thoughts of the modern Mississippi boatman. He lives in a silent, self-sufficient, introspective world, and as the months and years go by, and the tangled banks float past, so slowly he merges his identity with the Mississippi's water. He becomes, indeed, like the boats and barges, a part of the river. Having seen a little of this process for myself, I left my towboat one evening at dusk, and the motorboat dropped me at a disused landing stage in Arkansas, near a bridge and a lonely highway. I said good-by to my friends, shouldered my baggage, and set off up a dusty track over the levee; and at the top of the embankment I looked back. There was the tow still streaming by, her engines beating, her searchlight flickering and flashing and feeling the banks, like a restless finger; as if she could no more stop, or pause in her progress, than the river currents themselves, swirling under the piers of the bridge.

ও **12.** ৩

Southernmost City

E DROVE from this Old South, of the towboats and magnolia trees, into Florida. Many parts of this well-known state are characteristic of the agricultural South; but many parts (it seems almost silly to add) are not. One place that is decidedly alien in spirit to the Southern temperament is Collins Avenue in Miami Beach, a street of nightmarish hotels, each more feverishly grotesque than the last, pink and saffron and blue, with glass front and marble pillars, indoor fountains, marvelously uniformed porters, and a constant stream of wild visitors, like a flood of some barbarous beverage, forever moving in and out of their doors. Another uncharacteristic southern region is the great swamp of the Florida Everglades, steamy and impenetrable, alive with spoonbills and panthers and alligators, inhabited only by Seminole Indians whose colorful costumes you may sometimes glimpse along a soggy track through the bogs. But the rarest southern spot of them all lies at the very tip of Florida, where the Gulf of Mexico joins the Atlantic; for Key West, the southernmost place in the country, is the most cheerfully un-American city in the United States.

We were chased by brutal tropical storms when we drove down to Key West, and the skies were full of beautiful angry clouds. The way runs out of Miami, across a corner of the Everglades, and onto the Overseas Highway, the wonderful structure (built originally for a railway line) that links the scattered islands of the Florida Keys. For a hundred miles or more you drive this flying road, now high above the sea, now descending to some small mangrove island, cluttered with fishing stations and restaurants. All around you stretches the water, the Gulf on one side, the Atlantic on the other, infinitely blue, dotted with little shrubby islets, with sometimes a powerful motor-boat, tarpon rods a-cocked, streaming away to the fishing grounds. This is a scene that Ernest Hemingway loves and has described, and it is infused with a great empty blue melancholy. Soon it will lose its last traces of loneliness, for on almost all the islands' houses and hotels are being built; but when I was there (out of season) there was a powerfully remote feeling about the highway, as if it were taking us away far out to sea to Rockall or St. Helena. Indeed, Key West is built on an island, a coral island, commanding the Gulf and the entrance to the Caribbean, and it has retained an insular sense of isolation and foreignness.

The rain caught up with us as we entered the town, and with the wind bending the palm trees there was a feeling of desolation to the approach. There have been repeated attempts to make Key West a booming holiday resort. During the New Deal they built promenades and piers, and "workers of the Federal Writers' Project" produced a guidebook; but the flagstones of Roosevelt Boulevard are crumbling a little now, and grass is growing between the cracks; the many visitors who go to Key West in the summer evidently enjoy its persistent air of slightly piratical independence. We sensed this air at once, even in the teeming rain. Everywhere men were lazing about with no shirts on, and women, their hair streaming with the wet, were doing their shopping in swimsuits. In the middle of one busy street an old man was leaning over, very slowly, to pick up a water-logged coconut and shake it by his aged ear. The place was hot and steamy, but enlivened with a brassy foreign gaiety.

In this atmosphere intrigue has always flourished. The independence of Cuba (only ninety miles away) was hatched in Key West. Some of the great buccaneers of history visited the island, and undoubtedly buried their treasure among the keys. Wreckers first made the island rich, and there are accounts of the dazzling fleet of boats, sail crammed on sail, which regularly left Key West en masse when news of a wreck arrived. One story tells of a Key West parson who sighted a ship in distress through the open door of his church while in the middle of a sermon; still declaiming piously, he edged his way toward the door, making sure (by the hypnotic spell of his message) that he had a head start on his congregation before shouting the traditional "Wreck ashore!" and sprinting for the quayside. In the Prohibition Era Key West was a smugglers' delight, for they could sail their fast launches through a myriad of little islands, hiding among coral reefs and mangrove islets, and emerging at night to slip through with their contraband from Cuba. There is still a pleasantly conspiratorial manner to Key West, as if it is forever plotting *coups d'état* or succoring secret agents. A man who claimed, obscurely, to be a spy working for Scotland Yard warned me in our hotel there: "Be on your guard: you never know who *or what* you're talking to in Key West!"— advice which, I confess, sent a certain cold chill of apprehension down my spine. On the very day I arrived in Key West, a Swedish freighter was escorted into the harbor by American warships, on the Buchanesque grounds that is was taking Polish arms to Guatemala.

These cloak-and-dagger sympathies are partly fostered by the climate. Key West is the only truly tropical town in the United States; there is never frost there. It is well below the twenty-fifth parallel— about on line with Calcutta—and the streets are lavish with tropical foliage (hibiscus and bougainvillea, orange poinciana's, allamanda, banyan, tamarind, frangipani, mango, guava, coconuts, bananas and begonia). There are hosts of tropical fruit to eat, and splendid fish from the Gulf (tarpon, amberjack, barracuda, sailfish, marlin, redfish, jewfish, kingfish, chowder and grunts): those who know say that the 600 varieties of fish found in the waters round about, more than 100 are edible.

If you wander among the coiled ropes and huts and boxes of the harbor front, you may see the boats of the shrimping fleet, which sail each day to the vast new shrimping beds of the Gulf of Mexico. Or you may see turtles, shipped in by schooner from the Cayman Islands, in great storage tanks on the quay, wallowing and groping round and round, and occasionally coughing throatily. On the water big brown pelicans swim ponderously and snobbishly about, and cormorants brood on the tops of posts.

Through this environment, as you may suppose, the people of Key West move lightheartedly. It is a little city dedicated to easy living. At night along Duval Street a colorful crowd saunters and sits and gossips. Sailors from the submarine base spill out of the innumerable bars, swapping bawdy with the girls and cramming into burlesque houses that offer a variety of not wildly wicked entertainment. In little open-fronted cafés you can while the hours away listening to Cuban music on the radio, and eating pungent Cuban sandwiches. Patio restaurants, in the courtyards of old houses, offer immensely long and varied meals. You can eat turtle soup (if you can bear the memory of those coughing captives); turtle steak, rather like veal, or turtleburgers. You can sip good wines and talk to artists, profane seamen, baffled tourists from Indiana, idlers, scientists, and collectors of shells. Or you can wander through the streets in the half-light, enclosed in the sticky warmth of the atmosphere. Nearly all houses are wooden, and a little dilapidated (some of them were built by the ship's carpenters of sailing vessels). They are encrusted with balconies, unpainted, cool and shuttered. Unlikely trees surround them, and the dusty streets are lined with handsome palms. Now and then a giggle steals out from a shadowy corner, or tipsy sailor curses as he trips over the pavement, or there is a snatch of some voluble foreign tongue from an alleyway; or you suddenly notice on the porch of a house, rigid as a figure from an Egyptian tomb, an old lady on a rocking chair, staring at you disapprovingly; or a knot of big Negroes on a street corner, smoking cigars, suddenly breaks into deep guffaws of laughter. There is a smell of exotic fruits and tobacco; and the breath of a hot wind stirring the palms; and high above it all the winking red lights of the Navy's radio masts.

An association, but scarcely a mixing, of races contributes to all this seductive potpourri. About a quarter of the people of Key West are Cubans, who speak Spanish, eat funny Cuban food, take part in Cuban national lotteries, and watch programs from Cuba on their television sets. They send their children to a Cuban school, maintained by the Cuban Government upstairs at the Cuban Consulate (emblazoned with enormous Cuban emblems). On Sunday evenings there is cockfighting in Key West, and sometimes Cuban entertainers give performances.

There are also the "Conches." These are people of English origin who came to Key West by way of the Bahamas. They are simple folk, tall, bronzed, and good-looking, and they talk in a strong Cockney dialect. It is odd to ask a question of a raw-boned Caribbean fisherman, answering the briefest of shorts and the gaudiest of shirts, and be answered in a voice direct from the platform of a London bus. Some of these sunburned out-of-doors men sound such thorough Londoners that they might well be pushing barrows down Whitechapel Road, or hawking avocados in Oxford Street. The Key West Negroes also talk Cockney of a modified kind, softened by trade winds and sweetened by sapodilla, for they too came from the Bahamas. They look quite different, in bearing and in feature, from the ordinary American Negro, and feel far from the petty degradations of the South. I was told repeatedly in Key West that both Negroes and Conches preserved "certain old Cockney customs," a phrase instinct with street cries and dray horses, music halls and cabs, and King Edward VII; but my knowledge of old Cockney customs is limited, and try though I could, I could find no ebony Pearly Queens, nor hear the tinkle of a barrel organ down any palm-fringed alley.

We had an agreeable if exasperating stay in Key West. Our hotel, enjoying an out-of-season rest, was dominated by a spirit of gentle procrastination. It was huge and grandiose, built by the railway mogul, Henry Flagler, who constructed the original bridges of the

Overseas Highway (at a cost of some 700 lives, many lost in a hurricane) and once ran a train service all the way to Key West. Its vaulted halls were generally empty but for a couple of dark-eyed pageboys glued to the television set in the lobby, and it took a very long time (with much ringing of bells, indignant chivvying, and exchanges of mild national insults) before the tea arrived. Once while we were there a wedding reception was held in the hotel. The bride was small, perky, bird-like, and bright; the bridegroom long and gauche and taciturn. Their guests ranged from brilliantly uniformed officials, flown in from Havana, to hoary lobster fishermen in slough hats. There were innumerable dark girls in dressy frocks, very high heels, and hats with veils, and they wandered in pairs throughout the grounds, arm in arm, loudly chattering and eating cream slices. There was a splendid profusion of food, apparently available to all comers; and the festivities were joyous and prolonged.

At other times gentlemen would buttonhole me in the lobby with dark questions. Was I looking for rare fish? Had I spoken to Mr. Alvark? Would I be interested in some unique stamps from the Cayman Islands, brought in by turtle schooners? Was it right, what the papers were saying about convertibility? Did I realize that a deputation from Ecuador was arriving in Key West the next day? What did the British Government think about labor restrictions in Peru? They, most of them, had a wild gleam in their eye, and, having said their queer bit, shuffled away like disappointed saboteurs. Key West is full of such suspicions of secrecy.

But through it all there seeps the comforting philosophy of *mañana*. The city is full of people with nothing much to do, but a talent for lounging gracefully in doorways. If you stand on the waterfront on a sunny morning you will soon find other idlers wandering to your side to stare at the water with you. Every quayside fisherman has his audience. Every swimming pelican finds someone to exchange cockeyed glances with. Out at sea the warships steal silently by, and a few lazy birds flutter overhead, and somewhere in the distance there is the muffled chug of a fishing boat. Slow and old is the island city of Key West; also surreptitious, bland and turtlelike.

We left it with regret, and drove away toward Louisiana and into Texas, until we passed the invisible boundary, between Dallas and Fort Worth, and were in the West.

PART THREE

THE WEST

⌖ 13. ⌖

Go West

S O WE drove out of the South and into the West; from Louisiana into Texas; from one myth, as the cynics say, into another. The Old West (as we know it from the cinema) has long been dead, killed by the cars and the fencing of the open prairie; but often as we traveled through this great chunk of the American continent, from the Gulf to Montana, we detected a lingering spirit of frontier freedom, stronger in some parts than in others, some- times spurious, sometimes artificially cherished, but still potent and agreeable, like a haunting echo of old jovial melodies, or a last wisp of smoke swirling around a deserted station. Taos, New Mexico (let us say), is a different world from Cheyenne, Wyoming; the one sun-baked and antique, colorful with Indians and Spaniards, the other a bold cow-capital, with memories of the famous plainsmen and buffalo hunters. But in both towns, and in a thousand others in the wide states of the West, there is still a feeling of deep-rooted individualism that is a relic, like the citizen of Cranbury and Mr. Price in Natchez, of the days of the old America.

The unifying factor of the West is space, and from the beginning communications were the foundation of its society. In the pioneer days, parts of Nevada were supplied entirely by horseback over the Sierra Nevada. The passes were rugged. In winter they were so brutal that one group of pioneer travelers, finding themselves stranded and foodless on the Donner Pass, cast lots and ate each other. At Genoa, in Nevada, I visited the grave of "Snowshoes" Thompson, a heroic messenger who kept such isolated western stations supplied through many a harsh winter, moving alone with heavy loads over the snow-blocked passes. His grave, its inscription blessed with an endearing misspelling, is surmounted by crossed skis; nearby is an old barn where the most celebrated of Western newspapers, the *Territorial Enterprise*, had its origin, sometimes subsisting entirely on the quota of paper brought by Thompson over the mountains from California. In the mountains above Salt Lake City you may still see the track beaten by the flying horses of the Pony Express, during their breakneck progression with the mails from Missouri to California. (In this service Buffalo Bill Cody once rode 320 miles in twenty-one hours, exhausting twenty ponies during the excursion.) In the High Sierra west of Lake Tahoe, a party of Odd Fellow pioneers stopped for a rest at the top of a high pass and scratched their initials in the rocks. Being Odd Fellows, they scratched nothing else, and you can still see their marks, a decorous memorial to the tenacity of the early American traveler.

But it was the railroads that made the West, and for me it is still the great trains, rushing by with their huge freights, or streaming past a level crossing with a flash of white napkins and silver, that best represent the flavor of the place. We lodged one night at a small, cheap, cigar-stained hotel at a typical Western railway town, within sight of the lines, and within sound of the hoarse and throaty voices of the station porters. During the afternoon the friendly landlord said to me: "If you like trains, don't miss the Rocky Mountain Rocket. The Rocket comes through here every evening 8:19 on the minute, and if you like railroads, as I say, she's a sight to see." At 8:17 or so we crossed the road to the station. There was a little crowd waiting for the Rocket—a few travelers, with their bags and corsages; a few friends; and a motley collection of sightseers like ourselves, some with children, some with shopping bags, some lounging about chewing and sometimes expectorating. It was dusk, and the lights were coming on. Before long we heard a deep roar far in the distance, and the blast of a whistle, and then the clanging of he bell. Down the line we could see the beam of a powerful light. The travelers gathered their luggage, the children skipped, the loungers chewed the faster, a few extra passersby dropped into the station; and suddenly the Rocket was with us, four huge shining diesel units, big as houses, with the engineer leaning grandly out of his window; and a string of flashing coaches, all steel and aluminum; and the glimpse of padded sleepers; and black-faced porters jumping from the high coaches and grabbing the bags; and travelers looking indolently out of diner windows, sipping their coffee; and a chink of light, here and there, as somebody moved a window blind. The diesels roared. The conductors jumped aboard, the doors shut noiselessly, and off the great train went, like a long silver ship, cool, clean, glittering, and powerful. Soon it would be out of the plains, and climbing into the Colorado mountains.

Several of the American railroads run trains clean across the Rockies—or through them; in the winter there must be constant snow-plowing, and more than once a train has been stranded helplessly high in the mountains, and has had to be supplied with food by helicopter. Driving a train in the West is still no sinecure, despite the careful comfort of the cabs. In the winter there are blizzards and snowdrifts; in the summer the long monotonous deadening hours across the plains and deserts, in oppressive heat. In Nevada once I drove my car parallel with a freight train traveling westward to the Pacific coast, and followed it for half an hour or so across the desert. Its progress seemed irresistible and automatic. When we were close enough I could hear the pulsing of its diesel engines and the rattle of its hundred big freight trucks; but in the distance it seemed like some sinewy desert creature, earnestly driving itself across the countryside, impelled by a dark and silent impulse. The heat was atrocious, and the train seemed to simmer; sometimes I could just see, sitting impassively at their high windows, the engineer and his mate.

The railroads are still immensely important to the West, chiefly as freight carriers (the Southern Pacific Railroad, for instance, earns only about 6 percent of its substantial income from passenger traffic); but they are also emotionally significant to nearly all Westerners. From childhood, and by heritage, their lives have been so closely linked with the arrival of the Rocket, for generations the only connection between these distant communities and the comfortable East. The steam train, in particular, is a cherished symbol of the Old West. When one Western railroad replaced its steam locomotives by diesels, the company fitted to the new engines whistles especially designed to reproduce the old sad, beloved wail of the steam trains, so melancholy a sound on a lonely evening, but so redolent with nostalgia and romance.

Everywhere in the West there are memories of the brave days of railroading. Thousands of Chinese coolies were employed in laying some of the first tracks eastwards from the Pacific (wearing their wide straw hats, they slung their panniers across their shoulders and carried the soil of California or Arizona for all the world as if they were toting rice in Sinkiang); many of their descendants are still in the West, and often you will find the grocer in some dry desert city deep in a Chinese newspaper from San Francisco. Many a shanty town beside the lines reminds the traveler of the old railway camps, brawniest of settlements, where lived those rough armies of Irishmen and Orientals who laid the first lines. I paused for coffee once at a little place called Imlay, in the Nevada desert. This used to be a stopping-place for the transcontinental trains, where passengers could stretch their legs and have a meal while the engine was refueled. Now there is a club for railwaymen housed in one of its ornate and smoke-darkened Victorian buildings. As I sipped coffee there from a chipped china mug, talking to the buxom girl behind the counter and listening to the conversation of the railwaymen around me, I could all but smell the smoke of the big steam trains, and hear the puffing of the wood-burners outside the window. The legend of the American railroads, still so powerful, pervades much of the national folk art, from "Casey Jones" to "Chattanooga Choo Choo," and its fascination is infectious.

The West is also, of course, the land of the adventurer; not only the cowboy, and the Indian scout, but also the prospector—and the presence of the miner still contributes to the flavor of the place. I remember an inn in Utah, perched on the edge of a mountain valley, which was full of unshaven men in colorful shirts, some cleaning obscure bits of equipment, some examining documents, some washing their clothes on the balconies of their rooms, some in earnest conversation in the bar. They were uranium prospectors, all of them just on the point (if you believe their conversation) of finding deposits of simply unimaginable value. You can hardly drive through the West nowadays, without seeing a couple of these men in a jeep, loaded down with sleeping bags, shovels, cookers, and Geiger counters, bumping across a desert track, the dust flying behind them, in search of an automatic Klondike.

Great fortunes have already been made in this new gold rush, and all kinds of people have joined it; deep in an inaccessible canyon in Colorado, for example, two young women are working a claim, taking their stores in by pack train. All over the high Colorado such lonely adventurers are prospecting or extracting ore. It is the third time this barren region has been combed for minerals. First the search was for radium, after Madame Curie's discoveries in the 1890s. Then, during the First World War, prospectors looked for vanadium, a substance used in making steel alloys. Finally, in the last war, the uranium search began. The Atomic Energy Commission did much of the original prospecting, using a fleet of 200 trucks, 150 house trailers, 22 caterpillar tractors, water trucks, generators, air compressors, motor graders, and aircraft. The United States Geological Survey operated with similar copious *matériel.* But the isolated prospectors I came across on the plateau were nearly all working on their own account. Any American citizen can go prospecting for uranium, and many thousands do, selling their ore at fixed prices to government buying stations. You can buy a

Prospectors Location Kit for seventeen dollars—complete with boundary posts, and a stake to stick your claim on. Already there is a magazine devoted to the interests of these adventurers. A prosperous airline—"Serving the Uranium Centers of the West"—has established its fortunes on the uranium rush. Mr. Charles Steen, the first uranium millionaire, has become almost a national hero.

All over the uranium regions you can see little one-horse uranium mines—a shaft-head and a hut or two, just like the shattered shanties that stand on the Comstock Lode as memorials to the gold and silver bonanzas. For such operators there are profitable sidelines. There is a belief that the rays or gases emanating from uranium ore can cure various ailments. "When the human body is exposed to the bombardment of gamma rays, many of these rays pass completely through the body without any effect, but many collide with electrons of various cells of the body, knocking the electrons away from their atoms, this ionizing those cells." So says a brochure issued by one of the many uranium mines, which invite sufferers from rheumatism and other afflictions to sit in their underground tunnels and be bombarded.

Miraculous cures are reported. One mine claims that a crippled Irish settler was totally restored to health. Many others publish grateful letters reporting total cures, amazing reliefs, improvements when all hope had been abandoned, shattering experiences on the train home. Some of the more successful "health mines" seem to have given up the production of uranium altogether, and have installed hygienic waiting rooms with chintz curtains, dainty rest rooms, and well-padded lifts. Most of the companies try to give their operations an air of scientific respectability. One pamphlet, signed by a qualified geologist, says (with a disarming lack of academic stodge) that millions of years before the advent of man into Jefferson County, Montana, Old Mother Nature was creating her uranium zones. "Not on graven tablets, or on written or printed page, did the Old Dame leave an indelible record of the location of these health-giving gases and radioactive zones of mineralization, but instead, she left it to Man of today to locate that which She left behind for the future generations of the human race to use for their benefit. And Man in the dual role of Mr. E. C. Miles and Mr. Joseph Stoner of Helena, Montana, have been the medium of discovery of these rich deposits of radioactive minerals....Following the deposition of the Madison formation which refers to the last deposits of sedimentaries, a land mass was in evidence, and finally the mountain masses and the outliers which you see today in the mine's vicinity, appeared, and inside of this mass, there was entombed the rich, life-giving gases and rays which today benefit those which seek their properties and relief-giving characteristics at the MINERAL HILL URANIUM MINE."

There is something about all this that brings the wanderer very near the heyday of the West, when prospectors made their fortunes overnight in lonely gulches or squalid mining camps. At Deadwood, South Dakota (the home of Deadwood Dick, the Deadwood Gulch, the Deadwood Stage, Wild Bill Hickok, and Calamity Jane), I talked to an elderly woman in a shop about the town's spacious days— when the miners were greedily working all down the gulch; when the stage left each week with its cargo of gold for the perilous journey to Denver, through Buffalo Gap, Lame Johnny Creek, Red Canyon, Squaw Gap, past the threatening haunts of Peg-legged Bradley, Dunk Blackburn, Curley Grimes, and the other ruthless buccaneers of that legendary road. "How long ago it seems," I said with a sigh, looking around me at the counters full of Colgate's and home permanents, "it might almost be another world." The woman seemed a trifle put out. "Well, I don't know," she said testily. "I don't remember Wild Bill Hickok, but I remember Potato Creek Johnny well enough, and you wouldn't call me an old woman, would you, or perhaps you would?" So saying, she opened her handbag and produced a snapshot. It was of old Johnny himself, one of the best-remembered of the Deadwood prospectors, who made strike after strike, but never acquired a fortune. There he was, staring at me from the picture with bright, birdlike eyes, his face enshrouded in a vast tangled beard, on his head a crumpled black hat, his old shirt open at the neck, in his hand a large gold nugget, symbol of his fluctuating fortunes. "He was as nice an old fellow as you could meet," said the woman, replacing the photograph in her handbag with (I thought) the faint suspicion of a snuffle, "so don't you go saying he was like something from another world."

She was perfectly right. These beloved old adventurers lived in the recent past, and the rumbustious tradition of the American frontier was established in our grandfathers' time (Englishmen, of all classes, played a colorful part in the formation of the West: Deadwood Dick himself, who died in 1930, was born in England). I made a pilgrimage to Wild Bill Hickok's grave, on the side of a hill outside Deadwood, and found it respectable and well-cared-for. Hickok, who was marshal of the town, was murdered in a Deadwood tavern with a revolver shot in the back. This is his second burial place. I forget where he was first laid, but in Deadwood I came across the memoirs of one of the undertakers' men who had helped move the body to the cemetery on the hill. He first gave some agreeably horrific glimpses of life for an undertaker in the great days of Deadwood, when bodies were lying about all over the place, in smoky taverns or in lonely thickets, and then he described the reburial of Wild Bill. "When we dug up Wild Bill," he recorded laboriously, "he still looked natural as life. Only his hair and whiskers had grown. But the air done something to the corpse. The air made Bill *sink in, crumble, or something.* We buried him up on the mountain."

They were men of infinite, of scoundrelly, resource and courage, the Western pioneers, In the early days of the Black Hills gold rush, which brought the first prospectors to Deadwood Gulch, they were opposed not only by wild Indians, unknown territory, and a ferocious climate, but also by the United States Army, which was ordered to prevent the entry of white people into those Indian territories. The most moving monument to the frontiersmen is the Thoen Stone, preserved at Deadwood. It was found in the Black Hills in 1887, and commemorates the enterprise and fate of a group of prospectors who defied the Army, found some gold, but were annihilated by Indians. Only the stone remains on them, with this message scratched in ungainly letters on it: "Came to the hills in 1833. Seven of us, Del Lacompt, Ezra Kind, G. W. Wood, T. Brown, R. Kent,

Wm. King. Indian Crow all ded but me. Ezra Kind killed by Indians beyond the high hills. Got our gold June 1834. Our ponies all got by the Indians. I have lost my gun, and nothing to eat & Indians hunting me."

Few such individuals prospect for gold nowadays, for it is so expensive to extract it in any quantity; but the greatest gold mine on the American continent, the Homestake, is still active in the Black Hills, in territory haunted by the shade of many a shaggy fortune hunter. Homestake is a vast concern, dominating the town of Lead, its huge shaft-heads high above the town, its welfare club bright in the main street, its employment office smart and busy. Of all the big gold-mining companies, through which so many famous fortunes were made, only Homestake is still producing. I was taken down the mine by a knowledgeable engineer who had spent the greater part of his life with Homestake, and who now descended its shafts every day, to wander through its dark, lonely corridors and visit the different crannies, tucked away in the labyrinth, where work was in progress. We went down to the 4,000 foot level in a steel cage, dripping with water to prevent the overheating of its wooden supports, and found ourselves in a dank and silent gallery. There was an uncanny stillness about it. Now and again a solitary miner, in steel helmet and rimless spectacles, would walk to the lift swinging his electric light and ring the summoning bell; and then the lift would come clanging down, and there would be a brief exchange of words, and the clatter of its steel gate. Generally there was not a sound, and our own voices reverberated creepily down the corridors. We walked a mile or more. Sometimes the galleries were lit with electric light, sometimes they were dark, and we relied on our safety lamps. As we walked, the engineer explained some of the techniques of mining in the Black Hills. The rock we were beneath was some of the oldest in the world, and into this antique substance the Homestake miners had already driven shafts to the depth of 5,000 feet. Now they were exploring deeper still. Mining was in progress on twenty-seven different levels in side the hills above Lead. Usually the veins of ore were attacked from beneath, and the miners worked upwards, creating a great chamber in the rock. To begin with, the masses of ore drilled off its walls were left where they fell, and the miners climbed ever higher on top of them; eventually, when the "stope" was exhausted, the whole lot was extracted and sent up above by elevator shafts. A ton of gold, and this only after immensely complicated treatments (though this stingy yield does not prevent Homestake from making a steady annual profit of something over $4,000,000).

We talked long and leisurely as we walked through the mine, but still there was no sign or sound of activity. "It's a lonely place." Said I, "Who would have expected a gold mine to be so empty?" "This is normal enough," the engineer replied. "Don't you worry, there are plenty of people down here with us. During the war, now, that was different. The Government banned gold mining then, so that miners could go and do war work, and the old mine really *was* empty. There was lots of equipment about, but all standing idle in the dark. We had a few watchmen working here, they used to roam about sometimes to see how things were, but most of the time it was all empty, all 5,000 feet of it, all twenty-seven levels."

At last we heard far in the distance a rumble of machines, and presently we saw lights. My guide suddenly left the corridor and swung himself up a ladder, through a narrow crevice in the ceiling. I followed. The surrounding mud was thick and slippery, and at the top of the first ladder we twisted around on a small ledge of wet rock, and began climbing another. Finally, squeezing through a little chimney, we emerged in a huge, low, cavernous, dusty, bright-lit chamber. There was a terrible din. At one end of the place groups of men, their faces black with dust, were drilling with large and shuddering electric drills. Sweat ran heavily down their faces, and when they stopped to adjust the machines they wiped their foreheads with their sleeves. The rock was falling off in great flakes. Sometimes a man paused from his drilling and prized a mass out of the rock wall with a steel instrument; it made a horrible tearing noise, like a tooth coming out. The ore was dark and unattractive. "Where's the gold?" I asked. The engineer smiled kindly. "You can work down here for five years," he said, "and never see a streak of the stuff."

Nevertheless, the gold is there, and it was from this scrubby mountain that the Hearst family extracted its wealth. Up the shafts goes the nasty dirty ore, to be crunched in giant crushers, ground between steel balls, whirled around in circular vats, and pushed over vibrating screens. Finally the gold is taken to be refined in an unpretentious brick building guarded by armed company policemen; and there a handful of workers, through the months, accepts and handles unexcitedly a constant flow of unimaginable wealth. "What happens to the gold when it's ready?" I asked, with a vision of creaking harnesses and rocketing stage coaches. My informant looked a little cagey. "It all goes to Denver, to the mint. All gold has to be sold to the Government, at a fixed price." "Yes," I said, "but how does it get there?" "Oh, by train, you know." "Where from? There isn't a station here, is there?" He looked at once determined and apologetic. "No, but it goes somewhere else first, by truck." "How do you mean, somewhere else?" "Well, it goes to a station somewhere else. In Wyoming." He was a friendly and helpful man, but I had the impression that on this point he did not want to be pressed; so, changing the subject swiftly, I asked him if there were many Plymouth Brethren in Lead, and he answered with a fluency that seemed to betray relief. I may have imagined all this; but it seems only natural that this great gold mine, one of the biggest half-dozen in the world, should not be anxious to advertise the route by which its hard-won treasure leaves the mountains for the mint.

Villains as well as heroes were produced by the adventure of the West; little villains, like those unscrupulous prospectors who would push a rival unhesitatingly down any convenient mineshaft, big villains, like the great combines which thrust their way to pre-eminence. Through the competitive turmoil of the times, to dominate the economy and society of their regions. One of the great popular villains of this kind is the Anaconda Mining Company, a fabulous octopus of a firm which has its headquarters at Butte, Montana, on top of a hill made of copper. Until recently, at least, this mammoth company (with subsidiaries all over the United States and in South America) was regarded by many Americans as a symbol of all that was ruthless, thoughtless and unkindly in big business. Trade unionists loathed it; liberal journalists vilified it; the unfortunates who worked in its ill-ventilated copper mines, and lived in its unkempt filthy streets, cursed it without inhibitions. It is still no Fairy Godmother, but has been improved by these persistent criticisms and now provides its workers with some excellent welfare facilities. When I was in Butte, all the same, a strike was in progress, and the tall pit-shafts dotted all over the "richest hill on earth" were still and silent. The company is in almost total possession of the town. The best hotel belongs to it, and so does the best store. The press is owned by it. The power company is closely allied. It is quite impossible to escape Anaconda in Butte. When you eat, switch the light on, go to bed, or read the newspaper you are always contributing to its giant resources.

Butte, a dismal town, was once the roughest and brightest of the Western mining camps. Until a few years ago gambling was legal there, and there was a famous "prostitutes' line" ("Just over there," an Anaconda official remarked to me nostalgically, "you could almost see it from my window"). Now all is drab and dingy, and the few nightclubs, ablaze with tawdry light, are outside the town in a dreary little hamlet among the hills. You can still hear many different languages in the bars of Butte, and on the town boundary there is an official sign which says of the place: "She was a bold, unashamed, rootin', tootin', hell-roarin' camp in days gone by and still drinks her liquor straight." But there is an endless dull slovenliness about the town that is greatly depressing, and frequently you can see cracks in the streets, and green grass growing, and the signs of movement and stress that show a mine shaft is beneath. Anaconda arranged that the town boundary should avoid many of its pit-heads, to preclude certain taxations; but underground there are no such distinctions, and the whole of Butte's hill is warrened and honeycombed with copper mines.

Butte stands in open country, on the edge of the hills, like a scab on a fair skin, dominated by the worst excrescences of the profit motive. But even in this gruesome place the spirit of the West is apparent. The miners are a friendly, salty, brave, uninhibited people, rough enough in the streets on paydays, leathery of cheek and brusque of tongue, but infused with a frontier liberty; and it is queer and interesting to see how closely the miner is bound to his calling, though he is no longer hoping for bonanzas, but simply working for a wage. It will be a long time before the values of commercial Americanism totally swamp the West. Though the towns are spreading, and the old individualisms are mellowing, and you need a license to shoot the elk, it is still the great trains, and the uranium seekers in their battered jeeps, and the mines, and antelopes in the prairies, and such high-vaulted, tempestuous tokens that I remember most precisely from those regions.

৩ 14. ৩

Spaniards

RIGHT cheerful color, too, is a characteristic of the West, especially in those parts where the Spanish Empire once held sway; no imperialism was ever more gorgeous, or more dazzling in its glare and glitter. Driving through New Mexico one day I came across a rock, at a place called El Morro, on which many generations of travelers have carved their names. First the aboriginal Indians cut crude pictographs, of stilted human figures, bison, and the imprints of hands. More recently American emigrants, moving west, stopped at El Morrow for water and scratched their names—stout Anglo-Saxon names, conjuring up scenes of wagon trains, corn-cob pipes and grace before dinner (though one Anglo-Saxon, Lieutenant E. F. Beale, was on his way to Arizona for experiments with Arabian camels). Some of these signatures are carefully cut, some roughly; some with the decision of education, some childishly. But all are outshone by a magnificent inscription that stands in a place of honor on the rock, with flowery embellishments and exquisite lettering, the very essence of cultivation and aristocracy; this was place on the rock in 1605 by Don Juan de Oñate, leader of the first Spaniards to colonize the wild Indian country of the Southwest; and it stands as a symbol of the brilliant Spanish spirit, born of bigotry and savage cruelty, which still brightens the whole southern frontier of the United States. In Texas, Arizona, and New Mexico, the three Southwestern states, Spanish ways still prevail, though harried everywhere by the advancing American civilization from across the mountains.

The most complete and delightful Spanish enclave of all is to be found in the Sangre de Cristo Mountains, above Santa Fe. They are some of the most beautiful of the American mountains, an outcrop of the Rockies jutting out across the desert. From far away, to the traveler approaching through the arid wilderness, they seem a promise of mystery and lush enchantment. The desert around the Rio Grande River (here no more than a clear stream) is rolling and disjointed, and intersected by deep ravines, so that you bob along the tracks, now on the crest of a desert ridge, now deep in a shrubby gorge; but always ahead of you are the mountains, blue and beckoning, a frame of dark clouds around them and a few streaks of snow on their crests.

Clustered on the slopes of these mountains are a number of Spanish villages, where old customs are still alive and where Spanish is still generally spoken. There are roads leading to these villages now—tarmac roads to the bigger ones, dusty tracks to the smaller and remoter places—but they are still insulated by thought and tradition from the encroaching Americanism, and have a charming air of tranquil satisfaction. I remember in particular the village of Cordova, which is tucked away off the highway at a height of about 8,000 feet. The track which approaches it begins respectably enough, but soon lapses into ruts and rocky ledges, and becomes disagreeably steep; until it eventually leads you, with much roaring of engines and changing of gears, between narrow walls into the village. Cordova is built on a bluff. Below there is a little gully, with a stream running through it, covered in lush crops—wheat and chili, and orchards of apples and pears. The village is full of growing things, too. The houses are shuttered and cool, with verandas and small courtyards, and when we were there they were ablaze with hollyhocks. Innumerable children, with attendant puppies, hang about its alleys jabbering in Spanish, or sit dangling their bare feet from the top of its stone walls. Sometimes in the evening a couple of tough shepherd boys will drive their sheep through the little square, brandishing sticks, with a clatter of hoofs and a few high-pitched and ineffectual commands. Old men with battered hats saunter by on donkeys on their way to the tavern. Hens clutter up backyards, and careful housewives brush their porches or shake carpets out of their windows.

When we first skidded and roared our way in Cordova, we found ourselves (like every visitor) quickly surrounded by a heterogeneous crowd of children, idlers, and passing farmers, and from it there emerged a tall, shy man, with a dome-shaped head and an agreeable smile. He introduced himself as George Lopez, and asked us if we would care to see his woodcarvings, rather as a roué of tradition hawks his etchings. We went inside his house, by way of a spotless little hall (his wife pausing occasionally, as we went, to flick some dust from the polished wooden floor) and found ourselves in a small, low-ceilinged room, smelling of wood, which was cluttered up with wooden figures. Their spirit had come direct from Spain—Cordova is one of several villages where there still live heirs to the original land grants of the Spanish crown. Many of them were of religious subjects: oddly formalized saints, in bright colors, and Virgins of an appealing angular simplicity. Others were of country subjects—animals and trees and flowers—and some of these seemed to show traces of Indian influences. We bought a small object described as a Christmas tree; from its straight trunk there jutted large flat leaves, and on each leaf there sat a little mountain creature—a squirrel, a hare, and a chipmunk, and a bird or two. Lopez said he had thought of this design himself, and his wife beamed with a homely pride.

In these anachronistic villages, where such handicrafts still flourish despite the chain stores in the valley below, there lingers a misty, medieval intensity of religion. At Chimayo, in the foothills of the mountains, there is a small wood and adobe church which is a hallowed place of pilgrimage. It is entered through a rickety wooden gate, between two gnarled cottonwood trees and past the serried tombs of the family that built it. In an unpaved room at the back of the church there is a hole in the sand, which allegedly cannot be filled or emptied however hard sand is shoveled into it or taken out. This sand is supposed to have miraculous powers, and those who will apply it to their crippled legs or withered arms will find them cured. The walls of the church are crowded with discarded crutches, with fervent letters of gratitude in Spanish or limping English, with paper flowers and postcards of the Virgin. (Among the first American troops to fight in the Pacific war were many New Mexicans; and at the end of the war hundreds of them joined in a pilgrimage of thanks to Chimayo.)

Often, on little hillocks in this country, you will find small chapels, approached by winding, precipitous paths, like some Buddhist *chorten* in the Himalayas; and on the outskirts of many villages there are solitary crosses, facing (it seems) the cardinal points of the compass. I asked several times what these signs meant, and was told that they formed part of the mystery of the Penitentes. This lay religious order, of peculiar characteristics, came to New Mexico with the Franciscan friars from Spain, in the sixteenth century (having earlier crossed the Pyrenees from France). I had heard strange rumors about its rites, and inquired in Santa Fe about them. I was told to go to Truchas, on a commanding spur on the western slopes of the mountain, and to ask its inhabitants; for it was a center of Penitentes activity.

The village was all but deserted when I reached it. There had been a fiesta the day before, and almost the only people in sight were a few obese Spaniards, propped up in the sunshine against a wall, with bloodshot eyes and pale cheeks, their hats pushed to the backs of their heads, breathing heavily and looking distinctly uninformative. There was a man sitting on a torpid donkey, and from time to time, raising himself momentarily from his slumped position over the animal's neck, he would shout something blurred and incoherent in the direction of a small tavern; from where would come a muffled reply, at once testy and lethargic, as if the innkeeper were lying in bed with his boots on, and had to remove the blanket from over his head before his could answer.

However, there was a trim house not far away, with a veranda looking away over the desert below. (In the distance I could see the suspicion of smoke from Los Alamos, the laboratory town where the first atom bomb was designed.) Its owner was friendly and articulate. He had been a well-known Truchas character for many years; had represented the district in the New Mexico Congress at Santa Fe; and was an elder of the Order of Penitentes. He pointed out to me a low adobe building, surmounted by a cross, on the edge of the village. This was the *morada*, or lodge, of the Penitentes, where they held their ceremonies. I asked him what was unusual about their orders of service. Was it true, as I had heard in Santa Fe, that some of their rituals were cruel and bloody, and that the Passion was celebrated by the crucifixion of one of the members, high in the mountains? On these subjects, he replied, he was forbidden to speak, for the Penitentes were a secret fraternity; and he then shook hands, warmly enough, and returned to his house.

I went to the other end of the village and called at a small school maintained by the Presbyterian Church. The headmistress, partly inspired, perhaps, by some slight antagonism toward the Catholic Church, and partly by the fascination of the subject, was very willing to talk about the Penitentes. Certainly the rumors were true. She was not sure about the crucifixions, which had led in the past to the deaths of several members of the Order, but she knew a good deal about some other esoteric customs, and they were certainly still maintained. The high moment of the Penitentes years is their commemoration of the moment when the veil of the Temple was split. Then in the Catholic church of Truchas the lights are doused, and in the pitch darkness strange rites are performed. Great stones are rolled about the floor of the church, and there is a clashing of chains, and all over the village the noise can be heard. After the service harsh penances are performed by chosen members of the sect (they consider it an honor to be selected). Outside the *morada* on the night of

Good Friday, my informant had seen a man circling a cross on his knees, bearing on his back a huge tree trunk, the weight of which nearly floored him. In other years processions have been seen coming down from the mountains that included barebacked men whipping themselves as they walked; their instruments of flagellation were branches of a cactus called the yucca tree and their backs bled profusely; so did their bare feet as they stumbled over the rocky paths. Always in these processions one man represented Christ, carrying a heavy wooden cross on his bare back, and wearing a crown of thorns.

I asked the Presbyterian lady if the Catholic Church had anything to do with these ceremonies. "Of course they do," she said briskly. "It all goes on in the Catholic Church, doesn't it? Its Catholic priests take part in it sometimes." When I returned to Santa Fe I called at the office of the Archbishop (in a fine old Spanish house) and talked to one of his chaplains. Yes, he said, the Archbishop had extended recognition to the Penitentes, but in return for their abandoning their superstitious ways. If such things still went on in the mountains, they were preformed by dissident groups of the Order: and indeed, if I liked, I could call on the head of the fraternity and see for myself his devotion to the Church.

I had some trouble finding this elder's house. He lived in a poorish outskirt of town, and I groped my way, in the dusk, through a number of dusty streets with washing flapping in the gardens and many radios blaring. When I did find it, I was kindly received. The elder was a tall and handsome old Spaniard who was treated with some deference by the other unidentified men and women thronging his parlor. On the walls were many signed portraits of eminent Catholic clerics, in their vestments, and there was a framed declaration to the effect that the Order of Penitentes had been given the blessing of the Archbishopric. The elder assured me that all was now harmony between the Order and the Church. There were no more crucifixions in the mountains; but (said the elder warily) it was not beyond the realms of possibility that a few odd practices were still performed in distant corners of the Sangre de Cristos, by refractory members of the fraternity.

He himself had taken part in many such esoteric rites, in the old days, but had conscientiously abandoned them as the Church demanded. Nevertheless, I could not help feeling, as we talked under the saintly gaze of the prelates, that part of his heart, at least, was still with the midnight processions. Nor could I ever see the mountains again, as I crossed the stony desert, without imagining the poor man with the tree on his back, crawling around the cross, or hearing the ghastly clatter of the stones and the chains from the church on Good Friday.

ᴄᴜ 15. ᴥ

Pueblos and Navahos

IDE by side with the Spaniards of New Mexico live their predecessors, the Pueblo Indians. At Santa Fe you may see them in the shadow of the old palace of the Spanish Governors, squatting placid and impassive beside their wares—pottery and rugs and odd ornaments. They wear colorful blankets around their shoulders, and are cluttered with earrings and innumerable necklaces, not unlike carthorses in Regent's Park. Their faces are a trifle lumpish and immobile, and they have no wild animation of gesture; for these are agricultural Indians, who have lived in their settled villages for centuries, occasionally fighting back at marauding Navaho and Apache, but never roaming the wide desert looking for blood and booty. I was sitting in the lobby of a hotel at Taos, some way north of Santa Fe, when two men from a Pueblo tribe sauntered bashfully in, a little misty-eyed (for a fiesta was in progress) and walking hand in hand, for courage. They stood in the center of the lobby, surrounded by palm trees, in their blankets and turquoise necklaces; and it was as if two fossilized sprites from a distant past, stiffened by the slow process of petrification, had detached themselves from a rock somewhere and come in to see us. The Pueblos are a well-ordered extraordinary resilient people, good craftsmen and farmers; but they are too rooted in their ways, and too swamped by religious impositions, to possess much grace or splendor.

One of the most familiar sights in America is that of the most famous of the pueblos, at Taos; in country made celebrated by such diverse characters as Kit Carson and D. H. Lawrence, it stands a mile or two outside the old Spanish town, at the edge of the mountains, with green fields all about it and the desert proper not far away. The main part of it is a kind of adobe apartment block, a serried jumble of square buildings, all interconnecting, like a box of bricks, with few windows but many square doors, and with ladders propped from parapet to parapet. When the Spanish conquistadors came this way in the sixteenth century, looking for the Seven Cities of Cibola, they saw such pueblos as this high on the desert horizon, and mistook them, for a few excited hours, for distant castles and minarets and battlements, stocked with gold, treasures, and beautiful women. In fact, those who admire most fervently the culture of the Pueblo Indians can scarcely deny that this poor mud pile is dull work. The Pueblos produce some pleasant pottery; but no paintings brighten the walls of their drab structure; what sense of color it has comes from the mountains and the desert. There is no intricate woodwork, no graceful courtyard, no latticed window, no delicacy of design. As their devotees proudly claim, the Pueblo Indians continue to live much as they did at the time of Columbus; as squalidly as ever.

These poor people work their smallholdings, or sell their textiles and pottery, with an air of dispirited dottiness; or, vacant of expression, they stand around the pueblo hopelessly, like idlers outside an employment office; for sometimes they stagger tipsily down the road to the pueblo, not magnificently, like a rolling English drunkard, but furtively, as if they are going to be sick. When the occasion demands, it is true, some of them can put on quite a creditable war dance. A few Indians took part in the Taos fiesta while I was there, and enlivened its carnival procession. They ranged in age from five to forty, and wore extraordinary costumes of feathers and fittings, with necklaces, armlets, bangles, bracelets, ornamented trousers,

headbands, and innumerable bells. They walked placidly in the procession, out of step, among the usual Army lorries, policemen, floats
of various organizations, children on ponies, and bands; but from
time to time they would suddenly stop in their tracks, as if seized by
some appalling thought, and launch themselves into a ferocious
dance. There they would remain for a moment or two in paroxysms
of staccato movement, their bells jingling rhythmically, the little
Indians nearly bursting with effort, the older ones fierce and determined, before ending as abruptly as they began, and resuming their
shuffled march toward the refreshment stalls. Generally, though,
they are as dull of movement as of visage, and little of the noble savage remains in them.

I recall with particular odium a Corn Dance performed at the
Taos pueblo one August afternoon. It had been widely advertised,
and many cars streamed down the dusty road from the town. We
were met in the open yard of the pueblo by an Indian who told us
where to leave our car, and instructed us to report to a neighboring
office to pay the necessary parking fee. At the same time he advised
us that if we wanted to take photographs there would be an extra
charge. Thus welcomed, we wandered on, to find the dance already
in progress. We had been warned of the sacred significance of the
performance, and were hushed, as though we were approaching the
altar of St. Peter's, or honoring some sublime and kindly figure of
the Buddha. The pueblo performers, however, seemed to take their
devotions lightly. They were arranged in rows, dressed in elaborate
costumes, the details of which escape me, but which have left a vague
impression of feathered bath towels. A drum played in the background, and a male chorus droned a sad and repetitive dirge.
Holding small bunches of corn, the dancers shuffled and hopped
rhythmically round and round, often grimacing at each other.
Sometimes giggling, for all the world like the juniors at the kinder-
garten, pretending to be fairies and goblins, or senselessly enacting
one of the verses of A. A. Milne. Sometimes they wriggled, but not
lasciviously, and sometimes they skipped, and sometimes they
kicked halfheartedly. The watching tourists looked understandably

bored, but so impressed were they by the supposedly spiritual nature of the ceremony that most of them were rooted there, and had a distinctly chapter-one-verse-fourteen look on their faces.

It struck me that there were a great many more women participating in this dreary ritual than there were men, but my guidebook told me that participation in ceremonials was a communal duty and privilege. Were all the men dancing elsewhere, I wondered; or parading at some distant carnival; or struck by some epidemic; or hunting squirrels in the mountains? An Indian selling Coca-Cola at a nearby stall gave me my answer. They were away in their fields, and had ignored the summons to the Corn Dance. Did he mean that they had deliberately shirked their communal duty and privilege? Certainly, he answered blandly, most of them did; was it not a total waste of time? "Well," I said, consulting my guidebook, "but it says here that the rhythm of movement of such dances is summoned to express in utmost brilliancy the vibrant faith of a people in the deific order or the world and in the way the ancients devised for keeping man in harmony with his universe."

The Indian looked rather blank. That might be so, he said, and certainly his grandfather knew all about that stuff; but as for himself, and all his friends, and his wife, and her friends, well, they had not the faintest idea what the dance was all about, and if they could possibly avoid dancing it, they naturally would. I sympathized with them. The entire official life of the Pueblo revolves around such ceremonies, once, anyway, thought conducive to crop fertility and rain making; some experts say that the Pueblo Indians spend more than half their time propitiating rain gods, making offerings to supernatural powers, and in other such strenuous activities of appeasement. Into this structure of piety they apparently find it easy to inject the Christian God, introduced to them (not without inducements) by the savage Spanish pioneers. One pueblo, for example, celebrates midnight mass decorously enough on Christmas Day; and then immediately breaks into a riotously pagan fertility rite, all primitive drum beats and savage motions, around a figure of the infant Christ.

Not all the Indians of New Mexico are so tamed and sedentary as the Pueblo people. If you drive across the great deserts to the west, on your way to California or the Grand Canyon, you will often see away in the wilderness the little encampments of the Navaho Indians, or glimpse a Navaho sheepherder riding by on his tall mare. Most of the these Indians inhabit the Navaho reservation, 24,000 square miles of it, with less than 200 miles of paved roads. They are semi-nomadic herders, with large flocks of sheep. There are nearly 70,000 Navahos, and they are increasing at a rate of about 1,000 a year; their huge pasture land, much of it rocky and inhospitable, is rapidly becoming too small for them; and there are more Navahos now than there were when the white man first arrived in America.

They have never established anything that could be called a village. They build fairly permanent houses, of logs, mud, and sometimes of stone, but they frequently move about with their herds over huge tracts of land in New Mexico, Arizona, and Utah, from the tribal capital at Window Rock, New Mexico (with a fine council chamber, a guest house, paved roads, and official residences), to the remote desert country around Monument Valley, uninhabited except by a few traders and by the lonely itinerant herds of these sheep-grazers. Often, though you can see them in the towns when they are doing their shopping. A favorite Navaho rendezvous is the village of Ganado in Arizona, where the Presbyterians maintain a mission and a hospital. On the balcony of the trading post there you may meet them any morning. They have come to Ganado on foot, on horseback, or by truck across the desert, and between their shopping (in the store you can buy anything from a lipstick to a vacuum cleaner) they chat on the porch of the store, leaning gracefully against the lumber walls, or squatting beside the parapet.

They are a handsome, upright people, rather like gypsies of the old school, with fine aquiline features (sometimes with Oriental eyes) and expressions of confident independence; perhaps the most decorative and self-sufficient of all the American Indians. The men wear blue denim pants, secured by ornamental belts, with gay shirts, large felt hats, and cowboy boots. The women's costume has been dictated by history. In 1864 the Navahos, then a bold raiding tribe, were rounded up by the United States Government, and their sheep and goats were destroyed. For five years some 8,000 of them were imprisoned at Fort Sumner, in New Mexico; and during that time the Government considerately reclothed them in the fashion of the period. Thus to this day the Navaho women wear velvet blouses and long, full calico skirts, vividly colored. They have high-topped boots, and around their shoulder, as often as not, they wear a blanket, exactly as the mid-Victorian woman (in New York or in London) would wrap a shawl around her to keep out the treacherous city damp.

The Navahos have their religious ceremonials, too (many of them borrowed in ancient times from the pueblos) but their spirit has not been blunted by an excess of devotionals; nor have they been perverted by the exactions of the tourist industry. They are still strangers, still generally aloof from the white man, still alone with their herds in the expanse of the desert. I remember clearly an old man who sat sipping a cup of coffee in Mrs. Martin's Café at Ganado. I had been talking to a local politician who was standing for election as sheriff, and who was busy sticking up posters asking people to vote for him. I asked if he considered the Navaho vote important. "In this country," he replied, "it's the Indian vote we depend on. You want to see the Average Voter in this part of the world? Well, there he is," and he pointed to the old Navaho at the counter. He sat on a high stool, with his legs crunched beneath the counter, and he drank his coffee delicately, genteelly, with a little finger crooked. His hair was worn in plaits and tied with pieces of wool, and on top of it he sported a high-crowned conical hat. On his wrist were two turquoise bracelets, around his neck was silver necklace. His face was wrinkled, reflective, and composed. In spirit he looked infinitely nearer the totem pole than the polling booth; and indeed, sitting there at Mrs. Martin's counter in the Arizona desert, he seemed representative of all those old mysterious things, of nature and folklore, of forgotten cultures and practices, that the new Americanism can never satisfactorily replace.

७ 16. ७

More Indians

THESE were not the Indians who established the Indian legend. But the hard-riding, buffalo-hunting warriors also lived chiefly in the West, in the prairies bounded by the Rocky Mountains. Their names were Sioux, Cheyenne, Mandan, Blackfoot, Crow, Ute, Pawnee, and Osage; and their descendants are still in the West today, more fortunate than their eastern brothers in that their reservations stand in ancestral country. (To the east these Plains Indians were bounded by the forest lands of the woodsmen tribes— Cherokee, Fox, Choctaw, Iroquois; on the northwest coast were the fishing tribes; south of them the seed-gathering Indians of California; and in the southwest the Navahos, Pueblos, and the wild Apache, who lived in the desert, and who fought their last battle against the white men in the 1880s.)

I stopped for a doughnut once at a small ranching town in South Dakota and noticed a number of drunken Indians leaning about on doorposts. I inquired about them at the coffee shop, and was told that they came from a neighboring Sioux reservation. I might like to visit it, because at Fort Yates, its headquarters, I would see the celebrated Standing Rock, the symbol of the fighting Sioux, which they defended furiously in many a bloody skirmish. The stone belonged originally to the Arikara tribe, living in adjoining territory, but was stolen from them by the Sioux, who regarded it with great veneration. It was said to look like a seated Indian woman, and the story was that a chief's squaw developed such a jealousy of his second wife that one day she refused to move camp, sitting sulkily in front of the fire with her child while the tribal tepees were struck; whereupon, by some gross miscarriage of providential justice, she and her child were both turned to stone. Fort Yates is a collection of pleasant buildings surrounded by trees, a little tumbledown, like a British Army cantonment (if one may harp upon a subject) in some about-to-be-abandoned corner of the Empire. It was a hot afternoon when we reached it, and there were few people about; those we asked seemed notably vague about the Standing Rock, but eventually we found the relic, mounted on a pedestal on the outskirts of the settlement. Its resemblance to a sitting squaw was no more than rudimentary, but it was interesting to think that so much angry energy had been expended, and presumably so many brave lives lost, in defense of so stodgy a symbol.

As we looked at it a middle-aged Indian approached us. "You don't want to waste time with that thing," he said. "That's old business. We've forgotten all that now. Come with me, I'll show you something better." He led us down the path, and around a corner we found a large plaque in honor of all those Indians from the reservation who had fought in the Second World War. Their names included Percy Tree Top, Earl La Duke, F. Young Bear, Paul Young Eagle, Gilbert Two Bear, Evans Use Arrow, Lee Red Fox, Terry Many Wounds, Francis Hairychin, M. American Horse, Tom Holy Elk Face, and George Afraid of Hawk. Many of the American Indians had admirable war records. Their most remarkable contribution was in the field of communications, for in the Pacific several Indian native languages were used instead of codes. Few, indeed, were the Japanese scholars who understood the Navaho dialects, for example, and the Americans rightly thought it unlikely that many such lonely sages, summoned from scholarly backwaters or shady quadrangles, would be available among the island battlefields. So messages were simply translated into an Indian language, broadcast, and retranslated into English by an attendant brave at the other end. Many suitable languages were used, and they never used the same one on Tuesday as had bafflingly gone over the air (inherited from dusty pueblos or solitary desert tents) on Monday.

"Come with me," said our guide, "and I will show you the grave of the greatest Sioux warrior of all—Sitting Bull." We tramped down the road silently, past an old store with a few Indian children playing on its porch, through a tangled thicket of brambles, until we reached a little clearing. "It's not too clean now," said the Indian. "It's so long since he died, and we forget easily." The grave had evidently been opened, for the slab on top of it was displaced. I looked inside to see if any bones were visible, but there was nothing but a few old jam jars, left behind by picnickers or by placers of posies, long since withered. Sitting Bull was among the most famous of all the Indians, and a lifelong opponent of the white man. He was a great prophet and medicine man, and as chief of the Sioux he fought the battle of Little Big Horn, in which General Custer made his last stand. After that bloodthirsty triumph (more than 200 Americans were killed), Sitting Bull fled to Canada, to return later on the promise of a pardon. In 1890 he rejoined the Sioux in the guise of a Messiah (they were expecting one) and whipped them into such a frenzy of dissatisfaction that an uprising was imminent. Police were sent to put an end to it; there was some violence; and in the melee several policemen and Sitting Bull himself were killed. He was a shabby hero by then, with an itching palm; and the authorities, no doubt with the Custer debacle still in mind, buried him unceremoniously at Fort Yates, without marking his grave. There he lies still, to the best of anyone's knowledge, the roof of his sepulcher slipping a little, overgrown by scratchy briars, with only the jam jars to pay him respect.

Fort Yates is near the big Sioux reservation of the Cheyenne River, where about 4,000 Sioux live in scattered settlements, doing a little farming and raising cattle. It is beautiful, wide open country, rolling grassland intersected by green gullies, with occasional thickets and a few dusty, bumpy tracks. The reservation is a good sixty miles long, and forty miles deep, and is crossed by a highway and a railway line. I called at its headquarters, the Cheyenne Agency, and met the agent. His office was in a building pleasantly shaded by big trees, and chock-a-block full of Indians, sitting on the doorstep, looking at notice boards, chattering, laughing, asking innumerable questions, very like gypsies at a fair. The reservation has its own police and courts of justice, and the clerks and secretaries are all Sioux. Indeed, the aim of the United States Indian Service is to bring itself to an end, and there are very few white officials even in the great reservations.

The Indian tribes of America used to be classed as "domestic independent nations," and independent treaties were concluded with each of them (only the Seminole Indians, whose straw huts may sometimes be seen in the boggy fastnesses of the Florida Everglades, have never formally made their peace with Washington). To dispose of these troublesome people, the Federal Government first tried to concentrate them in the West—the advanced and talented nation of the Cherokees, for example, was forcibly removed from Tennessee and thereabouts to Oklahoma. Later the reservation system was established, and by 1870 all Indians except the Apache, who were still fighting under their bandit leader Geronimo, had been placed in reservations, and were forbidden to leave them. Every attempt was made to stifle Indian culture, to banish the native languages and crafts; but more recently the purpose (which had fluctuated wildly) has been to establish the Indians as citizens following their own mores and inheriting their own traditions. They have been full citizens since 1924, though until very recently Arizona and New Mexico, which tend to regard them rather as the South regards its Negroes, refused them the right to vote.

The agent was an intelligent and sympathetic man, not unlike the best kind of British colonial officer, and he discussed very freely the situation of the Indians on his reservation. In general, Indians throughout the United States are still poor (though the Osage Indians of Oklahoma occupy land so rich in oil that since 1900 the

138 *Jan Morris*

tribe has earned more than $300,000,000 from it). In the fifty-odd years before the war, the Indian population increased from about 240,000 to more than 400,000 but for one reason and another their lands shrank from about 138,000,000 acres to about 52,000,000 acres—and much of the land lost was good farming and timber country. Much of their present territory is sparse, dry land—on the Papago reservation in Arizona, for example, 200 acres is needed to support one cow. As a result, in recent years the average Indian farmer's income has been about a fifth of the average white farmer's.

Indians can, of course, leave their reservations if they like and find work elsewhere, but many of them are handicapped by poor education. The more scattered and remote tribes, like the Navahos, do not insist too firmly on their children's attendance at school, and because they see relatively few white people, they often speak their own languages rather than English. Some tribes take decidedly unkindly to the advent of new schools. The Seminoles, for example, would not have one at all until the 1930s. Though there are three kinds of schools on the Indian reservations—schools run by the Indian service, ordinary public schools, and private or mission schools—there are still many Indian children who are simply out of reach of a classroom. Indians also suffer from poor health, especially from tuberculosis, infant diseases, and pneumonia. On the Papago reservation, a quarter of the babies die within a year; nearly half die before they are seven. The life expectancy is seventeen years.

Much of the Cheyenne Creek reservation is leased as cattle graz- ing ground to non Indians; the few Indian villages are small and poor. The agent showed me a map and suggested that I drive to one of the more remote settlements—Cherry Creek, near the Cheyenne River, where there was a federal school, but which was a long way from white civilization: it was eighty or ninety miles from the agency, and the last thirty miles of the route lay along dusty tracks. We stopped at the last town on the paved road, called Dupree, to have some lunch. The main street ran at right angles to the highway, and was very rough and bumpy; the pavements included the remains of the old boardwalk, the raised wooden passageway which was so familiar a feature of the frontier towns. There were a few Indians about and one or two cowboys. (Not far from the town was a characteristic spectacle of the modern West. They were improving the highway and the construction workers had established a little township of caravans and huts and tents, surrounded by parked bulldozers and earth-removers, clouded in dust, with some washing streaming in the breeze. These are the new American nomads, moving willingly wherever there is work to be found, whether it is building a dam in New York State or cutting a highway through some remote Arizona canyon. Often, in distant country districts, you will meet a cavalcade of them; trucks and cars and caravans, and the huge grotesque implements, all bumps and appendages, with which the Americans build their marvelous roads.)

We struck south from Dupree on a dirt road, across a featureless country. There were few people in sight; only an occasional farmer in an unenclosed field, or sometimes a rancher on horseback. The country was green and spacious, and looked limitless. Before long we reached Cherry Creek, an isolated hamlet far out of the prairies. There were a few dilapidated Sioux huts, pleasantly situated on the top of a ridge; and a fine new white school building, with swings outside it. We introduced ourselves to the schoolmaster, a good-looking young Creek Indian from Oklahoma, who was understandably proud of his school. Throughout our conversations (conducted during a tour of the classrooms, the cupboards, the kitchen, the dining room, various corridors, closets, corners, landings, and cubbyholes) we were jostled and crowded by a packed crowd of little Indians, boys and girls, with solemn round brown faces and bright dark eyes. Some of them looked sickly, some not very bright, some like little moles, some like young foxes; but almost all were infinitely attractive; his wife, a gay and gracious Indian girl who was busy cooking doughnuts; and an elderly lady who had just arrived, apparently not greatly disconcerted at the idea of living in a caravan in an isolated Indian village on the Great Plains.

We wandered around the village, pursued by the more determined scholars. A few Indian women were washing clothes at a nearby well; by a happy geological stroke the well provides constant warm water, which makes the scrubbing easier. Outside the schoolmaster's house there was a toy car and a tricycle; next door lived a white American and his wife, who ran the trading post. Up on the hill we called at a Sioux hut where two weathered men were sitting with two jolly old women. We sat on the ground or on low stools, and chatted pleasantly, the Indian's command of English being limited, but their general bearing affable. I asked the men what knowledge they had of the Indian wars, fought in those regions not so very long ago. They answered with slow and restrained smiles (chiefly, I suspect, because they had never heard of the wars) and seemed to think it gently amusing, no more, when I suggested that their grandfathers might have taken a few white scalps in their time. There was no pretense about these Indians; they were far from the tourist routes, almost as simple in their outlook as they must have been in the days of the powwows and the slaughters.

As we sat and talked we noticed a large cloud of dark smoke across a neighboring ridge, and before long a miscellaneous crowd of Indians of all ages ran out of the schoolhouse and the other buildings in the village and piled into a few old cars and trucks that were standing about. It was a bush fire. Soon there was a general frenzied movement away from the village. Our old Sioux friends got their hats. One or two horsemen galloped out of the village; little boys jumped up and down with excitement, and we leaped into the car and drove helter-skelter down a brutal track toward the smoke.

So we clattered off, men, boys, dogs and all, across the dried bed of a stream, swerving through a thicket of trees, along a heavily rutted path, until we found ourselves high on the open prairie, with a great wall of smoke in front of us. A few white ranchers had been first on the scene, and they were trying to prevent the fire from spreading too far by denuding a strip of ground, around the perimeter of the blaze, of all its grass. An athletic young man in a wide hat was running along with a blazing torch, stooping now and again to set fire to the grass. His little blaze was bounded on one side by the track, but it spread so fast in the dry prairie grass that he could barely outrun it. The fire had spread over wide acres of land and the heat was intense. What with the smoke, and the blank prairie, the wrinkled ranchers, the Indians, the horses, the battered cars, and the smell of burning grass, this was a scene that might have been extracted from some pictorial textbook of the West. But there was nothing we could do, so we turned the car around and made our way westward across the open lands of the reservation, maples and disorientated, but pleasantly wandering and meandering along little beaten paths and gullies. The smoke behind us, now biblical in its posture, guided us roughly for thirty miles or more, and we eventually arrived at the hamlet of Hartley, one of the few places to be recorded in my American gazetteer as having a population of one.

The Indians are an odd, anachronistic part of the American body politic, in an uncomfortable state of half-integration. At Haskell Institute, their best-known institute of higher education (chiefly for vocational training) they gave me a copy of their magazine, including portraits of all the students. They are a fascinating study. Here is a girl from the Cherokee nation with a Scottish name and with all the plush attributes of the modern American girl; her hair carefully waved, her make-up impeccable, her smile poised and conscious, her cardigan worn with a careful casualness, a single strand of artificial pearls at her neck, an elegant watch on her wrist. Here, on the other hand, is a young man so ferocious of appearance that the scalping knife seems practically in his hand; his nose is hawked, according to tradition, his eyes flash, his eyebrows are heavy and threatening, his hair curls in a menacing quiff, his lips are thick but cruel, and his expression is one of unalloyed brutality. What a queer, mixed-up, mongrel, misused, ill-understood people these original Americans have become! They have their Football Queen at Haskell, their Pep Club, their Beau Brummel Society, their Katy Koeds, and even their Indian Club (where they dress up in feathers). But they seem to resist the racial melting pot more subtly and more resiliently than any of the enormous racial groups that have flooded into America during the last century; and there is about Haskell, despite the devotion of its skilled and kindly white staff, a feeling of melancholy and disenchantment.

For the Indian is still not as other Americans are. He is a man apart, a figure from the past, an old enemy, separate and different. Not long ago this induced among white Americans, a blind passion for extermination; now the mood is rather one of repentant patronage, for the treatment of the Indians has long been on the sensitive national conscience. Time has mellowed the old enmities; even the cinema makes heroes of its Indians nowadays. On the banks of the Fox River, in Illinois, there is a monumental statue by Lorado Taft of the great Fox chieftain Black Hawk; he was a persistent and dangerous enemy of the white man, but today many hundreds of tourists visit his statue, to gaze with veneration, no less, at his stolid face as it stares out toward the West. There is even a statue of poor Sitting Bull, on the banks of the Missouri River in South Dakota, protected against vandals by a cage of wire netting. It is fashionable and interesting to claim Indian blood (among white people, that is; statisticians say that 25 percent of the American Negroes could make such a claim, if they had the mind). In the Indian country, of course, many white ranchers can truthfully declare, as did one cheerful dark-skinned loafer I met in Oregon: "I'm no Indian, but I guess I'm kinda Indianified." But among another class of person Indian connections carry a status of allure rather akin to the alleged gypsy origins of F. E. Smith. I remember a smart socialite in Chicago, living in a beautiful lakeshore house, substantiating her claims to kinship with Pocahontas by showing us an entire room devoted to Pocahontas relics; and, indeed, she bore an extraordinary resemblance to that beautiful pagan.

Poor Indians! The hunters deprived of their limitless lands; the salmon-fishers working in canning factories; the Pueblos gaped at by tourists and patronized by gushing sociologists; the Navaho sitting at the wayside, like desert barrow-boys, hawking their blankets and their trinkets. The New Yorker expressed it well in one of its trenchant cartoons. Two Indians are squatting forlornly beside their wares, a few unenticing pots and trays, and one says bleakly to the other, like a sad spokesman for his people: "Being a chief in this day and age is a hollow thing."

Dams, Bridges, and Bones

*I*T IS science that has done this to the Indians, taming their prairies and humbling their befeathered warriors; and science, in its most spectacular forms, is still a dominant social force in the West, harnessing rivers, reclaiming deserts, altering the face of the land and the lives of all its people.

Take a road northwest out of Kingman, Arizona, through the scrubby desert that surrounds the Colorado River, and before long you will see science applied to nature at its most magnificent. The road passed first through gold-mining country; little dusty tracks lead off into the blue Cerbat Mountains, and sometimes in their foothills you can see, imprecisely, the cluttered buildings of a mining camp, or read on a crooked notice beside the road the high-sounding name of some small hopeful enterprise. There are no towns for fifty miles or more, only an occasional cocky shambles of a shack and a gas station out in the wilderness; but a side-turning goes to a mining village hideously named Chloride. On either side the mountains rise, a desert plain intervening, sometimes red, sometimes a startling purple, and alone in this human landscape crouch a few shriveled cactus trees. Presently the highway enters the hills, and winds over the dry dusty rises, doubling on its tracks, and twisting, and falling precipitously; and sometimes far below you can see a brown sluggish mess of slow water—the Colorado River, already 150 miles from its moment of glory, the Grand Canyon. Up and down the road goes, across interminable ridges, hot and dirty-looking, the only sign of life an occasional little cheerful donkey trotting along a hillside. The mountains are higher now, but the air is heavier, and you are beginning to wish you had driven straight through into the orange groves of California; until suddenly, in the narrowest of canyons, squeezed in between glowering ridges, high above the river, like a towering white fortress or the wall of the Potala without its prayer banners, proud, gleaming and monumental, appears the Boulder Dam. I would fly to America again tomorrow, and make the long hard journey across the continent, and spend an uncomfortable night in a second-rate hotel, for five more minutes beside it.

The dam is necessarily very narrow, and immensely deep (the deepest, I believe, that has ever been built); and the armies of pylons that march away from it, carrying power to California and its factories, are built willy-nilly up the side of the surrounding hills; they stand at grotesque angles from the ground, sometimes hanging horizontally over the gorge, sometimes so drunkenly leaning that they ought to sway, sometimes just a trifle out of true, so that you look at them twice and feel a little giddy. What with this queer crooked menagerie of steel objects, and the road running through the canyon, and the powerhouse in its depths, and the enormous face of the dam itself shining through it all, Boulder gives an extraordinary impression of jumbled brilliance; and to this effect an air of mystery is added by the constant unwavering hum of the turbines below, the only sound (with the dull thudding of water) disturbing the silence of the hills.

From the top of the dam you can see through the canyon to the open desert beyond, and there stands a lake so blue as to be almost ridiculous. It was created by the building of the dam and is the largest man-made lake on earth. (We bathed in it and found its floor lined with thick and foul-smelling mud. One of the purposes of the lake was to absorb the millions of tons of silt carried downstream by the Colorado River, which cuts and swathes its way through the crumbly desert hills; much of this muck is trapped in the lake, and dictates the consistency of its floor, though a great deal escapes and is piling up rather ominously against the northern face of the dam.) All around is a great recreation area, for hikers and picnickers and yachtsmen and swimmers, all a by-product, as it were, of this marvelous structure.

Boulder, with its bold lines, its excitement, its size, and its ability to give pleasure as well as utility, is characteristic of those vast monuments of American engineering which set the national pace and best reflect the national predilection for power. I never drove along a great American highway without experiencing a sensual pleasure, as if I were being carried away by the irresistible thrust and drive of the country. They are so wide and spacious, those great turnpikes and freeways, so sweeping and overbearing, so imperious in their stride. In any European country they would be called military highways, for they, are strategic arteries, carrying great quantities of goods, and capable of transporting whole armies swiftly across many states. They are not all in the spacious West. The most famous of them indeed, is the Pennsylvania Turnpike, which is described by its controlling authorities, without false modesty, as The World's Greatest Highway, The Highway of Tomorrow Serving You Today, a Gateway to Pennsylvania's Travel Wonderlands, and The Highway That Restored Pleasure to Modern Driving. You pay to use this road, but once having passed the toll booth you may drive at seventy miles an hour, with never a pause, from one side of Pennsylvania to the other. The road runs clean through the Allegheny Mountains (one of the historic barriers to American expansion) by a system of tunnels; it crosses three big rivers, the Allegheny, the Beaver, and the Susquehanna; 378 structures carry other roads over or under it, and there are twenty-four places of exit; nowhere on the entire highway, even among the hills, is there a single spot where a driver cannot see 1,000 feet in front of him. There are restaurants, and gas stations at frequent intervals, and so carefully is the whole system planned that the authorities have even dictated the correct length of the frank-furter sausages to be served at the wayside cafes. The turnpike has its own police force, equipped with wireless and radar, and its own authorized breakdown service. A series of microwave relay stations ensures radio communications throughout the length of the road.

Then there are the masterly bridges of America. Everyone knows the Golden Gate, which stands so slim and serene across the entrance to San Francisco Bay; but there are scores of others rivaling it in beauty. I remember with excitement my first experience of the Delaware Memorial Bridge, which carries the New Jersey Turnpike across the Delaware River. The road is running smoothly across a flat, colorless landscape when it is overcome by a sudden and dis-concerting spasm. It twists abruptly, shudders a little like a cat about to pounce, and then soars gloriously into the air on the thinnest of concrete supports. Almost before you know it you are high above the river, with the bridge white and shimmering all around you; and in a moment or two you are sweeping downwards in a graceful curve to be deposited gently on the Delaware shore. Such a bridge is one of the blessings of the automobile age, for a train could never sur-mount its gradients, and a horse would probably prefer to swim.

In Florida I crossed the wide expanse of Tampa Bay in an elderly puffing car-ferry, which made the voyage hourly from Piney Point to St. Petersburg (a city of old ladies, sunning themselves on benches, and probably playing clock golf before lunch). It was a beautiful sunny day and we labored gently across, vibrating heavily and wheezing; and as we moved there slowly came into view across the water the distant silhouette of an unfinished bridge. It spanned the whole bay, about fifteen miles wide. From each shore there jutted a low causeway, on stilts, and clustered here and there were little groups of cranes and derricks and hoists. In the middle of the bay—with the open Gulf of Mexico beyond it—the structure rose abruptly, to allow the passage of big ships; and in the very center there was a gap, where the two advancing structures had not yet met, as if two fingers, stretched out from the shore, were straining to touch each other, but could not, and had fallen back disheartened. A small coastal steamer, belching black smoke, passed beneath the distant struts as we watched, and presently the ferry jolted into its dock, there was a clanging of steel plates and a tooting of horns, and we drove ashore.

The atomic era has already begun in America (I stood at the dockside at New London, Connecticut, when the strange bulbous uncouth form of the *Nautilus*, the first atomic vehicle, slid improbably into the water) and sometimes, hidden away in lonely places, or deposited in some arid waste, you may come across one of the great centers of nuclear research and production.

There is an atomic reactor, for example, at a place called Arco, in Idaho; it stands in the middle of a volcanic desert, surrounded by distant dim hills, and littered with black crags and ridges of lava. Here they made the engine for the *Nautilus*, in a mock submarine housed in a concrete building, though it is 2,000 miles from the sea, in the center of the continental mass, with endless deserts and plains and hills between it and the Atlantic, and the Rocky Mountains blocking the way to the Pacific. The reactor buildings are far from the highway and that part of the desert is closed to the public, but you can see, settled squatly on the plain, a square white building like a brick, which houses some of the more significant devices. Around it are a few straggled houses and structures, but it is the squareness and whiteness of it that stands out, and you can see it for many miles along the highway, and ponder for many minutes (if you are that way inclined) on the oddity of its presence there.

Los Alamos, where they first penetrated the ghastly secrets of the atomic explosion, is in another, brighter, gayer desert, in New Mexico, within sight of those gracious mountains where the Penitentes indulge their mystic tastes. You can see the smoke of it above the ridges, but it is a secret city, and unless you have friends, or good reason, you are not allowed to pass the guarded gates that stand a couple of miles outside the laboratory area. Los Alamos has been a mystery for so long that it has become a tourist attraction, and many visitors drive down to peer through its iron portals. Two French visitors who went there recently reported that the entrance was guarded by tanks and surrounded by antitank barriers. When I went, there were only a few languid, apologetic policemen, with revolvers at their hips, who said how very sorry they were that I could go no farther, and urged me to remember the names of any friends I had inside the barrier, who could give me authority to enter. The antitank obstacles, I am told by New Mexicans, are only gates to stop the cattle wandering. All the same, Los Alamos has its secrets still; the atom bomb was hatched there, and the hydrogen bomb, and who knows what is happening now in its desert hollow? During the first hushed activities of the Manhattan Project, when lorries drove through the night across the empty ridges to Los Alamos, and consignment of strange workers arrived to labor there, and when secretive scientists from several nations began to appear in Santa Fe, the local belief was that a new weapon being designed was something vast and round, that could be rolled across the countryside squashing everything within reach; now the wiseacres admit that anything being cooked at Los Alamos today is beyond the reach even of their fluid imaginations.

Oak Ridge is at once the most compelling and the most suggestive of these atomic spectacles. They built it in lonely heath country in Anderson County, Tennessee, and I saw it for the first time on a lowering drizzly day in early spring. If you are driving there from the north you see first the small and unpleasing township which was built during the war to house the Oak Ridge workers. Though it has some grandiose signs outside it, describing it as the cradle of the atomic era, it is a depressing place, a cross between an army barracks and a lumber camp, with buildings of a dishearteningly temporary feeling, all peeling and cracking, as if they are not worth mending. There are a few shops and a hotel; and some long dormitory blocks that made me shudder slightly, so close were they in spirit if not in antiquity to the Cavalry Barracks at Aldershot; and an interesting museum where you may see a huge mechanical arm, used for handling radioactive materials, sweep out with the authority of a sledge hammer and pick up from the ground, softly and sweetly, with infinite gentleness, a small but speckled egg.

Around the corner the blighted domesticity evaporates. The heath is bleaker and more desolate, and presently through a gap in the high ground beside the road you can see the atomic plant. For me, on that gray, wet morning, the impact of it was alarming. The sprawling plant lay in the gloomy hollow, all colorless, faceless, and anonymous, surrounded by high fences of barbed wire. Rank upon rank of low buildings stretched away out of sight, and smoke drifted and scattered from many tall chimneys. There it lay, silently; there was no sign of human life, but only this vast factory, like something dead, shut in and secretive, closed to the world, like a prison or an asylum. There was a hush about it, and a deathlike blankness; and it was this supine feeling that made it eerie, for no doubt behind its characterless walls thousands of pleasant people were busy making bits of bombs, knocking off at the evening whistle, and driving down to their dull town for an evening's bridge or a visit to the pictures.

America, and especially its western states, is littered with projects of such extravagant importance, and everywhere big new things are being done: wide roads are slapped across the countryside; graceful bridges soar across the rivers; there are new airports everywhere, new skyscrapers, new dams, whole new suburbs. Great river systems are being harnessed, as the Tennessee was harnessed years ago. In the Columbia Basin, for example (where the superb Grand Coulee Dam stands), there is rising a wide intricate network of dams, canals, reservoirs, pumping stations, and powerhouses, providing not only immense supplies of electricity, but also channeled water to irrigate large areas of sparse and wasted land. Often in the West you can see signs of the spreading fertility that follows such works; in a valley between dry brown hills for instance, where a few first fields are ten-tatively sprouting and the road runs for a time between delicious green patches before plunging back into aridity. With an eye to that incalculable commercial advantage called "goodwill," the Americans always make provision for the passerby who likes to observe works of construction, even to cutting convenient eyeholes in the wooded walls that surround building lots. One warm summer's day I stopped to observe the construction of a new dam. The river valley above it had already been stripped of life and it lay there shaved of trees and shrubs and farmhouses, with an even mark, like a contour line, marking the permissible limit of vegetation on its slopes. On the big pile of earth and stone that would one day be the dam, elaborate machines were busily moving, scrambling over the rubble, picking up soil and dumping it, pushing mounds out of the way, and suddenly scurrying off into the distance to perform some obscure separation out of sight (for all the world, at that distance, like singularly well-behaved beetles, off to perform a natural function).

The construction company had obligingly placed a little hut on an eminence overlooking the dam site, for the benefit of the idle traveler, with pictures showing the course of the work, and a big model to demonstrate its purpose. A man in uniform was there to explain it all, and very willingly he chatted. He was a local man, and had watched the progress of the dam since its inception. How long ago, I asked, did the people living in the valley know that one day they would have to move? He considered for a few moments.

"Let me see, now. I was born in a farmhouse just beyond that ridge there—all gone now, of course, but it was a good old place—and I remember as a boy being told the old place was going to be pulled down because of the dam. Let me see, that must have been 1916 or '17—1917, I should say, I remember it quite clearly, the war was on and they said the old place was going to be pulled down."

"Good gracious me," I said, "all that time ago! So they had plenty of time to get ready."

"Oh yes, we had twenty years and more, and then they fixed us up with a house in the town there, you must have passed through it, on the left hand side it is, very comfortable. Oh yes, it was quite a break though, the family always lived in the valley, you know. Yes, my grandfather and grandmother were buried down there, to begin with."

"Oh, they're not there now," he said, eyeing me as if I were something of a simpleton. "They moved all them cemeteries. Two whole cemeteries they moved, dug 'em over the hill there. They couldn't leave graves down there, you know, it wouldn't be decent.

They shifted the whole lot, gravestones and all, over the hill. Yes, there was my granddad, and my Uncle Joe, and a cousin or two—moved 'em all, couldn't leave them there—it wouldn't be right!"

I left him trying to remember if Aunt Martha had been buried there too, and drove away wondering at the omniscience of these engineers, who harness the elements and bridge the great streams, split the atom, and throw their roads across the continent, and yet (if only for the goodwill) manage to remember Granddad's bones.

∾ 18. ∾

Mormons

*A*LMOST the first to introduce the benevolences of science to the western frontiers were the Mormons, the original American masters of irrigation, whose home in Utah is still a showplace of induced fertility.

The Mormons like to say that they obey the most catholic and least contentious admonition of Saint Paul: "Whatsoever things are true, whatsoever things are holy, whatsoever things are just, whatsoever things are pure, whatsoever things are lovely, whatsoever things are of good report; if there be any virtue, and if there be any praise, think on these things." They have a reputation for eccentricity, and certainly some basis of their belief are marked by a decided oddness; but I have never encountered a community so generally contented, so prosperous, confident, and well-disposed. The Mormons long ago gave up polygamy, in return for the granting of statehood to their territory of Utah; but they believe that no man can go to heaven without his family, and that the accumulated piety of the generations is spiritually important, so that Utah is notable for a lively happiness of home life. They are by no means a morose or solemn sect, though alcohol, coffee, and tobacco are officially forbidden. They are fond of music and dancing and bright colors, and their recent architecture is delicate and agreeable. (There was a time when Mormon ladies greatly outnumbered their menfolk; so they devised a special form of the cotillion, that gracious and elaborate dance, to allow every gentleman two partners at a go.)

I came in to the Mormon country from the west, after a day of desert driving. The first sign of Mormon activity was a series of irrigation canals, making the country (between dry hills) green and pleasant. There were rows of poplars, planted to act as windbreakers; neat barns; small farmhouses, rather in the English manner; and innumerable haystacks, each surmounted by a strange crooked derrick for hoisting the hay, which is very characteristic of the Utah countryside.

The first town was Delta, a small place with a double row of shops and a wide street, clean and well kept. There was a new Mormon chapel and assembly hall, with a spire as slim as a needle, and a portico with four slender white columns. I asked the hotel-keeper if he was a Mormon. "Sure I am," he answered cheerfully, "we all are around here mostly; and if you ask me, anyone who ain't don't know what he's missing!" He told me about the community activities of the place—activities which, though scarcely to my own taste, certainly sounded worthy and well intentioned. The Mormons set great store by voluntary work for the common good. They operate mines and factories, for example, and cultivate land, chiefly by voluntary labor; the projects provide work for those who need it, and the profits go to a great welfare fund. (Sometimes Utah even relies upon voluntary executioners. A criminal condemned to death may, if he chooses, be executed by a firing squad instead of by hanging; and a team of volunteer riflemen then carries out the sentence, shooting through slits in a canvas screen at a range of twenty-five feet.) "Talk about the Welfare State!" said my informant. "We've had one for a hundred years! Did you ever see a disgruntled Mormon? Or a happier place than Utah?" The Mormons believe strongly in good education, and for years maintained their own excellent schools. They believe in proselytizing, and have missions in (among other places) Argentina, Australia, Brazil, England, Guatemala, Denmark, Germany, Finland, France, Japan, Mexico, Holland, New Zealand, Norway, Samoa, South Africa, Sweden, Switzerland, Tahiti, Tonga, and Uruguay.

Partly because even the sins of ignorant ancestors can be expiated by present conduct, they are keenly interested in the past, and in forebears and origins (only their motives being different from those of the ladies of Charleston or Nantucket). One of their older convictions is that in ancient times the American continent, especially South America, was inhabited by a race of extremely early Christians. The dates of their dynasties are obscure; but the founder of the Latter-Day Saints, Joseph Smith, was guided by a spiritual personage named Moroni who had been, in his earthly existence, a prophet among these archaic Americans. A Mormon girl happened to tell me that her father was out of town that week, doing a series of lectures. "He lectures about South America," she said, "and of course he's very busy." "He's lived in South America, has he?" said I, wondering a little, for the family ran a modest grocery store. "Oh no, he hasn't—but *all our folks lived there, you know, in the olden days!*"

She was referring to Moroni's people, and accepted without question all the peculiarities of history and circumstance which are entwined in this strange Mormon theory. This is typical of the Mormons. They are an eminently practical people, good planners and agriculturists and social organizers. The visitor, inevitably impressed by the results of their faith, is tempted to slur over its more unlikely tenets on the grounds that so happy a society more than makes up for a few implausibilities. But the Mormons will have none of this. Not only do they readily agree that Mormonism triumphantly succeeds, but they also insist that all its claims are literally true.

To those whose visions less glazed by faith, the origins of the church seem enshrouded in dubious vagueness. In 1823 Joseph Smith, the founder (then aged eighteen), was visited by angels at his home in New York State, and was told of some gold plates buried in a nearby hill, which concerned the history of the ancient Christian

Americans and would become "a new witness for Christ." After many exchanges with divine messengers and advisers, he dug them up, found them to be written in Egyptian, Chaldaic, Assyriac, and Arabic, and set about translating them. The consequent writings constitute one of the sacred books of the Mormons.

Smith later had some witnesses to the existence of the plates. Three friends, of exceedingly religious temperament, joined him in praying fervently that the plates, removed by the messenger, should be shown to all of them. One, Martin Harris, withdrew after a period of prayer because he felt that his presence was impeding the process. Before long the other three were visited by an angel, who showed them the plates, turned over the leaves, and announced that Smith's translation was an excellent one. Meanwhile Harris had gone elsewhere to pray by himself, and Smith joined him. Again, the prayers were answered. "The same vision was opened to our view (wrote Smith), at least it was again opened to me, and I once more beheld and heard the same things; whilst at the same time Martin Harris cried out, apparently in an ecstasy of joy, ''Tis enough, 'tis enough! Mine eyes have beheld; mine eyes have beheld!' and jumping up he shouted 'Hosanna,' blessing God, and otherwise rejoicing exceedingly."

Later twelve other witnesses said that they had actually handled the plates, apparently while they were in Smith's possession, and they signed a testimonial saying: "This we bear record with words of soberness, that the said Smith has shown unto us, for we have seen and hefted, and know of a surety that the same Smith has got the plates of which we have spoken!" These testimonials are taken very seriously by Mormons who are of course aware that many Gentiles (as they call the rest of us) regard the story of the plates with some degree of skepticism. But they do not all agree about the eventual fate of the plates. Some say that they are now in divine hands, others that they were returned to their original cache in the hillside (a sparse and scrubby little hill in New York State) never to be disturbed again until a divinely appointed hour.

Whatever the truth of these obscure matters, Smith's followers were infused with a resolve that brought them, after cruel persecutions and harsh journeys, across the mountains to Salt Lake City, where their splendid leader Brigham Young looked out across the desert and made his celebrated pronouncement: "This is the place!" The phrase has become a slogan, at once sacred and patriotic, encountered everywhere across Utah: and when you drive across the border into naughty Nevada, you find near the state line a gaudy, neon-lit, clinking hooting gambling saloon which has applied the words to its own premises. When we drove into Salt Lake City, past the incredible waste fastness of the Great Salt Lake, we could see across the plain to the mountains which the Mormons traveled with such hardship (dismantling their ox wagons on the eastern slopes, manhandling them across the range, and reassembling them on the other side).

It is a handsome and spacious city, dominated in every way by the huge sacred edifices of Mormonism. On Sunday morning a green Temple Square, in the center of the place, is gay and animated, full of people in colorful clothes on their way to service, or to listen to the enormous Mormon choir whose Sunday services are broadcast throughout the nation. The chief building, the Temple, is vast and Gothic, with six pinnacled towers, one surmounted by a gold figure of Moroni, unfortunately at such an elevation that it is difficult to see what such an ancient American prophet looked like. The Temple is not open to the public, only a few spiritually eminent Mormons are allowed to enter it. Nearby, among the landscaped gardens dotted with memorials and monuments, is the Tabernacle, a massive domed building largely made of wood, with a famous organ.

To hear this great instrument, we went to a recital there and enjoyed a characteristically Mormon half-hour. The Latter-Day Saints are talented publicists and we were welcomed by a smooth young man who made a little speech about the precepts of the Church. The program was an odd mixture of the classical, the sentimental, and the homegrown. There was some Handel and some Bach, played thunderingly; a piece called "The Thrush," which set the old ladies of the audience smiling winsomely; a scherzo composed by the organist; an old melody arranged by the organist; and the favorite Mormon hymn, "Come, Come ye Saints." During my stay in Utah I came to know this hymn well and to like it. It was written during the march of the Mormons westward across the continent, in the 1840s, and it has a fine jovial exuberance: "Why should we mourn, or think our lot is hard? 'Tis not so; all is right!" But carefully though I have listened to it and tried to analyze its shape, I remain baffled by the complicated balance of its rhythms, which always seem to be coming to one conclusion, but inevitably break away to another.

There is a little museum near the Tabernacle, with some interesting things in it, and some mementos full of curious nostalgia; a 'cello, for example, brought by one of the pioneers with the ox trains, and some desert crickets, preserved under glass, of the kind that almost destroyed the Mormons' first crop after the establishment of Salt Lake City. (The crops were saved by a swarm of seagulls, which arrived miraculously in the nick of time, ate up all the crickets, and are commemorated by a tall memorial pillar near the Temple.) The first cabin in Salt Lake City is preserved behind iron railings and protected by a classical pergola. There is also a war memorial. The Mormon pioneers naturally made magnificent fighting men. I was once driving down almost as lonely a highway as you could find in America, across a stretch of the Nevada desert, hot, empty, forbidding, when I saw a small monument beside the road; it commemorated the young Mormon volunteers who had fought in the war against Mexico in 1846. The Mormons had begun their slow journey westward into Utah when the war broke out, and they were asked by the Federal Government to provide 500 young men for the war. The men instantly volunteered and made a famous forced march southwards in the heat of summer, from Council Bluffs, in Iowa, to San Diego on the southern Californian coast, across some of the hardest and hottest country in America, with a speed and cohesion that astonished the professional soldiers. They had passed down my own road (before the road was there) and as I stood beside the monument I could all but see the pious columns of the Saints streaming across the desert in this *tour de force*.

On summer nights there are film shows in the gardens of Temple Square. Hollywood once made a film of the life of Brigham Young, and this is shown by earnest Mormon operators to silent crowds of tourists, sitting on deck chairs, strolling by in the shadows of the plane trees, sprawling on the grass. An efficient publicity organization has its offices in the square and issues slick, shiny booklets about Mormonism and its buildings, and answers questions with automatic courtesy, like a slot machine responding to pennies. This organized self-advertisement is conducted partly, no doubt, because the Mormons are such avid missionaries, and partly because the great tourist traffic which now finds its way to Temple Square contributes usefully to the prosperity of the place. The Mormon Church is financed chiefly by tithes; every member contributes a part of his income to the central funds, administered in a big building in the classical manner, suitably dignified with broad steps, Ionian columns, and an air of unfathomable probity. "But take a look around you," a man remarked to me one evening as we stood at the gates of Temple Square, "and it all belongs to us. See that hotel, the best in the city? That's ours. See that one there, the second best? That's ours. Buy a paper, sir? It's ours. Listen to the radio? It's ours. Want to open a bank account? We can fix it. Yes, sir, don't worry, we know all about making money!"

Indeed, the Latter-Day Saints, who founded Salt Lake City, still firmly control it. Even if you wander away from Temple Square, which is the fulcrum of the city, you will constantly find yourself up against smaller sacred edifices, statues of Brigham Young declaiming "This is the place!" emblems of Mormonism, the offices of Mormon-owned companies, Mormon pamphlets, Mormon music, and the talkative Mormons themselves, who live their lives with persistent sprightliness.

Whenever I think of Salt Lake City, with the dome of its state capitol and the pinnacles of the Temple shinning there beneath the mountains, I think of bright clothes and urgent smiles; the sickly harmonies of the old melody, as played by the organist at the Tabernacle; the strains of his vast choir seeping across the square on

Sunday morning; this unquenchable cheerfulness of the people; the general air of satisfied competence; and the extraordinary blandness of the old lady who told me one fine summer morning that for high religious purposes she had been tracing the course of her ancestry, and had succeeded in establishing it back to 64 B.C., "only a few years," as she rightly remarked, "before Caesar went to England, but of course, the ancient Americans had been civilized for centuries, as the blessed prophet Moroni told our founder—that's him, that's the prophet Moroni, right up there on the Temple tower—see?"—and I looked again, shading my eyes against the sun, but could perceive only the vague outline of that antique saint, holding what looked like a trumpet.

A Lively Ghost

I DROVE from Utah into Nevada, for I wanted to see a famous ghost town there and to sample its unusual pleasures. It is worth visiting these abandoned towns of the West, for you can trace in the crumbling ruins of their cabins some of the old excitement of the region, when a wild multitude of adventurers was looking for gold, fighting feuds, drinking ghastly brews, making fortunes, and ruining women among the dusty hills. Some such skeletal towns are quite isolated and forgotten. I drove for many hours along rough tracks, through uninhabited hills, to reach the site of an old mining center called Aurora, on the eastern frontier of California. This had its heyday in the 1860s, but until recently a couple of resilient prospectors were still extracting a little gold, by simple means, from the surrounding land. The shells of their shacks are still there, with sagging staircases and holed ceilings, and a few shreds of flowered wallpaper; and the body of an old-fashioned car with no tires is rusting away in a gully. For the rest, there are only the suggestions of vanished occupation—fragmentary walls and piles of bricks, flagstones sprouting thistles, and doorsteps hidden in the undergrowth. In this place, now totally deserted, Mark Twain began his career as a reporter at a time when the news from Aurora was read avidly throughout the mining regions, and had its effect upon the price of gold, upon private fortunes and public funds, even upon the state of peace and the chances of war. Much of America has this feeling of impermanency, partly because people are always prepared to move, and have no roots in the towns where they live, and are just as prepared to make money in San Diego as they are in Buffalo. But it is not always so poignantly obvious as it is in the dead towns, which so recently enjoyed their days of consequence.

Sometimes, like great mansions in England, they are preserved as curiosities, and so, with a tightening of the belt and a grimace, manage to potter on through the years as remembrances of things past. Central City, in Colorado, has achieved this sad protraction. It is tucked away in the Rockies above Denver, and has a stream running through it from which, if you are conscientious and have time to spend, you may still extract a few dollars' worth of gold any day you please. The hillsides flash with deposits of mica, which deceived many a poor prospector, in the old days, and is still called "fool's gold." But the town is surrounded by the decaying remains of mines, long ago worked out, and has rows of quaint Western houses and saloons, and an old Opera House in which distinguished companies now perform, during a summer season, to audiences composed of dutiful tourists and the sizable local intelligentsia. The Victorianism of the place is its present fortune. Shop names are written in ornate lettering; houses that would hardly deserve a second glance in some dingy London outskirt are displayed as historic attractions. The Old West, which seems so very old to the Western American, smacks strongly of Aunt Agatha to the wandering Englishman. Central City is a museum piece, interesting enough as a memorial to the mining pioneers, but stultified and fossilized.

There is one ghost town, however, which has managed, despite the tourists and the sanctity of age, to retain something of its old rumbustious heartiness. Virginia City, Nevada, was the capital city of the Comstock Lode, and for a decade or more it was one of the most exciting cities on earth. It was built high on a hill range near the western frontier of the state; around its ridge stretches an enchanting green plain, made fertile by irrigation, beautified with rows of tall poplars, bounded on one side by the desert, on the other by the brilliant peaks of the Sierra Nevada. Immense fortunes were made in Virginia City in its palmy days, and it was a large and luxurious metropolis. The International Hotel was famous for its food and for its elevator, the first to be installed between Chicago and San Francisco. Paris couturiers had branch houses there, so plentiful was the cash and so ambitious the inhabitants, and whole ships were chartered to bring European furniture and fripperies for the mansions built by the gold magnates. A celebrated railroad, the Virginia and Truckee, wound its way up the hills to Virginia City, conveying in its elegant canary colored carriages many an eminent financier from San Francisco, and taking back in guarded trucks the troves of gold extracted from the neighboring mountains. At the big Opera House scores of eminent artists performed at one time or another; more for the money, I suspect, than for the critical acumen of the audience. The *Territorial Enterprise* was the most distinguished newspaper of the West, and a national force not only because of the wealth that lay underneath it, so to speak, but also because of the trenchancy of its comments. Virginia City must have been the gaudiest and rowdiest of towns, full of saloons and gambling houses and brothels; enlivened by romances, brutal murders, and the affairs of celebrated courtesans; rolling in gold, fame, and notoriety; so important that the discovery of a single deposit at Virginia City caused Bismarck to abandon the silver standard—and all this among the forsaken hills of Nevada, a land of freebooters, Indians, and desert creatures.

Virginia City is still a vivacious and florid place chiefly because it happens to be in Nevada. Of all the states of the wide West, Nevada retains most completely and most easily the old frontier liberalism of the region. Gambling is legal in Nevada, and divorce is easy. It is a place of hard drinking and all-night gambling, a state with no speed limit for cars and a flexible outlook on the value of existence (a croupier who recently murdered a customer by knocking him down and jumping on his head was sentenced to six months' imprisonment and is probably back on the job by now). All the symbols of the West are more intrusive in Nevada than elsewhere. It is the least populous of the American states, and the great trains sweep majestically across its expanses of empty desert. It is a place of insufferable summer heat; at Death Valley, just over the California border, temperatures have been recorded higher than anything known in Asia, and only two degrees Fahrenheit lower than the highest ever recorded anywhere (at Azizia, in Libya). Mines are everywhere, and often and again you can see on the side of a distant hill the cabin of some lonely operator. There are many Indians: one tribe, the Paiute, lives on the shores of Pyramid Lake, a secluded place of dazzling beauty, once abounding with rare fish, with swarms of white pelicans flying over its depths and settling on its jagged rocks. Nevada is a colorful, open-air, easygoing state; and it makes its living by gambling, for every town has its garish casinos, and Las Vegas, the crowning symbol of the state, is one great blinding and nightmarish tribute to the gamblers' gods.

It is gambling that has kept Virginia City so boisterously alive—gambling and the presence there of a stormy lover of the West, Mr. Lucius Beebe, who edits a revived version of the *Territorial Enterprise* and lives grandly in a small Victorian mansion, keeping Rolls-Royces and St. Bernards. When we first drove along the narrow main street of Virginia City, a blurred composium of bright saloons, with the clatter of a piano, disastrously ill-tuned, echoing among the alleys, we chose a likely hotel and had our bags moved through its tiny front parlor, up its narrow stairs, and into a front room boldly named "Julia Bullette" after the most famous of the town's nineteenth-century madams. Virginia City has many such hostelries, smelling slightly of dust and old bricks but agreeably instinct with memories of robust pioneers and their adventures. Almost before we had settled in (first opening the windows to let out some of the prospecting aridity, then closing them again to keep out the piano), Mr. Beebe was aware of our presence, by bush telegraph; and before long he was showing us the town, wearing a hat with a flat crown and a very broad brim, a shirt with a wide and handsome check, an elegant pin-striped suit, and a waistcoat embellished with a splendid gold watch chain. Mr. Beebe is a fine sight at any time, but is at his best when he strides into a gambling house with his St. Bernard at his heels; pausing for a moment beside a roulette wheel to throw a handful of silver dollars on the table with a satisfying clang; shrugging his shoulders with a cheerful nonchalance when he loses the whole lot; bending an ear to a tattered prospector from the hills who has some slight financial worry; raising a negligent hand of greeting to an acquaintance here and there; listening patiently to report of the activities of a man who plans to get even with him for something he wrote in the paper last week; ushering his guest into the dimness of the bar with a truly Bostonian courtesy, before hitching his frame on to a bar-side stool and ordering an extremely large whisky.

He has managed to make Virginia City a greatly profitable affair, without entirely destroying the magnificent natural brassiness which never deserted the town, even in its inglorious decades of neglect. Many tourists are attracted to it by its manner of rather musty wickedness, and the shops are booming. A man dressed as Buffalo Bill, with authentic mustache and goatee, and a cowboy hat, runs a place that is part museum, part antique shop, crammed with old clothes and mining mementos, with frilled bloomers hanging from its walls, and all kinds of oddities displayed on tables. The Opera House, despite its blackened decrepitude, is open to the public again; its walls flutter with hundreds of old posters, and familiar names spring out as you pass along the line—Jenny Lind, an indefatigable performer to Western audiences; Edmund Keen, and many another well-remembered virtuoso. The *Territorial Enterprise* flourishes again, after a few years of oblivion. Huge posters proclaim its value throughout the surrounding hills, and everywhere in the town you see its old-fashioned masthead and glimpse a few lines, on the news agent's stand, about a vendetta, or an effrontery, or a brazen boast— matters which appeal to Mr. Beebe, its publisher, and admirably reflect the tenor of the town. The paper circulates widely, for it has a curiosity value, besides some good writing by friendly contributors of distinction; and because Mr. Beebe has been, in his time, a well-known Eastern bon vivant and observer of society affairs, it is crammed with advertisements for night clubs and scents, expensive cars and splendid hotels, which read queerly among the tumble-down enticements of Virginia City.

Very little has been rebuilt in the town, despite its revived prosperity. Main Street is still lined with false fronts, the pompous facades of the shops belying their poky premises. On the walls there are still visible advertisements for forgotten remedies of startling efficacy. Part of the station is still there to see, though the marvelous old trains run no more; one old engine stands forlornly in main street of Carson City, the capital of Nevada, a few miles to the north; and in another piece of rolling stock, wheel-less and pitiable, you may eat a memorial hot dog, and wash it down with a sad funereal coffee. From the saloons on Main Street you can look down on the richly Gothic church, built by a gold magnate when the galleries of his mine underran the old one; and far in the distance, down a sandy gulch, you can glimpse the place where they buried Miss Bullette, who was eventually murdered by a thief and taken to her unconsecrated grave in pomp by all the men, and none of the women, of that rampaging community.

In the summer season the gambling houses are crammed with drastically assorted crowds—ranchers in wide hats and shirts with pearl buttons, visitors from Iowa in loud shirts, impending divorcees from Reno and Las Vegas, a schoolmistress or two (most adventurous of Americans), a few hairy locals and mountaineers, and Mr. Beebe strolling expansively through the throng. You may gamble in many different ways, entrusting your cast to the roulette wheel or slipping your dime into a machine, pulling the handle, and waiting for your winnings to emerge. Numbed indeed are the faces of those unfortunates who find themselves hypnotized by this last device; there they stand, hour after hour, inserting the coin, pulling the handle, inserting the coin, pulling the handle, catching their meager winnings as they fall from their hole in a little paper cup provided for the purpose. Sometimes they win a jackpot, and are handed a voucher for thirty dollars or so. More often they squander the hours away listlessly, with never more than momentary fluctuations in their capital, confident that the machines are honest (for the state controls gambling with paternal care), and performing the necessary actions with a heavy rhythm. In the bigger gambling towns of Nevada you may see these people at any hour of the day or night, sweating in the raging heat of noonday or dismally alone at night, clutching their little paper cups, their eyes glued dully to the machines, inserting the coin, pulling the handle, while the hours crawl by.

But sometimes, too, you may observe a gambling session in the legendary style: the groups of anxious betters, grouped around the roulette table, not disposed with the elegance of Monte Carlo, but in a rougher, lustier pattern, and the hard-faced croupier of tradition, impassive at the head of the board. I remember clearly the appearance of one of the most famous of Nevada's croupiers, descended directly from the great Western gamblers of the gold rushes. He is a tall man who wears a check shirt, open at the neck; narrow trousers sustained by a belt with an ornate buckle; and a black eyeshade. His face is withered and wrinkled like a tortoise; his nose hooked and slightly crooked; his eyes sharp and pale; his mouth thin but humorous, conveying an impression of unyielding bonhomie; his ears long and protruding; his tall, thin neck entwined with a mesh of muscles and sinews, like Laocoön and the snake. Coldly and knowingly this man presides over the game, with precise efficiency, taking or paying mechanically with never a flicker of emotion, only the slightest hint of a nod, or the suspicion of a gesture, or the embryo trace of a beckon, in the direction of the management. In front of him the piles of big silver dollars (common currency in Nevada) glitter like stage properties; and once in a decade there passes through his hands a dollar made of gold, withdrawn with heart-searchings from beneath some indigent mountaineer's mattress.

It is hard to escape the spell of such a gay and resilient society. Nevada has its hideous aspects, its rows of garish neon signs, its dubious citizens, its occasional hypocrisies, its willingness to live on human frailties and temptations. But is has its likable excesses, too, and many kindly people among its bars, mines, and ranches. And however mild your temperament, cherished in Cheltenham or in shady Cotswold vicarage, you will scarcely evade some small tingle of excitement, like a giggle from the corner of the garden, as you drive through the desert for an evening at the Golden Nugget.

ᘓ 20. ᘔ

Creatures of the West

EVADA is so predominantly desert that much of it is uninhabitable even by animals; but if you drive northwards, toward the Great Plains, you can sometimes imagine what a paradise of animal life the West must have been before the eastern Juggernaut rolled in. Occasionally you may even still see the buffalo (or the bison, as he should really be called). "Keep your eyes open on the left," said the warden of a reserve in Wyoming, "and you may see a few of them near the road. Don't go near them, now, they turn nasty sometimes." Sure enough, there they were, not in the endless black seething herds that the old plainsmen hunted, but pottering about in twos or threes, with their hunched shoulders and matted hair, looking bored and brainless. Some were strolling through the clumps of trees scattered about the open plain, and rubbing their thick hides on the trunks; some were sitting about like cows, chewing.

A restaurant beside the road offered "buffaloburgers" for lunch and I stopped to ask how it was that these animals, so scrupulously preserved from extinction, should be available for this sad metamorphosis. I was told that since they breed fairly prolifically and cannot roam elsewhere they are outgrowing their limits; so for an unfortunate minority, whack! and there is a crate of buffaloburgers. This is an astonishing fact, for in 1889 the original mighty herds of buffalo, which positively blackened the Great Plains during the migratory season, had been reduced to 541 head, and most of those were in zoos or private preserves. Thanks to the American strain of historical romanticism, the beast has made a remarkable recovery, and there are now about 9,000 bison in the United States, most of them as free, and all of them as stupid, as the ones we saw in Wyoming.

Apart from their physical presence, the heritage of the buffaloes is always alive in the West. In the Great Plains you may sometimes see a big dusty depression in the ground that is pointed out to you as an old buffalo wallow. After rain, when these holes were filled with water, the buffaloes used to splash in them and roll about in the mud at the bottom—not for the pleasure of the exercise, but because they wanted to cake themselves with a covering of dried mud to form an armor against the attacks of insects. Then there is a cliff in Colorado that is shown to the inquiring traveler as the scene of a great disaster in the heyday of the buffalo herds. One day, it seems, a vast concourse of buffaloes was moving slowly and relentlessly forward in the face of a terrible blizzard. They could see practically nothing, so thick was the driven snow, and when the first animals of the herd reached the edge of the cliff they were unable to stop in time and plunged over it, to be killed at the foot of the precipice fifty feet below. So tightly packed together were the other creatures, and so slow of intelligence, that one by one their ranks reached the edge of the cliff and were pushed over it. For years their bones lay there, several feet deep, and it is said that 100,000 buffaloes died in the tragedy.

Indeed, the very roads you drive along, and the railroad tracks, were probably originally stamped out by the buffalo herds. The first white men to cross the Allegheny Mountains found a way through them by following the trails of the buffaloes; for the herds apparently wandered regularly across the hills, the last wild bison east of the

Alleghenies surviving until 1801. Farther west the buffalo herds had known for generations where best to cross the big rivers, and they had done so in such countless multitudes that they had worn smooth passages down the bluffs to the fords—gentle enough, very often, for the unwieldy covered wagons that followed them. When the transcontinental expresses travel beside a western river (as they frequently do, most colorfully, on the railway posters) they are often following a buffalo route; the bison liked to journey within reach of a river, and they were skilled at finding shortcuts between streams, which were later useful to pioneers making portages.

It is difficult to conceive nowadays, in the empty prairies or among the scattered survivors of the buffalo population, how many of these animals lived in the Great Plains in the days of their prime. Some experts believe there were about sixty million, most of them forming one huge herd which wandered from Texas to Canada. A traveler in the 1870s encountered a group of bison which was fifty miles long and twenty-five miles wide; he thought there were probably four million animals in it. Often the prairies were black with them, and they held up traffic on the railways and occasionally, by swimming in the rivers, seriously delayed the passage of steamboats too. Buffalo families (led by a cow) wandered widely within the loose society of their herd, especially in the summer when they were looking for fresh grazing grounds. They often traveled 400 miles or more for good pasturage, gathering again for safety and for comfort when the winter came. Thus before its settlement the American West was alive with those creatures, sometimes in herds of unbelievable size, sometimes in small groups, traveling the length and breadth of the prairies, crossing mountain ranges, beating out routes, fighting off wolves and coyotes, breeding hardily and unaffected by the severe fluctuations of the western climate. But it took only half a century to reduce them to a handful of pathetic survivors.

The Americans are still idealists, and have developed an active conscience about the barbarities of their grandfathers; Indians are, as we have seen, one target of their repentance, and buffaloes are another. Though Buffalo Bill is still a popular hero, many are the virtuous who deplore his record of 4,280 buffaloes in eighteen months. And indeed the nineteenth-century American hunted the buffalo with a senseless and insatiable appetite. It was true that for the pioneer, as for the Indian, the carcass of a bison was extraordinarily useful, providing staple foods and delicacies; hair for blankets; hides for tents, clothes, and shoes. Later, too, there developed a great commercial demand for buffalo robes and heads. But often the creatures were slaughtered simply for a rather bestial kind of blood sport, and in the second half of the century the commercial hunters were able to kill them so easily, and worked so ruthlessly, that many herds were swiftly and totally exterminated. When buffaloes were plentiful, people shot them simply for fun; out of train windows, for example, as they crossed the Great Plains, with no hope of recovering the bodies, only the transient and dubious pleasure of seeing the animals fall. Later, when they were beginning to disappear, the professional hunters pursued the last herds mercilessly, standing watch at water holes so that sooner or later the beasts would be forced to come within rifle-range. When the buffaloes themselves had gone, fortunes were made out of the bones which lay in almost endless profusion all over the prairies. Trainloads of these remains were shipped out of Dodge City, Kansas, the buffalo capital, to be made into fertilizer.

There were excuses for all this carnage. The bold plainsmen of the frontier times naturally did not think in terms of conservation, neither their temperament (to which we owe the opening of the West) nor their circumstances demanding any such caution. Certainly they felt no sentimental qualms about animal life, which, like themselves, must simply comply with natural laws about the survival of the fittest. (Though Americans in general have not inherited the frontiersman's realistic attitude toward animals, they have never become reconciled to mountains, which were fearful obstacles to the pioneers, and which are still to most Americans things to be avoided unless properly tamed.) Moreover, besides the economic value of dead buffaloes there were some political arguments for killing them off. The Indians depended upon the herds for their sustenance, their homes, and to a large degree their continuing indigenous culture, because their ornaments and tokens were made from various parts of the bison. This was before the days of reservations. The Indian tribes were still fighting the United States Army in the field, and the American Indian Problem was as much military as social. There was therefore a school of thought in Washington, fostered by some of the generals, which believed wholeheartedly in the speedy destruction of the buffalo herds. The Indians would be deprived of their raw materials, it was argued; their warlike activities would be suppressed; their resilient peculiarities would fade; civilization would be greatly advanced. When a bill for the protection of the buffalo was presented in Washington in the 1870s (in one recent season 75,000 animals had been killed within seventy-five miles of Dodge City) President Grant refused to sign it. The sooner the buffalo vanished, the sooner the Indian would be forced into more reasonable behavior.

Anyway, the American conscience has saved the buffalo. There are at least twelve times as many now as there were at the beginning of this century, and they still have their fervent lobbyists. Some livestock men foresee a new branch of their industry if the buffalo becomes readily available again. Its meat is good, and there are still uses for its hide and hair. People have already tried crossing the buffalo with a cow and the yak: they called the resulting organisms cattalos and yakalos, but they were not wildly successful. Now one enterprising rancher is trying to breed musk oxen, having captured a few specimens during a determined campaign in the Canadian Arctic; and elsewhere in the United States reindeer are being bred. If these farsighted venturers have their way, America will be populated with such great beasts again; and the wild buffalo of the past, so dominant a figure in America's days of adventure, will graze quietly with improbable colleagues in many a peaceful field.

Some of the other western animals still flourish, though the prairie no longer teems with an endless abundance of game. There are many antelope in the Great Plains, tame and placid for most of the year for they are protected, suddenly and understandably shy when the first shot of the hunting season is fired. In some dry hills a few burros linger on, deserted by those unshaven prospectors, slung with shovels and knapsacks, who used to spur them so confidently toward the big bonanzas. Black and brown bears are common enough. In some of the national parks their commercial instincts have ruined them; for they line the motor roads, bereft of grace and independence, begging for food like actors who have sunk through drawing-room comedy and music hall to the chilly corners of Shaftesbury Avenue. Tourists are often injured because they insist on feeding these tasteless animals by hand, and it is amusing to watch the park rangers when a bear turns up, for example, on the terrace of a resort hotel; at once protective and educational, interrupting their discourses about feeding habits to shoo a child away and scold its blushing parents, and holding the audience in an obedient ring around the wretched animal; which, calmly gobbling a sugar bun, sits on its haunches in the limelight like a nasty old man out of the woods.

Occasionally in the West you come across a colony of prairie dogs. I had always imagined these to be coyotes until, in Wyoming, I was shown one of their cities. It was a warren of small burrows, each with a small mound of earth in front of it, spread over a wide area of flat prairie ground; and when, after a long delay, one of its inhabitants ventured to poke a quivering head out of its hole, I saw that it was a little rodent like a hamster or a dormouse, bright-eyed and alert. Such a city supports an advanced and sensitive society, presided over, it is said, by an individual animal to whom some nineteenth-century naturalists gave the Orwellian title of The Big Dog. Its inhabitants post watchmen on top of their mounds to give warning of any approaching dangers. When a peril materializes, these sentries make a sort of whistling noise, somewhat resembling, as the explorers Lewis and Clark succinctly put it, "tweet, tweet, tweet!" before making a mad dash for the burrow and disappearing. "They're friendly little things," said our guide in Wyoming. "You wouldn't believe it, but they have little owls living down those burrows with them, tiny owls, sharing their burrows. You wouldn't hardly believe it." He was right. I did not believe it. But later I looked up the prairie dog in my encyclopedia, and sure enough tiny owls *do* cohabitate those burrows, subsisting mysteriously, so the book says, on "insects and crayfish."

In relatively limited quantities (by the fabulous standards of the old Indian country) there is still a variety of game in the West. A hunting map of Utah, for example, shows the presence of bears, elk, mountain lions, bobcats, antelopes, deer, rabbits, quail, duck, sage grouse, geese, pheasant, and mourning dove. Thirty-six different species of duck visit the state, and six species of geese. But it is no longer a hunter's free-for-all. There are strictly limited seasons, there is sometimes a limit on numbers, and many creatures are protected (in South Dakota they include frogs). In the deer season it is a common experience to be stopped by enforcement officers who want to see if there are any slaughtered animals in the boot of the car; and everywhere along the country roads cars pass by with loads of jovial hunters, and the carcasses of deer affixed to their radiators, their haunches protruding on one side, their antlers, poignantly, on the other. So many men go shooting in the deer season, and so many of them are such abysmal shots, that rigid regulations are decreed to prevent accidents. Some states, for example, oblige hunters to wear red caps and red jerkins; others forbid the wearing of any checkered colors. The newspapers, with a saccharine piety not uncommon among the provincial American press, join in the safety campaign assiduously. One journal, I remember, published a photograph of a very stout Westerner in the middle of a forest clearing, laboriously stooping to tie up his shoelace. "Don't shoot!" admonished the newspaper. "This is not a deer!"

But of all the creatures of the West, the horse is king. He forms so integral a part of the Western pattern, and has contributed so powerfully to the Western myth, that it is sometimes difficult to remember that he is not indigenous to the country, but was a Spanish importation. As Sir Thomas Browne observed: "How *America* abounded with Beasts of prey, and noxious Animals, yet contained not in it that necessary Creature, a Horse, is very strange." There are some wild horses in the West now, hunted by "mustangers" for conversion into dog meat; and there are countless brave domestic horses, on every ranch and Indian reservation, haughtily carrying Paiute farmers along the shores of Pyramid Lake, or, gay and sweating, dashing across the churned mud at many a rural rodeo. Cowboys are everywhere still, often dressed (just like the pictures) in elegant shirts with tight sleeves and many buttons, and in high decorated boots. In the bars of almost any small western town you may find these handsome men, talking in their slow and dreamy drawl, or drinking alone, their hats on the backs of their heads, looking away into a nonexistent distance with an expression of total and enviable vacuity. When they ride (with an easy and unorthodox grace) they and their horses are one; there is no master and servant relationship, no arrogance of breeding, no formalities of snobbery; the two animals, equal in rank and very similar in nature, simply perform as an entity.

In Montana once I found the road blocked for a mile or more by a mass of sheep. Some were moving very slowly, some were nibbling the sparse grass beside the highway, some were sitting down, and one or two seemed to be fast asleep. At the head of this leisurely procession were two cowboys, mounted on fine black horses. The men were very weather-beaten, dirty and bearded, with their tangled hair escaping from their hats and their fingernails black and broken. They had been rounding up the sheep in the surrounding mountains, to bring them down for shearing and to escape the coming winter snows. "We been fourteen days in the hills," said one, "and seven days on the move. Sheep ain't very fast movers. Boy! shall I be glad of a bed!

"As for this horse," he added affectionately, "all he wants is a good hot cup of coffee and a place to put his feet up! Ain't that right, boy?"

PART FOUR

THE PACIFIC COAST

∾ **21.** ∽

On Hollywood

$\mathcal{L}$ ONG AFTER the Industrial Revolution in England the Pacific coast of the United States remained unspoiled and idyllic, all the way from the forests of Washington state to the Spanish shore of southern California. Times have abruptly changed, for at its most delectable point, where the mountains come down to the sea, the Americans have built Los Angeles, and for most people that hectic complexity has become representative of the region. I have never experienced a less pleasing contrast than the one which overwhelms the traveler, in his innocence, as he journeys out of Nevada across California and into the frenetic bustle of Los Angeles.

The city sprawls from the sea for many miles inland, an enormous mess of related townships, criss-crossed by big busy roads, blotched by dingy quarters of poor whites and Mexicans, given its reputation of fabulous peculiarity by the mansions of the film magnates and the glamorous streets of shops and hotels that surround the studios of Hollywood. The business area of Los Angeles is drab and ugly; the long line of the beaches has been spoiled by relentless exploitation, so that the beautiful semi-tropical coast, so warm and inviting, is alive with a riotous mass of feverish architecture, tarnished and corrupted by the touch of a jazzy civilization.

The pressure of life in this place is wearying, and many of its people are therefore touchy and unfriendly, not even bothering (as often as not) to summon that veneer of standard charm dictated by the American theorists of success. Irritable faces are everywhere, and hurried, waspish movements. Only the police force, one of the best in America, manages to maintain the easy courtesy one would expect of a people so happily placed geographically, and with so gracious a historical background.

Nevertheless, there is a fascination about Los Angeles, emanating chiefly from the film studios, that is not easily escaped. It arises partly, of course, because of the extreme notability of its inhabitants. I once arrived at Mary Pickford's house in response to an invitation to tea. Miss Pickford, though no longer acting, is a powerful force in the financial structure of Hollywood, and her mansion, a pleasing white house in a country-house garden, is excessively grand. I was greeted by her manager, but by a misunderstanding he had not been told of the invitation. His manner, I thought, was a trifle forbidding. Might he see my credentials, please? Yes, yes, a visiting card was all very well, but how could he tell that I was who I purported to be? Did I not realize that Pickford was a very, very important person indeed? "Tell me," he said, "would you expect to go straight in and see the Foreign Secretary, back home? Do you realize people try and get in this house just to *touch* Miss Pickford? She is a *fabulous* personality, and we have to be very, *very* careful who comes in here." I was ushered into the garden where Miss Pickford was drinking China tea, given her by Madame Chiang Kai-shek, with a young Episcopalian clergyman and a celebrated surgeon from Texas.

∽∾

The fascination lies in the fact that this aura of unnatural despotism surrounds people who are intimately familiar to us, whose faces we know precisely, whose very boudoirs we have, as often as not, entered in the course of some dancing comedy. It was greatly interesting to me, if not moving, to enter the very room where Walt

Disney's chattering chipmunks were conceived. Disney's studios are large and beautifully tended with gardens and lawns and streets named after cartoon characters: but for me the best of it was to hear a friendly artist say: "I've always loved the chipmunks, ever since we first drew them." These two little creatures, who live together in a tree trunk, talk to each other in a wild flow of unintelligible language, very fast and squeaky. I asked Disney if they were really saying anything comprehensible. "Well, we began by recording a conversation, speeding it up very fast, and then playing it backwards, so you couldn't really make much sense of that. But lately we've played it the right way about, and if you listen very carefully you can sometimes get the meaning of it." Two little American animals (their very species is unknown to millions of their admirers) sent out to distant and exotic places to talk an alien language backwards!

The stars, poor things, can scarcely resist the temptations of global celebrity. Beverly Hills, the district they have built for themselves on the hillside, stretching away out of the perpetual mists of Los Angeles into the heavenly sunshine above, is a caricature of a stockbrokers' suburb, enlivened by illusions of greater grandeur. The streets are neat and symmetrical, lined with handsome trees. The garden gates are dainty, often suggestive of gnomes and thatched summerhouses. The houses are rarely blatant, but generally decorous, and usually of Olde Worlde inclinations. On the higher reaches of the hill, where the flowers are more brilliant and the air more stimulating, the houses lose some of their restraint, but most of Beverly Hills is eminently genteel, in appearance anyway. The bigger and more established the star, the more he tends to see himself as a magnate rather than an artist, and the more hierarchical his household becomes, and the more dignified and manorial his residence. How unbecoming they must think it, these constitutional monarchs of Hollywood, when the tourist guides set up their stands on the pavements, and tote their brazen signs: "See where the Stars Live: Maps and Guide Books 50 cents! Every Star's Home Marked!"

I watched one of the most feudal of all Hollywood actors in action in a studio, and was amused to see the corrosive effect of many long years as a celebrated profile. How he posed and postured! How regularly, when he muffed his lines, did he stare petulantly toward the door, as if to imply that some poor stagehand, standing morosely there, had disturbed the flow of his words with a stifled cough or a shifting of feet! With what consummate tact the director gave his instructions, so circuitously worded that no suggestion of command could be read into them; and purposely designed to allow that aging hero, with a flourish of impatience, to disobey them in the required manner! "Do we really need all these people on the set at once?" said the profile irritably. "I mean they don't appear in this frame, do they! Forgive me, but I really can't see why these people should hang around. *Would* you mind?" (here a sudden intense flash of the famous smile) "—*would* you mind leaving us, my dears?" And with what grimaces of tired and tolerant distaste those two good subsidiary actors left the set, the little man with the wrinkled face, the tall lady who portrays to perfection the fussy schoolmaster's wife, with a wink to the director from the man, a mock flounce and tossing of skirts from the woman—lost, all lost, on that dull conceited actor behind them, smoothing his graying mustache with one hand, thumbing his script with the other, with the air of a man who is expecting to find spelling mistakes!

However, I confess that despite the presence of such unattractive phenomena, I enjoyed my glimpse of Hollywood and its people. I sat one evening in a smart and famous restaurant with Mr. Edmund Gwenn, the doyen of English actors in the place, and one of the best-loved of its inhabitants; and past us, down the passage between the tables, came a dazzling procession of handsome men, and girls in wonderful dresses shimmering with fine brocades, sparkling with diamonds, their furs as crisp as snow, their manner of festivity flaunting and irresistible. I do not know what sordid proceedings were hatched at Chasen's that night, nor what forbidden intimacies were performed afterwards, nor how crucial were the contracts discussed. But many of those ambitious young celebrities paused very pleasantly to pay their respects to Mr. Gwenn, with a smile or a light remark, and to shake hands agreeably and unhurriedly with me. Some of their faces are as familiar in Baghdad as in Stoke Newington; but only occasionally did I see one racked by the blasé complacency I expected. On the technical side of film productions, in particular, there are many bright, able, and accommodating people. You may meet them anywhere as you stroll about the studios, the English artist working for Disney, with his north-country bounce, his cheerful cockiness, and his excellent tweeds; the young cameraman from Brazil, with a roving eye and a wittily disjointed style of conversation; the writer from Yale, not too cynical about his professional tasks, but deeply engaged nevertheless, in the corner of the studio, with the manuscript of a book on the metaphysicals. I shall never forget the grave pleasure with which one of the greatest art directors accepted his winnings at a game of bingo in a club at Santa Monica, on the sea; the prize was one dollar, and he wondered anxiously (whispering about it to his wife and to me) whether he ought to go and collect it, or whether it would be presumptuous to expect the master of ceremonies to bring it to him; and he sat there indecisively until it was brought to him at last, a silver dollar at the bottom of a goldfish bowl, and he picked it out seriously and slipped it into his pocket, very pleased indeed.

The wealth of Los Angeles, and especially Beverly Hills, is incalculable. It was brought sharply home to me by the manager of an actor who suffered from recurrent illness, and was thereby handicapped in the making of films and the accretion of money. "Poor fellow," this man said, "he's going through a bad time. I don't mean he's starving, or anything like that, you know. He can manage. He gets by. He can make—poor chap, it's hard to watch—he can make one film in the year—$90,000 or so—he manages—but it's a bad time for him, a very bad time." This was an actor never particularly well known, a familiar face without a name; and his situation emphasized the simply fabulous resources of the top stars—wealth beyond the imagination of the old gold prospectors, and by no means to be sniffed at by many a small and moth-eaten republic. The streets of Beverly Hills are among the most glittering in America; the shops packed with delectable items, the hotels piled deep with carpets, the boulevards wide and embellished with fine palms. Around the fringes of Los Angeles there is much dinginess, and some of the streets that link the business section with the sea are paragons of drab monotony; but Beverly Hills oozes opulence, well-being, and good preservation.

Not all this money comes from films. The high company and glamour of Hollywood has lured many rich men to its precincts who have nothing to do with the cinema; and Los Angeles itself, in area the largest city on earth, is booming with industry. Several of the American oil millionaires live in Beverly Hills, as much courted by the film community as the stars are pestered by their fans. I went to a cocktail party at the house of one of these tycoons. His was a mansion built in the Spanish style, with shutters and porches and creepers, and large slim dogs standing languidly near the door. In the hall, I remember, there was a large book-rest, like a lectern without its eagle, and on it, opened at the letter O, this making a fairly symmetrical ornament, was a gigantic leather-bound copy of *Webster's Dictionary*. The room in which the party was already nosily proceeding was crammed with the heads of wild animals—not just the odd elk's head, or a few scattered antelope, but close, serried ranks of larger and more ferocious creatures—lions and rhinoceros and hippopotami—pushed in together, jowl to jowl, tusk to tusk, so that one beady eye seemed to run into the next, and shaggy matted ears were all but entangled with neighboring horns. Our host, a genial and robust person, was standing at the bar, built of dark oak in one corner of the room, telling a funny story to the barman. "Hi, there! Come on in!" said he, pushing me a potent martini, "You know the general, don't you!"—and still with one arm on the bar he waved cheerfully in the direction of an elderly man whose very word, only a few years before, had been enough to summon an army or launch a campaign. So the evening began, and I found myself wandering a trifle dazed among the animals and the celebrities; the film stars, bronzed or beautiful; the captains of industry, in dark double-breasted suits, wonderfully suggestive of stocks and oil wells and astronomical incomes; the leopards; the public figures from a few years back, whose faces once looked at us from the cover of *Time* magazine, who have written their memoirs and ground their axes, and who have now withdrawn to California, with their plump wives in pale-blue cocktail dresses, and their sons on leave from Fort Knox, to mingle eminently with the party crowds, and express their ponderous opinions of the strategic value of the Pescadores.

"And where are you off to next?" asked a benign plutocrat, wearing shoes of crocodile skin.

"Seattle," I replied, "for a couple of days. I'm taking the train there tomorrow."

"Ha!" said he, "don't take the train. I'm going there tomorrow myself, on my way to visit my oil wells in Alaska, and I'm taking my private plane. Why don't you come along? It's very comfortable—it's a DC-3, boosted up, of course, I've put my own engines in, we should make it in three hours. Okay? See you at the airport."

And so saying he wandered off, to flirt heavily with a nearby actress, and dig a friendly admiral wickedly in the ribs.

So I did, and left Los Angeles suitably. We arrived at the airport in three different cars—the millionaire, his private secretary, and I— each with our uniformed chauffeur. There stood the airplane, gleaming in the peculiar combination of colors. It was decorated with the flags of every territory it had crossed, and with the names of the various seas, and the millionaire's monogram was prominently displayed on its nose. There stood the pilot, and the co-pilot, and the steward, and the crates of good food, and the bottles and the siphons, and the napkins decorated with the millionaire's initials. There waited the various secretaries, and managers, and couriers, with last-minute advice about the state of stocks, and a few whispered queries, and a briefcase full of papers.

We climbed aboard, and were soon roaring across the airfield. I noticed on the tarmac a powerful fighter aircraft of lethal aspect, clearly capable of great speeds and formidable impact. "That belongs to Jimmy Stewart," said my millionaire, leaning across my seat and offering me a cigar from a silver box. "Remember him in *Rear Window?* He's *very* fond of aviation."

ᴄ **22.** ᴐ

Motor-living

*I*F IT is this kind of thing that gives Los Angeles its aura of affluent individualism, its air of frenzy stems directly from its position as undisputed capital of the world of the automobile. They make the cars in Detroit; but they use them, more than anywhere else on earth, in southern California, where almost everyone has a car, where the undergraduate expects one as his due, and the high school boy's popularity may depend upon the color of his convertible. The American civilization is inextricably enmeshed with the internal combustion engine. ("Now we're the upper-middle class district," said my guide as he took me round the suburbs of Portland, Oregon, "moving up out of the Oldsmobiles into the Buicks"—and sure enough, Buicks there were, by every curb, with only an occasional Oldsmobile standing sheepishly in a garage.) To observe this phenomenon at its most advanced, you must go to southern California.

It is an old joke that the Americans are soon going to lose the use of their legs, and eventually have them reduced to vestigial remnants, like the feet of whales; but it is true that few Americans will walk anywhere if they can help it, either for practical purpose or for

186

pleasure. You can do your banking from your car, without leaving the driving seat, by choosing a bank with a "curbside teller." You can post your letters in postboxes that protrude to the level of your car window. You can watch a film from your car in a "drive-in" cinema. At many stores you can be served in your car. At innumerable restaurants waitresses will hitch trays to the car door, so that you can eat without moving. In Florida there is even a "drive-in" church, where two or three may gather together sitting in their Chevrolets. There is no more characteristic gesture of American life than the casual rolling-down of the car window and the emergence of a hand, to grasp a hot dog or a theater ticket, a pound of apples or an evening paper, a check book or a bottle of cider from a roadside stall.

Imagine yourself, for a moment, as a traveling motorist in America. Setting off in the morning (let us say) you pull in to a petrol station for a tank of petrol. "Regular?" says the attendant, meaning the cheaper kind; and the answer he gets depends upon the locality. In New Jersey, where so much oil is refined, petrol is likely to be cheap. In Colorado, on the other hand, it can be nearly twice as expensive. If you are lucky, you may pass through a region which is enjoying a price war, and find yourself faced with a succession of scrawled blackboards, each offering petrol at more ludicrously inadequate rates, until (if you have patience) you may fill your tank practically for nothing. "Okay," says the attendant, wiping his hands to receive the money; but in the meantime he had not only delivered the petrol; he has checked the oil and the tires, cleaned the windscreen, filled the radiator, inspected the batteries. If it is desert country, he has topped up the water bag you carry slung over your front bumper. If you needed maps, he has produced them free from the office. He may have given your small son a lollipop from the stock he carries in his pocket. He has certainly asked you where you are from, and told you about how he was stationed outside of Norwich with the Air Force, and how he liked the pubs, but he wouldn't go back for anything all the same, and he hoped the food situation is better now. He expects no tip, but smiles the standard American smile (so universally pleasant as to be enigmatic), and waves to the children through the back window as you drive away.

So you are off. The road is likely to be smooth and wide, and you are tempted to speed, not least because almost everyone else on the road is speeding already. The limit varies, according to the state you are in. Nevada, as we have seen, has none except in cities. In some other places you are theoretically limited to fifty miles an hour. If you go too fast, you may be stopped by the traditional "speed cop," with his howling sirens and trenchant manner, and given a little yellow ticket. It is more likely nowadays that you will be intercepted by radar. Notices will warn you beforehand—"Watch your Speed! Checked by radar!"—and your progress with be picked up by instruments mounted beside the road or in other cars, infallibly recording your speed and probably photographing your number plate.

Take no risks on the roads, especially in southern California. The American is a dashing driver, and often a reckless one; and statistics have shown that it is thirty-two times safer to fly in an American aircraft than it is to drive on an American road. Whatever you do, avoid the low-priced car driven by the single young man; he is probably a salesman, oppressed by the prosaic nature of his calling, and he likes to devise unutterable dangers on the road, as a relief to the monotony. If you see a woman driving, with small children in the back of the car, keep with her: she is probably just as skillful as the men, and, with all her responsibilities concentrated on four wheels, she is prudent too.

Do not be ensnared by the numbers and plates on other cars, which are a constant distraction. Every state has different number plates, often prettily colored, and with fancy slogans like "Minnesota: Land of 10,000 Lakes"; "Illinois: Land o' Lincoln"; "New Mexico: Land of Enchantment"; "New York: The Empire State." If it is near the turn of the year these slogans are even more diverting, for they are often changed, and it is amusing to see what horror Arkansas, for example, has perpetrated *this* time. There are many other odd things to see on the passing cars. Some people invent slogans of their own. "Official Car," says a pompous plate, aping the senatorial manner, and adds in smaller print: "Tax payer." Another popular one, during my stay in America, was: "Don't Blame Me! I voted Democratic!" Often motorists buy stickers to record the states and "scenic wonders" they have visited, and their rear windows are a gaudy mess of colored posters, with reproductions of decorative hanging bridges, Puritans, geysers, bears, country houses, the Capitol, Indians, caves, and rhymes like:

> There's always a welcome, early or late,
> From old Minnesota, the North Star State.
> In the land of the lake and the tall fir tree
> Joy is awaiting both you and me.

The whole makes a pattern of souvenirs that is not only dangerous, in that it blocks the view through the car windows, but is often aesthetically indigestible.

In any small town en route you may buy an excellent cup of coffee; but be careful how you park the car. It is generally illegal to cross the road and park the car on the other side in the direction you are traveling. It is usually unpopular, in places where cars are parked at right angles to the curb, to swing around and cross to the opposite side of the road. Once you have found a place you must have a nickel or a dime for the parking meter; put the coin in the slot, and the machine records how long you have been standing there. If you overstay the limit a red flag will show, and the chances are that a slowly wandering policeman will happen by, and pause to examine the evidence, and then, laboriously extracting a notebook from his recesses, will take the number of your car in triplicate, and affix a notice to your windscreen instructing you to pay a small fine by such-and-such a time. It is a painless process, for you need not appear in court; indeed in some places you can pay the fine there and then, by wrapping your dollar in your police ticket, and depositing it in a box conveniently affixed to a neighboring lamppost. In a small town in Kansas my ticket, apologizing profusely for the trouble I was being caused, instructed me to place the fine on a tray; and there I found change, in case I had only a five-dollar bill. It is an admirable device, the parking meter, relieving policemen of unnecessary duties, involving the minimum of paperwork and administration, and making it easy for the motorist to comply with the law and have his coffee too.

Most of the big American roads are most skillfully signed. Large notices suggest the safe speeds for corners, and if you test them you will find that they are exactly right for the average American car, so powerful on the straight, so lumpish on the corners; go slower than they suggest, and you will be wasting time, go faster and you will feel the care heel over, and hear the tires scream disconcertingly. (They scream more easily than European tires, anyway, thus giving the impression, when some gentle old lady drives cautiously around a bend, that she is making for the Presbyterian Church with an uncharacteristic abandon.) If there is a dangerous curve, or an obstacle, huge boards scream at you with bright colors or checkered patterns, not singly or in pairs, but in long rows, for several hundred yards, so that you can hardly escape their impact.

If you are color-blind, you may have difficulty with the traffic lights, for you cannot rely on the relative positions of the colors. In England I know that when the light is shining in the top hole, I must stop; and that when it shines in the bottom hole, I may go. In America there are no such certainties. Sometimes the red light is at the top, sometimes at the bottom; sometimes it is not red at all; sometimes there is no amber light. Whatever the system, there will soon be a riotous hooting of horns behind if you fail to move when you may, for the American driver has none of the fatalistic patience of the British. In San Antonio, Texas, I once found myself (in common with everyone else) faced with peculiar traffic light problems; for the whole system had gone wrong, and the lights were flashing and winking crazily, shining in the wrong order, staying for interminable minutes at red before changing momentarily to green, sometimes coming on all at once, sometimes going out all at once, till the whole city was dizzy, and portly businessmen were lying back in their driving seats in heavy hilarity. "That's Texas for you," my companion remarked, "they always overdo a good joke."

Presently it is time for lunch, and you may care to try a drive-in restaurant. Steering warily into a kind of covered stall, you blow your horn (trying not to make it sound peremptory), and soon there emerges from the central building a waitress. She is likely to be plain, but heavily prepared. Her heels are high, her skirts a little short, her nylons excellent, her manner experienced. She takes your order, and soon reappears with the food, on a metal tray which fits neatly on the door. Milk in a carton (let us say); ham and eggs on a horrid disposable plate, which makes the ham taste insidiously of cardboard; bread automatically sliced; coffee in a cardboard cup; lump sugar wrapped in hygienic paper. If you want a dessert, there are many ice creams on the menu, and always several varieties of pie; the fruit pie is a national dish—cf. the menu of the *Monarch*—and pie *à la mode* (meaning pie with ice cream) is a universal favorite. When you want to pay the bill, blow your horn again, and soon the waitress will be with you once more, smiling prettily, and examining the tip without much bashfulness as she takes the tray back to the kitchen.

When the dusk comes down, and you begin to feel the fatigue of travel, you may like to relax for an hour or two at a drive-in cinema. If you are near the town in southern California you are sure to come across one—a big stadium with a high wall, overshadowed by the screen, with the gigantic silent figures of the actors easily visible from the road. You buy your ticket without leaving the car, and maneuver your way into a convenient position. On posts dotted around the arena are loudspeakers attached to wires; reach out of the window for one of these, place it on the seat beside you, and there you are. At first it may seem a little queer having the voice beside you and the figure far away on the screen; but you will soon get used to it, mentally arranging (according to your temperament) either that Miss Monroe is really in the car with you, or that Mr. Frankie Laine's voice is up there with his larynx. It is a wonderful way to see a film, for if you are really bored you can go to sleep in the back seat, leaving your wife to endure its banalities; and from time to time, in the best drive-ins, somebody comes round with a tray of refreshments, and knocks politely on your window. You can take your dinner with you, if you like, and eat sausages while the cowboy gets his man. Moreover, you can talk when you please, and put your feet up, and wear the most wildly extravagant of hats without being hissed at from the row behind. Only one thing can be said against the drive-in cinema; on a dark, lonely evening, in the flat and open country-side that surrounds so many American towns, there is something creepy about the sight of those silent figures on the screen, singing their silent songs, whispering their silent intimacies, hurling their soundless imprecations, as the motorist drives by outside.

Finally, at the end of your day, you decide to put up for the night. Just beyond the drive-in cinema, toward the center of the town, you will find the motels. There are rows of them, each with its neon sign, its oddities of architecture or decoration, its illuminated notice announcing a vacancy. Some are long terraces; some are a series of huts, like bathing cabins. Some veering toward the pretentious, and going in for swimming pools and television, are liable to be expensive; others patently frequented by cockroaches and secret lovers, are certain to be cheap. You take your choice, register at a little office, and drive to your own front door. There is no service (and no tipping), and you may have to walk down the road for a meal. But your room is probably clean and comfortable, if not luxurious, and your car is parked freely and conveniently directly outside your window.

There will certainly be a shower, and very possibly a bath. If it is a good motel, all kinds of small attentions will be paid you. The evening newspaper will be provided, and a small library will be placed beside your bed. There will be a new pair of bedroom slippers, made of a thick paperlike substance, and an unused fabric device for cleaning your shoes. Coat hangers without number hang in the wardrobe. There is a radio, and perhaps a television set. Nests of plastic cups are in the bathroom, and cakes of soap in healthful packaging. The tumblers may be enshrouded in cellophane, and the lavatory seat (as likely as not) will have a paper wrapping across to testify to its cleanliness. Some motels, with a thought to the early traveler, provide coffee for the morning. It comes in powder form in a little cardboard cup, together with milk powder, sugar, and a cardboard spoon; and in the morning, in the cruel dawn, you have only to add hot water to this mixture (from the tap) to have a peculiarly repulsive and effective beverage.

So you sink into your soft, squashy bed, while the night traffic roars by; and in the morning, so gentle is the civilization of the automobile, you need only walk a pace or two across the carpeted floor before you can sink refreshed into the welcoming driving seat. But this manner of life, so highly refined by the southern Californians, is only a beginning. One city is installing conveyor belts to carry pedestrians along its shopping streets; they will step from their cars first onto a slow-moving belt, then onto a faster one and so proceed in elegant ease along the boulevards. Already the Californians need rarely walk; soon, if this is any kind of portent, they will have no opportunity.

ت **23.** ک

San Francisco

Y OU do not have to travel far up the Pacific coast to en-
counter the very antithesis of this motor society. San
Francisco is famous as the most glittering, glistening, and
cosmopolitan of American cities; but I found there an integrity and
earnestness of thought that reminded me of the life my grandfather
led at the turn of the century, on the intellectual fringes of country
society near the Welsh border. I was once flying over San Francisco
Bay with my host in northern California, an eminent businessman
with all kinds of knowledgeable interests, from mountaineering to
typography. Below us stretched the fine wide expanse of water that
divides San Francisco from the Bay cities of Oakland and Berkeley.
And around it the hills were brown, and speckled with white houses;
on an eminence to our right there was a series of tall radio masts. To
the west, where the Bay joins the Pacific, the ineffably beautiful
Golden Gate Bridge was softened by the sea mist; and perched on the
hills beside it was San Francisco, crowned by a few skyscrapers, a
mass of white buildings tumbling down the hillside, and stretching
away to the ocean as far as the eye could see.

My friend leaned across me, more delicately than the Los Angeles
millionaire had leaned. "Now *there*," he observed, "he might very

well have put in there. You see that bay down there, this side of the hill, where that little ridge comes down? That would be almost perfect—sheltered by the hill, d'you see, and out of the tide, but not too far inside the Golden Gate. They must have rowed in, you understand—they couldn't sail directly in through there, and that would have done them perfectly. You can scarcely imagine a more suitable place, can you?"

He was saying all this half to himself, and with an expression of great earnestness; and, primed though I was by earlier experience, it was some few moments before I realized that he was talking about Sir Francis Drake, who sailed down the Pacific coast in 1579, in the course of his voyage around the world. Nobody knows, it seems, whether or not he discovered and entered San Francisco Bay, and among a minority of San Franciscans It has become a perennial intellectual exercise to worry out the facts, to conjecture the progress of his voyage and the needs of his quartermasters, to examine the chances and argue the likelihoods, to search through old documents and estimate the worth of those few records left by members of Drake's company. My companion, thus considering a possible sheltering place, was behaving rather as Mr. S. D. Roberts might, if he were taking a bus down Baker Street and pondering the situation of No. 221B.

This agreeable preoccupation with a problem at once academic and romantic is characteristic of the faintly old-fashioned intellectual activity of some cultured San Franciscans. They examine such a matter with tremendous thoroughness and enthusiasm, and pursue it if possible to a well-documented end. The Drake question, for example (which is extraordinarily fascinating, especially in surroundings so redolent of golden adventure), has been considered by San Franciscans in the minutest detail. The evidence that Drake ever put into San Francisco Bay is by no means conclusive. There is no doubt that he sailed down the Pacific coast, and a nearly contemporary record says that he put into a "fair and good Baye," a "convenient and fit harborough," where he beached and careened his ship. Before leaving this haven, says the record, he erected a plate claiming possession of that country in the name of Queen Elizabeth, and naming it Nova Albion.

Until 1936 the historians, antiquarians, and loyal Californians argued the point of the basis of this inadequate knowledge. It is perfectly possible that Drake sailed right past the Golden Gate without detecting the magnificent harbor inside it. San Francisco is often shrouded in a thick sea mist; the entrance is narrow; the Bay itself curves southward, so that you cannot appreciate its magnitude for the sea. On the other hand, if he did penetrate the Bay the fact is not likely to have been publicized. Drake's voyage was of crucial strategic importance, and to give away to the Spaniards the existence of so fine a haven would have been so careless as to be criminal; about like publishing, let us say, technical details of one of the smaller hydrogen bombs. The admiral's own journal and his charts were handed over to the Queen, and a full account of his voyage was never published. The only contemporary descriptions are generally thought to be unreliable.

So for half a century the San Franciscans contented themselves with hypothesis. Could he have brought the *Golden Hind* into the Bay, supposing that he had indeed found its entrance? What course would he have followed inside the Gate? Many are the citizens who have tried, over the years to re-enact the Captain-General's arrival, struggling through the vicious currents of the Golden Gate in heavy rowing boats or sailing skiffs, laboriously progressing, in the interest of history, toward some sheltered inlet or likely creek. Many are those who, flying back from a conference in Portland or a half-term celebration at Andover, have leaned over their neighbor to peer through the window and murmur: "Perfectly possible! Almost an ideal spot, don't you think?"

In 1936, however, a scholarly bombshell burst, disintegrating many a rigid opinion. In the library of the University of California at Berkeley I was taken to a table in the middle of a room, placed there reverently like a shrine, and shown an old and battered brass plate, preserved under glass. There was a small hole in it, about the size of a sixpence, and on the hoary surface of the metal I could just make out the following inscription:

> BEE IT KNOWNE VNTO ALL MEN BY THESE PRESENTS
> JUNE 17 1579
> BY THE GRACE OF GOD AND IN THE NAME OF HERR
> MAIESTY QUEEN ELIZABETH OF ENGLAND AND HERR
> SVCCESSORS FOREVER I TAKE POSSESSION OF THIS
> KINGDOM WHOSE KING AND PEOPLE FREELY RESIGNE
> THEIR RIGHT AND TITLE IN THE WHOLE LAND VNTO HERR
> MAIESTIES KEEPING NOW NAMED BY ME AN TO BEE
> KNOWNE VNTO ALL MEN AS NOVA ALBION.
> FRANCIS DRAKE

Here was evidence indeed! Just 375 years after drake sailed down the coast, this plate was found near the shores of San Francisco Bay. It was not on the beach, and had certainly been moved recently; but it would appear to prove, if genuine, that Drake had at least landed in the close vicinity of San Francisco, if not actually inside the Golden Gate. People naturally took the first news of this plate with a distinct pinch of salt. The thing looked old enough, but its patina might easily be faked. The inscription was authentically Elizabethan in sense and in manner, and corresponded with what was already known about Drake's landing; but at any time during the past century an informed hoaxer might have composed such a message.

San Franciscans are not the people to take such phenomena lightly. They subjected the plate to the most intensive scientific and scholarly examination. First they tried to narrow the possible limits of its age. It was not, for example, made of rolled brass (which would have proved it to be modern); nor did it contain any other ingredients that were unknown to metallurgists of Drake's time. Its mucky coating had not been recently applied, and seemed to be a natural covering which had been formed slowly over many years. There were tissues in the cracks which appeared to show that the plate had been lying on the ground for some time. Into the hole in the brass the scholars exactly fitted an Elizabethan sixpence, such as the old adventurers habitually used as a substitute for the royal seal. The cleverest and most confident researchers in America would not hazard an exact date for the plate; but it was generally agreed that it was more than a century old; and before 1836 not enough was known about Drake's voyage to make such a counterfeit possible (and anyway the virtual nonexistence of San Francisco at that time would make the purpose of such a fake singularly obscure).

So on the whole San Franciscans accept the plate as genuine, and believe it to prove that Drake beached the *Golden Hind* somewhere near their enchanted city. The conclusions of the scholars and scientists exactly suited their temperament; for while the fundamental evidence has become firmer, their Drake problem remains unsolved in detail. They still do not know precisely where he landed, and can spend their Saturday afternoons examining again the contours of the Bay and imagining that weather-beaten warship, with its great captain writing sonnets in his cabin, straining out of the mist into the shelter of the hills.

It is not only in historical matters that San Franciscans employ this thoroughgoing approach. Their whole city gives the impression of being well ordered, neatly filed and classified. In some ways, it is true, San Francisco is a topsy-turvy place, built on the flanks of impossibly steep hills, so that driving home is an adventure, and walking back from the theater in high heels or long skirts an hilarious impossibility. (When a furniture van recently ran away down one of these hills, it reached a speed of 100 m.p.h. in its breakneck progression toward the sea.) It is a city, too, of many races, jumbled in narrow streets and crowded quarters, Chinese and Mexicans and Italians, and sailors barging by from the quaysides; with the beloved cable cars scurrying up the hills and swaying perilously around the corners; and cluttered wharfside restaurants, all mixed up with fishing boats and wayside stalls, and smelling of prawns, lobsters, and the succulent abalone; and gay gardens perched on the flanks of hills, with dainty shambles of artist' houses all around; and beautiful, elegant shopping streets suddenly degenerating into alleys, full of swarthy grocers and newspapers in Chinese. But though it has all this lovable profusion of facets, San Francisco still feels competent, self-possessed and mannerly; a city with the seams of its stockings straight, and no buttons undone. It is also a kindly city, where few people carry chips on their shoulders. I once parked my car, with a sleeping baby in the back seat, outside the door of my hotel in the center of the city. Two policemen approached me, and one asked me rather brusquely what I was doing, parking the car there, right in the middle of the traffic, couldn't I see I was obstructing the street, why, the cable cars couldn't get by, and where was my license, anyway? I was just about to reply when I was interrupted by a sudden appalling noise from the baby, who was sitting up in his cot, nebulous draperies falling about him, howling like a banshee. The policeman's jaw dropped (as the novelists say); and his companion turned to him with an air of infinite reproach. "There now, Ed," said he, "why d'you have to shout at the guy? Look what you've done— *you've woken the baby!*"

A powerful contributor to San Franciscan methods, and at the same time a characteristic product of them is the California Academy of Sciences, a splendid institution with a wide popular membership. (You may become a regular member for $10 a year, and a life member for a deposit of $250; but to be classed as a Benefactor of the Academy you must put down no less than $50,000, which is a lot of money even by Californian standards.) The Academy maintains a planetarium housed in a building in Golden Gate Park—a park famous for a garden in which devoted gardeners of pragmatic tastes have planted specimens of every plant mentioned in Shakespeare's plays. The planetarium is probably the finest in the world, and was the first of comparable complexity to be built in the United States. Its story is another lesson in the unwearying resolve of intellectual San Francisco.

The device known as the planetarium, which simulates to order the movement of the heavenly bodies, was invented soon after the first war by Dr. Bauersfeld, of the Zeiss company at Jena. Between the wars the company built twenty-seven of them, and six were brought to America, where they occupy a place in the public mind halfway between a scientific lecture and a striptease. The last war came, the Zeiss people turned their attention to more urgent matters, and by the time the California Academy of Sciences had raised enough money to buy its own planetarium, Jena was in Russian hands and there was no planetarium to buy.

This was maddening, for the campaign to raise funds had lasted for many years, and plans were already far advanced for the building to be erected in Golden Gate Park. For a moment or two the academicians were stymied. However, their spirits quickly recovered. During the war the Academy had repaired and manufactured optical parts for the United States Navy. This, in itself, was odd. It had happened that the curator of paleontology had been interested in such matters, as a hobby, and had become an authority of optical instruments. All his fossils were therefore moved out of his department, and an instrument workshop was substituted. The curator of paleontology soon recruited willing help. The curator of herpetology, for instance, learned the trade quickly; the curator of ichthyology became a repairer of binoculars. Amateur telescope makers were recruited for their skill with glass, and soon fifty people were working where the fossils had so long dreamed their empty dreams.

The Academy authorities, faced with the extinction of Zeiss as a supplier of planetaria, suddenly remembered this reservoir of optical knowledge; and, looking at each other with a wild surmise, rushed off to Los Angeles to examine the Zeiss instrument there. They came back next day and reported to their trustees that the problem was solved: the California Academy of Sciences would make its own planetarium.

They launched the project with unorthodox enthusiasm. Working drawings were made on the backs of enevelopes; suggestions were considered from the most unlikely quarters; the designers had no detailed plans of the Zeiss instruments, so they struck off boldly in altogether new directions. The instrument is so complicated as to be frightening. More than thirty separate projectors throw the image of 3,800 stars on the dome of the building, and the machine portrays the motions of sun, moon, and visible planets at any period of any century. There are 321 different lenses in the machine, and 158 gears. I cannot begin to describe the intricacy of the automatic card system which insured that the right stars were correctly tabulated, nor the minute labor with which each single star was represented on the plates of the projector.

But it was all done, and almost all of it within the Academy buildings. Only the big castings and the main base of the instrument were made outside (by a shipbuilding company). After four years of work the planetarium was complete, and it was in many ways superior to the Zeiss model. The San Francisco instrument, for example, can work itself entirely automatically if the need arises. A tape recording will give the accompanying lecture; an electric device will dim the house lights, turn on the stars, move the planets and usher in the dawn; and finally the tape recorder will say politely to its audience: "Thanks, come again." The Germans used copper foil in which to punch the holes that represented stars, but the San Franciscans thought of a better substance; they coated glass with a very thin layer of aluminum, and managed to make the stars look much more realistic. The German moon was simply a white disk; the San Franciscans project an actual photograph of the moon on to the dome. Thus by a combination of inspired makeshift and liberal knowledge they achieved their object; and a marvelous instrument it is.

There is a flavor to this cultivated avidity that Englishmen sometimes find jarring, especially if they like their learning to be easy-going and their culture inclining slightly to the dilettantish. San Franciscans' libraries are apt to be very perfect in their condition and composition, very conscious of distinction and completeness, and the thought of educated San Franciscans strikes some visitors as a little intolerant of stray ends and loose components, inconsistencies and improbabilities. But San Francisco is scarcely a century old. Its culture is young, and its bland sophistication only a recent acquisition. Another half century and it will be the queenliest of cities, as wise as any Athens, as beautiful as any Paris, as instinct with unconscious assurance as St. James' Street on a summer morning, with the sentries moving grandly outside the Palace, and the calm men in bowler hats strolling down to a long lunch.

ఌ 24. ఌ

The Sierra Club

HE GEOGRAPHICAL position of the city is delectable. On one
side is the Pacific, with a gentle range of hills running along
its shore; on the other a lush and friendly plain leads away to
the Sierra Nevada, one of the noblest mountain ranges in the world.
The Sierra is a playground for San Francisco, for it is not far away by
car, and it contains a multitude of wonderful things. There is Mount
Whitney, the highest peak in the United States, a stately mountain
always flecked with snow, overlooking the dusty expanses of eastern
California and Nevada: from its summit, 14,495 feet high, you can
all but see Death Valley, 280 feet below sea level, the lowest and
hottest place on the American continent. There are splendid forests
in the Sierra, some of them given added magnificence by the presence of the Giant Sequoia, greatest of trees. There are innumerable
limpid lakes, high among the mountains, and many savage and inaccessible canyons.

The spirit in which this marvelous country is approached is as
characteristic of cultivated San Francisco as the story of the planetarium. Conscious that it could all too easily be spoiled, San Franciscans,
defend its scenery and its flavor with academic resolution, easily

rationalizing their motives in well-written treatises, setting up efficient and prosperous organizations to resist change, just as in other matters they will accept innovations with eager but tabulated appetite.

My wife and I spent some days with a San Francisco family on the shore of Echo Lake, one of the smaller but easily accessible lakes of the Sierra. They had a chalet there, and we lived a delightful open-air existence, spilling out of the house into tents erected on the bare rock around it, lounging on the balcony in the sunshine, walking in the wilderness country that encloses the lake, or scrambling up the high crags that overlook it. A number of San Franciscan families have such small houses on the lake, and they have taken great pains to preserve its sense of remoteness and isolation. There is for example, no road around the lake; to reach the houses at its upper end you must either walk through the pine trees along its banks, or take a motorboat. There are no telephones, either, and messages must be left for collection at the landing stage. At the southern extremity of the lake there is a pleasant clutter of buildings and outhouses: a grocery store, a post office, boat repairers, and handymen's huts; and beside them, especially on a Friday evening, there is much cheerful bustle when the husbands come out from the city to join their families; big cars disgorge their comfortable drivers, in sports shirts and holiday hats, and there is a whirring and a screaming of motorboat engines, and a plethora of welcoming daughters, and a splashing of spray and hoisting of suitcases. Elsewhere around the lake all is sylvan calm; and at night, when there is only silence and the twinkling of a few scattered lights, you might well be a hundred miles from a road, and a thousand from the Golden Gate.

Many San Francisco businessmen send their families to some such place as this for the whole of the summer, driving out themselves for weekends. Our hosts were fairly characteristic, in this respect, of well-to-do San Franciscans. The family ran three cars: one for the husband, one for the wife, and one (a battered old shooting-brake) for general family purposes. This makes visits to Echo Lake very simple. Mother and daughter Sue (a glamorous and nylonned fourteen) can set up home there for the entire summer holiday; the elder son, reaching that age of Americanism when social activity assumes an excruciating importance, can use one car to make his frequent journeys between the lake and the city; father can use the other to escape, each Friday, from the compulsions of accountancy. No wonder this handsome family, even in the autumn, looks bronzed and healthily windswept.

The oldest and most distinguished of the societies devoted to the preservation of the High Sierra is the Sierra Club of San Francisco. It was founded in 1892 under the inspiration of John Muir, the naturalist. Muir was introduced to the Sierra Nevada by his trade: he was then working as a sheepherder, and he took his flocks to graze in the indescribably beautiful Tuolumne Meadows, near the Yosemite Valley. He was seized with a desire to protect this high seclusion—as he put it, "to do something for wildness"; and so the club was formed. It has been immensely influential. It was largely because of the efforts of the Sierra Club that the Yosemite Valley, the most spectacular of the Sierra canyons, was preserved as a national park. Many mountain trails were established, and many mountain huts built, opening the Sierra to an altogether new class of wanderer. The club has helped to preserve forests, and to restock fishless waters. It has contributed to all kinds of exploration and scientific study in the Sierra. Many of the most forbidding peaks on the continent have been climbed by its members, and many of the lesser-known high regions have been mapped by its cartographers. During the war Sierra Club mountaineers played a crucial part in the designing of American mountain equipment and the training of mountain divisions. (The names of these mountaineers are instructive: they were Raffi Bedayn, Dave Brower, Chester Errett, Charles Hanks, Milton Hildebrand, Solon Lindsey, Richard Leonard, Phil von Lubken, Einar Nilsson, Rolf Pundt, Jack Riegelhuth, and Bestor Robinson.)

All this is done with a fine professional efficiency; but there still hangs about some of the club's activities a gentle fragrance of the 1900s, just as, on the murals that decorate San Francisco's celebrated Bohemian Club, members are depicted in plus fours and cloth caps. Since 1901 the Sierra Club has organized annual outings into the mountains. A member wrote of the first outing: "The trip was made interesting by the obstacles to be surmounted, and it was a sight to see dignified college professors, wily limbs of the law, deft doctors, and reverend clergymen joking gleefully in rolling rocks, lifting logs, and shoveling snow to make way for the commissary." Nowadays the obstacles to be surmounted are carefully graded. You may choose, for example, if you are young and indigent, to go on a Knapsack Trip, carrying your own food on your back, walking, and pitching camp yourself. Or you may prefer a Burro Trip; donkeys will then carry your goods for you, an as a result your wanderings are more closely confined to trails. Those who are both well-heeled and energetic can do a High Trip, lavishly attended by people to do the chores, but moving camp from time to time during a four-week trip; or a Saddle Trip, in which horses carry both you and your possessions, and minions do all the cooking and packing (the minions are sometimes the sons of members, earning their way; my host's son had spent the previous summer acting as boatman on the swift currents of the Colorado River). Finally, if you are a very dignified professor, or an excessively reverend clergyman, you can stay at Base Camp, living at a central headquarters staffed with cooks and "activity leaders," and thence going mildly out, day by day, into the wilderness.

There is an ominous sound to one phrase in the regulations for the Saddle Trips. Each member is allowed fifty pounds of dunnage; but, say the regulations, "riders able to play musical instruments may have them transported in addition." What desperate prospects are opened up by this phrase! With the elderly attorney strumming at his guitar and clearing his wizened throat, before embarking upon some outdoor epic or comic novelty; with the rest of the party preparing their smiles, or clapping their thighs; and no one more enthusiastic than the young lawyer from the same office, and no one more impatient than some other anxious performer, already taking advantage of the shadow of the trees to tighten the strings of his ukulele. It is all part of the flavor of the Sierra Club, and of San

Francisco itself; and, when encountered, it is found to be graced with a pleasant simplicity. All the same, it is at once amusing and alarming to think of those eminent divines tramping the Sierra and singing, in a cracked but determined unison:

Up in the mountains, free as air,
High, high, high!
Finding new life and ideals there.
High, high, high!
We're Sierra club hikers out for the fun
Of hiking from dawn to the set of sun
With a song in our hearts when the day is done.
High, high, high!

Here, I think, the Sierra Club parts company with those scholarly and respectable English societies graced by the bearded membership of my grandfather: for it is difficult to imagine the vicar of Nether Broughton or old Dr. Crithersby contributing to such a sing-song as they stooped to examine the flora of the Shropshire hills, or progressed toward some little-known Saxon lintel.

But there is among most Americans a predilection for the communal, a survival, no doubt, from emigrant and pioneer days; and the Sierra Club is no exception. Somewhere among the remarkable technical achievements, the lavish publications, the distinguished membership, there is a faint but persistent hint of the youth hostel. As long ago as 1903 Mount Whitney was climbed by a Sierra Club party numbering 103, a circumstance which would seem to detract from the mystic satisfaction of reaching the summit; and two years later 61 people stood on the top of Mount Rainier—"the largest recorded party," says the Club convincingly, "to make the climb in any one day." The Sierra Club has an eminent mountaineering record, and one of its early supporters was Edward Whymper of the Matterhorn; now something called the Hundred Peaks Award is awarded by the Southern California Chapter's Desert Peaks Section to members who climb 100 peaks between Pehachapi Pass and the Mexican border. The compelling drive and thirst for success of most

Americans does not offer march easily with the serenity of the mountains.

Indeed, there can be few places of comparable grandeur so ghastly to visit as the Yosemite Valley on a holiday. From the east a narrow tortuous road leads over the mountains from Leevining, beside the delicious blue expanse of Mono Lake; and along this highway the cars move almost bumper to bumper, with a constant whining of engines, and incessant stoppings and goings, so tiring for the nerves that if you so much as slow down to look at a deer in the woods there is a blaring of horns behind you, passed on like some hideous talisman from car to car through the mountains, until far in the distance behind you there may be heard a last faint echo of exasperation.

The valley itself is one of the most magnificent places in America: a canyon dominated by rock slabs of enormous size, with waterfalls gushing from the edges of precipices and falling hundreds of feet in slivers and plumes of white. But on a holiday the magic of the scene is totally destroyed. Cars in their hundreds are lined in awesome array in the car parks. Policemen control the traffic, for all the world as if it were the intersection of Park Avenue and 52nd Street. Milling crowds in open shirts and floral frocks buy their picture postcards and send letters home (if you are too lazy to write, you can probably buy one already written for you, full of such phrases as "Yosemite is one of the major scenic wonders of the nation, and we certainly are glad we motored here through the incredible beauties of the Sierra with the trees looking beautiful in their summer foliage."). The congestion is terrible, the constant unrelenting movement of the tourists wearisome in the extreme, and the predominant atmosphere sticky, jaded, but determined.

This is a characteristic paradox of the West Coast: for within sight of these multitudes there are crags and mountain meadows almost unvisited from one decade to the next; and the tasteless crowds of Yosemite often drive on to visit San Francisco, most radiant and sublime of American cities, where the Sierra Club continues its efforts to "do something for wildness."

∽ 25. ∾

Lumber

ROM CALIFORNIA we traveled northward into Oregon and Washington state. The coast road, often narrow and unfrequented, winds its way along beautiful cliffs, with meadows on one side and the blue Pacific on the other; it is a rocky coastline like Cornwall's, but softened by the green fields which sometime slide beneath the cliffs, too, and stretch down to the very beaches. Not far from San Francisco the road passes an old Russian settlement, established in 1812 (a great year for the Russians) as a center for fur trading, but abandoned soon afterwards. There is a church with a bulbous steeple, a fine wooden house that belonged to the garrison commander, and a stockade overlooking the ocean; the whole surrounded by fields, with hummingbirds darting about the bushes, an odd and piquant memorial to an ill-starred colonial venture. Soon the character of the country changes. Woods begin to creep down to the road from the higher ground to the east, and before long on each inlet of the sea there are sawmills belching smoke, with piles of tree trunks awaiting attention, and the smell of shavings and wet wood. This is the country of the lumber industry, which dominates the economy of the Pacific Northwest and dictates the character of the northern Pacific coast.

The most famous of the Pacific trees is the Coast Redwood, *sequoia sempervirens*. In conversation in San Francisco you cannot escape the eventual intrusion of this tree, because a pervasive *mystique* has arisen around it. Scholarly societies fight to protect the chastity of its woods. Wealthy philanthropists compete to finance its preservation. Countless tourists, avid at once for the gigantic and the educational, flock to stare at its trunk and awe their unhappy children with details of its antiquity. A great section of the country has been christened the "Redwood Empire," and as you travel north you can scarcely fail to notice when your road suffers the inevitable metamorphosis and becomes the "Redwood Highway." There is no more beautiful tree than the Coast Redwood; immensely tall, straight, slender and gracious, its branches intertwining high above you to form a dark and luscious canopy. There is something magical about a grove of these great trees, so vast, old, and silent. But unless you are a passionate subscriber to the Save-the-Redwood League, there comes a time as you motor north when each successive grove of redwoods (usually piously christened after the benefactors responsible for its preservation) begins to look astonishingly like the one before; until, having savored the mystery of these ancient things for a good many miles, and paused in their shadow for several cups of coffee, and dutifully left the road to visit the oldest and the tallest and the most historic trees, you detect in your reaction some slight affinity with that of the less scrupulous Pacific lumberman, who would dearly like to chop all the redwoods down and turn them into planks.

All the same, there is an extraordinary fascination about their age. In several places in the Redwood Empire there are trunks of redwood trees that have been sliced across to display their age rings; and marked on the wood are the years represented by each ring, and a few contemporary events to illustrate the slow but irresistible growth of the thing. You may find, for instance, that the tree you are examining was a sapling in King Alfred's time; was a stalwart young redwood at the time of the Norman Conquest; entered middle age with the Renaissance; advanced into dotage with the Age of Reason;

and died a few years ago, eleven or twelve centuries old, having experienced nothing through all the vicissitudes of history but a fire or two (duly dated on the rings), the winds and the rain of the Oregon forests, and the ultimate sharp cleavage of the saw.

There were once sequoia trees all over the world, but most of them were exterminated in the glacial age, leaving only fossils to be picked up in Cornwall, France, Russia, or Alaska. Until recently naturalists thought that only the two American species of the genus were left—the *sequoia sempervirens* of the Pacific Northwest and the *sequoia gigantea* of the Sierra Nevada. The former are the tallest living things—up to 364 feet high; the latter are the biggest and oldest—thirty-five feet thick sometimes, and 3,500 years old. (The *sequoia gigantea* was originally named, by British scientists, *sequoia Wellingtonia*, at a time when scarcely an Englishman had set eyes on one. "Emperors and kings and princes have their plants," it was said, "and we must not forget to place in the highest rank among them our own great warrior.") However, an odd thing happened a few years ago. A young botanist employed by the Chinese Government penetrated to a village in Szechwan where, he had been told, there was a very big tree. He found that it was, in fact, a very big tree indeed, and he hastily took cuttings of it. Analyzed by astonished pundits, these cuttings proved that the tree was a third kind of sequoia, as much a living fossil as the coelacanth (that impudent fish which defied all the rules of natural science by emerging from the Indian Ocean in a condition several millennia out of date). Since then many specimens of this tree, the Dawn Redwood (*Metasequoia*), have been found in the remote valley of central China, and some have been transplanted elsewhere.

In the old days the Pacific lumbermen did their best to eliminate the Coast Redwood, swathing their way through its forests with terrible abandon, leaving devastated area behind them, buying up forests, chopping them down, and moving on ruthlessly to other regions. Thousands upon thousands of the redwoods were cut, dragged through the woods by teams of oxen, and floated down the forest streams to the coast, where the sawmills seized them and did their duty. "We may not know how to grow them," says one lumberman to another in a cartoon I was shown in Oregon, "but we sure know how to cut 'em down!" It was, of course, this process of blind extermination that led to the foundation of the various redwood preserves; but hard economics have now convinced most of the lumber companies that conservation is as important in forestry as it is in agriculture; and only a few minor, unrepentant operators are still demolishing the woods with the old carefree robustness.

I was the guest of one of the most enlightened redwood lumber companies at Fort Bragg, in northern California. This is a company town par excellence, all but wholly owned by the Union Lumber Company. Its streets are crowded with prosperous lumberjacks, big men in check shirts and boots, and with cheerful wives wearing headscarves. Like English ladies at a point-to-point. The company store, the town's chief emporium, is a square building made of redwood, with a little of the manner of a frontier trading post, and a Scandinavian standard of neatness and convenience. There is a company train, a little diesel car nicknamed *The Skunk* (because of its strange fumes), which chatters off each morning through the surrounding hills and woods to join the main line forty miles away. Down by the sea there are the remains of a jetty, for until the 1920s the company used to ship its lumber by sea to San Francisco, and schooners and steamers used to stand off shore while the wood was loaded by pulleys.

Near the company offices there is a little museum. The lumber industry is pleasantly interested in its own history, and this gentle preoccupation with the past casts a sometimes misleading aura of detachment around the activities of the different companies. The beginning of the Pacific lumber trade occurred not much more than a century ago, and the work of the early lumberman is still easy to imagine. The Union lumberjacks often find pieces of old equipment, abandoned in the woods by their predecessors when they moved on to new territory—old steam donkeys, with tall black chimneys, standing rusty but statuesque among the trees; axes and hammers of antique design, and big wooden wheels on which the sawed trunks were transported. Sometimes deep in the woods, miles from anywhere, you come across a shattered and decaying house, with the remains of a flower garden, and a front gate tottering on its hinges. This was once a ranch, where the lumber company's oxen were raised and grazed, and toughened for the task of dragging immensely heavy logs through the thick undergrowth of the redwood forests. The Union people are still selling wood cut by the pioneers in the 1850s. Occasionally, when logs were cast into a stream to float down to the mills, they sank, or were entangled in foliage, or for other reasons failed to make the journey; these logs are still being retrieved, none the worse for the 100 years' hiatus between their chopping and their milling, and if you buy a redwood plank you may well be handling lumber cut by some of the first white inhabitants of the Northwest.

Nevertheless, the big lumber companies have modernized and mechanized their activities with impressive thoroughness. Nowadays few lumbermen live in the old remote lumber camps, in brawling and boozing comity; they prefer to live domestically in maisonettes, driving into the forests each morning in their own fine cars, along jungly lanes. Once in the woods, they cut their trees with power saws, and the logs are pulled by tractors to a central clearing place. There enormous lorries are waiting for them. They have driven up the forest roads with their trailers carried pick-a-back behind the cab, to save tires and make the driving easier; now these trailers are lifted off by cranes, coupled up, and loaded with logs, until the whole machine bends and creaks with the strain, but starts up nonetheless with a roar and a puff of exhaust smoke, and pounds off through the woods to the mills. Most big lumber companies have private roads into the woods, and this means that the lorries can carry a heavier load than is legally allowed elsewhere. On the Union Lumber Company's roads they travel, for one reason and another, on the left-hand side of the road instead of the right; and it can be disconcerting for the unwary and ill-oriented motorist, plodding around a corner, to find himself faced by a gargantuan lorry with a mountain of logs, careening toward him at great speed on the wrong side of the highway.

The mills keep huge stockpiles of wood, because logging stops in the winter, and there must be a supply of raw material to keep the plant active during the cold months. A fascinating variety of machines converts these logs, when required, into planks. A powerful jet of water, for example, strips the trunk of its bark; the water gushing out of a nozzle with a roar, while two metal claws like lobsters' pluck the log from a conveyor belt and revolve it to ensure that no snatches of bark escape the jet. The log is then placed on a mobile platform which is whisked up and down on lines, with an unfortunate operator sitting precariously on it like a young man showing off at a fair. On each of these precipitous movements the log comes into contact with the blade of a saw, which strips off a plank as a bacon slicer cuts a rasher. The noise is indescribable, and the master sawyer, who stands at the controls beside the saw, gives his instructions with an odd, enigmatical sign language, the twitch of a finger, almost the contraction of a muscle, conveying some such meaning as: "Bring the blade forward two inches, Bert." There is a delightful smell inside the mill, despite the profusion of machinery; and because much skill is required in processing and grading the wood, as well as in the forests, the industry has the quality of a craft, and commands much the same loyalty.

The flavor of Fort Bragg is very agreeable. Though the company has (for instance) its own airplane, it is still a family concern governed by inherited principles. I stayed in its guesthouse, an unpretentious Victorian redwood structure built by the company's founder. The bathrooms were of unusual magnificence, but otherwise the house was appealingly old-fashioned and middle-class, akin more closely to society in the English shires than to the rough frontier environment in which it presumably made it debut. The business office of the company is also comfortably nostalgic, with polished wooden counters and grills, like a country bank, and small wood-paneled rooms for the executives. The young manager (heir to the family firm) wore a thick tartan shirt without a tie when I called on him there, and on his feet were high-ankled lumberjack's boots. Like most of his contemporaries in the Pacific lumber industry, he has learned every facet of the business, and pursues its affairs keenly but (mercifully) not so boringly as some of his counterparts to the east.

Another young man of influence at Fort Bragg is the chief forester, a disciple of the celebrated Emanuel Fritz, the greatest authority on the redwoods. As the industry has grasped the meaning of conservation, so the professional forester has assumed new importance in its hierarchies. Most big lumber companies now consider their trees as a crop, to be cut in rotation, taking care that a fresh supply is coming along; in future you will not often see those wide drab wildernesses that were the sure mark, in the past, of the indiscriminate passage of lumbermen. Nowadays the forests are either cropped selectively, or in strips, leaving islands of trees to reseed the ground; and great care is taken when timber is withdrawn from the woods to ensure that young trees are not damaged in the process. There is an accepted standard of conservation, and forests that reach it are granted certificates recognizing them as "tree farms." The Union forester took me through miles of tangled woodland to visit a section of forest he was cherishing with particular care. There he had thinned a grove of redwood trees, carefully removing those that were economically useless or especially ripe for chopping, and leaving the others with much more light and space. The redwood lumbermen are still cutting virgin timber, but they will soon be moving on to second growth; so there is especial significance to such essays in artificial cultivation. We stood in silence in his grove, a clearing of light in the dark forest: he thinking of trees in terms at once practical and affectionate, and murmuring now and then: "I should have got rid of *that* old so-and-so!"; I allowing myself for an unguarded moment to plunge into a mystical reverie, much concerned with the fundamentals of Life, Death, and Purpose. (It was true that I had recently read some literature of the Save-the-Redwoods League; but it was the haunting silence of the trees, the somberness of the surroundings, and the overpowering sense of antiquity, that had this disconcerting effect on me.)

⌒⌒⌒

The Pacific Northwest is in a period of change. Vast engineering projects are altering the character of its economy. The Grand Coulee Dam, with its associated works, is providing great quantities of electric power and is irrigating thousands of square miles of unproductive land. The lumber industry, too, is feeling the impact of scientific progress. I was lunching one day in Seattle with a well-known lumberman, talking not of this and that (for such is not the custom with American businessmen) but specifically about the future of the forest industries. Suddenly he reached for the briefcase that lay beside him, and sweeping a few knives and mustard pots heedlessly onto the floor he emptied upon the table an ill-assorted collection of objects. There were small pots of various fluids; a bottle of sugar; some molasses; a cake of wax; a square piece of brown textile; a little box boldly labeled "Rabbit Food"; several pieces of cardboard; and some plastic ashtrays. "D'you know what they have in common?" said he. "They're all made of wood!"

For years the lumber people have tried to make good use of all the waste materials of wood—bark and shavings in particular—and in Europe progress was hastened by the need for synthetics during the war. Now the Americans are catching up, and the bigger firms are spending large sums of money on research; the huge metal incinerators in which they burn their waste have become marks of shame. "Mark my words," said my friend at Seattle, who turned out to be an enthusiast on the subject, "before many years are out the waste product will be more important than the wood." Certainly, despite the obvious fact that wood is no longer used for many of its traditional purposes, the lumbermen show no sign of despondency about the future. By the nature of their calling, they think in terms of generations. In the early days, one generation of tree was all they could envisage. Now the tree farms are organized with a view to logging trees in 50 or 100 years' time. Whereas in the old days most of the wood cut was of great age, soon it will be rare to buy lumber more than a century old; and eventually to buy wood not especially grown for lumbering will be as unusual as to buy a chicken not reared for domestic purposes. Progress is affecting the forests as it affects the very nature of the Pacific coast, once so rugged and untamed, now contentedly sinking, almost everywhere, into genial commercialism. Sometimes there are setbacks, though. Tractors have not proved altogether suitable for hauling felled logs out of the wood, for their tracks cause much damage to young trees and shrubbery. Thus, though the redwood bark is turned into ashtrays, and the forest firefighters jump to their targets by parachute, and the great machines whine through the day at the sawmills, we may yet see teams of horses in the woods again, and hear the forgotten cries of their drivers.

And whatever changes occur, the fight continues between the lovers of trees and the lovers of lumber. However enlightened and cautious the lumbermen, there will always be men and societies to oppose the felling of trees, and there will always be woodsmen to give them characteristic answers. I remember a forester in California discussing, with a gentle degree of asperity, a little too well, and which particularly objected to the damage caused by the removal of felled logs. "Now I put it to you," he said, pointing to a colossal cross-section of a redwood tree, as big as a room, cut with enormous labor and soon to be laboriously transported out of the forests to the mills. "I put it to you as a fair and impartial observer, how can you get a thing like that out of here without disturbing a few of the ferns?"

ल 26. ७

Northwest Extremity

T THE northern end of this timber country the land and the sea become inextricably mixed, and the map is a mass of small blue streaks, patches, and fingers, where the inlets and lagoons of the Pacific eat their way into Washington state. The stalwart center of this region is Seattle, standing on the edge of Puget Sound, and to grasp the watery affinities of the place you can best approach it by ferryboat, across the sound from Bremerton.

Some of the ferries are very grand, for they play an important part in the life of Puget Sound. It is difficult to drive about this district, for the roads are constantly being intercepted by protrusions of the sea; so here the ferryboats, whose steam whistles elsewhere all too often have a dying ring, are still in their heyday. Some of them are streamlined and look like electric irons; some are double-deckers; a few are ferries of the old school, with black upright funnels and much clanking of the metal parts. Onto one of these craft we loaded the car at Bremerton (a naval base, with the gray masts of warships standing above its rooftops) and it took us tortuously through various cool winding waterways into the sound and across to Seattle.

This big city has few beauties of structure, but its position on the water's edge is splendid. As the ferry creeps around the corner of an outlying island the city edges into view: a cluster of skyscrapers, in the universal American manner, like mother buildings surrounded by their broods; and a long row of warehouses and cranes; a ship steaming out for Japan, Alaska, or Honolulu: a few tall radio masts; the endlessly busy comings and goings of the waterfront, tugs and ferries and big diesel trucks; the puff of smoke from a train, the distant hooting of a whistle; and above and behind it, beyond wooded ridges, the graceful snow peak of Mount Rainier, Seattle's Fujiyama. Of all the great cities of the United States, only San Francisco has a natural setting to compare with this.

But if from the sea, in the half-light of evening, it has a certain delicacy of manner, Seattle is by no means a ladylike city. It still has some of the elemental brutality of the Klondike days, when the gold-diggers in their hopeful thousands sailed from here to Alaska. Its people are bold and bluff; and its police are probably as rough-and-ready as any in America. I stopped my car for a moment outside a hotel in the city in order to ask for a room; but when I returned to collect my bags, without even pausing to register, some passing constable had seen it there, and had interrupted his awful progress to fine me five dollars for unlawful parking; terrible indeed are the penalties of Seattle, and inexorable its enforcements of the law (only the very agile visitor, calming his conscience, can skip on into the next state without paying his fines). The push, rush, and bustle of Seattle is at once daunting and invigorating; its waterfront is less colorful and exotic than it used to be, but the city is still the *de facto* capital of Alaska, and many are the ships that sail north to Anchorage. It is only suitable that nowadays Seattle, a brawny place, should build bombers; on the road to the east you pass the plant, one of the biggest in the world, and may see some of its latest products standing there gleaming and pompous, rather like the Cranbury fire engines.

Seattle is so particularly brash and booming that it is difficult to realize, as you stand in its deafening main streets, that it is the center of a region of idyllic peace and enchantment. Along the neighboring Pacific shore, peopled by fishermen, oystermen, lumberjacks, and Indians, is a sea area enshrouded in mists and mystery, like some Norse coastline of antiquity. I drove out one day to the very tip of this shore, to the extreme northwestern point of the United States. The road runs along the edge of the Olympic Peninsula, an area deliberately preserved as wilderness, with lofty and inaccessible mountains and impenetrable stands of timber. This was the last part of the United States to be properly explored, and there are a few romantics who claim that some of it is unknown country still. Certainly as you drive along its fringes on a day of fog and drizzle it still has a magnetic and secretive quality about it, like the Himalayan foothills in the monsoon.

On one side, then, is this rugged mountain region; on the other, the Strait of Juan de Fuca. (This was named for a lie, for the Greek seaman de Fuca never did succeed, I need hardly say, in forcing his alleged passage down the strait, across the continent, and into the Atlantic.) Almost within sight is the city of Victoria, on Vancouver Island, the most doggedly British city in Canada, where ladies in floral silk and restrained hats sip their afternoon tea beneath portraits of the English military or nobility, or guard their treasures from Kashmir and Khartoum, or open their air-mail edition of *The Times* in scrupulously chronological order—Canadian citizens, most of them, but *plus royalistes que le roi*. On the American shore of the strait the coastline is dotted with lumber mills, surrounded by their huge contributory rafts of logs, tucked away in secluded coves below the level of the road, beside the streams that flow out of the mountains. Beside one of these mills (when I drove past) two dignified steam engines stood back to back, snorting little, encrusted with brass ornamentation, while their elderly crews sprawled on benches inside a nearby shed, drinking fizzy lemonade out of bottles. Sometimes, out in the strait, you may see the small black outline of a tug, training through a choppy sea with its long line of logs; and sometimes from an unsuspected lane a battered car emerges from the woods with a complement of gay lumberjacks in loud shirts.

There are still lumber camps in these forests, drenched by the frequent rains; for there are few towns nearby, and nowhere convenient for families to live.

At the end of the peninsula, where the strait meets the Pacific Ocean, stands the small fishing port of Neah Bay. In spirit it is directly related to Venice, Louisiana, that small sticky village where the Mississippi meets the sea; for both are extremities, where the traveler can go no farther, and both have the character of the absolute. The road swings into Neah Bay around the edge of a pebbly beach, and you find yourself abruptly among its meager rows of wooden houses. It is a damp place; its nature is impregnated with the rain, so that the roads seem muddy even when they are dry, and the trees on the surrounding hills smell wet and fresh, and the waters of the bay are constantly churned with raindrops. The attractively bleak and remote quality of the settlement is due to the fact that it forms part of the Makkah Indian reservation, and is thus relatively immune to the diseases of commerce. There is one inn, a good old wooden house overlooking the water, whose landlord runs fishing boats and whose landlady may have a box full of gray kittens in her kitchen. At the end of the jetty is the Fisherman's Cooperative, partly a store, partly a market where the fishermen pool their catch for an agreed price. Out in the bay are the fishing boats, the *raison d'être* of the place, row upon row of trim diesel craft, with intricate riggings and neat cabins, and a few hardy fishermen fiddling with ropes or greasing their engines in the rain. They sail far out to sea and up the Canadian coast in their search for salmon, red snapper, and halibut; but their profits are not always dazzling (nor are their jobs, in these small boats, for such employees as the plutocrat skippers of Grimsby, who earn more in their early thirties than Admirals of the Fleet).

The Indians of these parts have never been among the indigent, for their country has always given them plenty to eat. In fact, of all the American Indians they have been the most consistently prosperous. They have always fished for salmon and shot their deer, elk, and mountain goat among the Olympic Mountains. Even the climate has been kind to them, for though it is wet, it is also mild; and a century ago many of the men were able to wear the economical summer costume of nothing whatsoever. Some of the northwest Indians are extremely skillful with their boats. One tribe used to harpoon whales in the open sea, and may (who knows?) even have preceded the Basques as pioneers of the trade.

They are still prosperous, within reason, for their reservations include some splendid stands of timber. In the days of cutthroat lumbering these Indians were ruthlessly cheated of their rights; today they are generally treated fairly, and consequently live comfortably enough. They are a taciturn and rather surly people, plain of countenance and unimaginative of dress; but in the days of their eminence, when the trade of the western fur trade was making itself felt in the peninsula, they produced fine woodcarving and enjoyed a lively culture.

Some outsiders have joined them in their outpost. Many of the fishermen are white Americans. I met one who was a schoolmaster for most of the year, and who came to Neah Bay in his vacations, to take his powerful diesel boat to sea, three or four nights at a time, and thus supplement his modest academic income. One sometimes sees servicemen in uniform sipping their slow coffees in the village. The Pacific coast is powerfully defended against attack (Seattle is about equidistant from Pearl Harbor and New York, and the airfields around these western centers are understandably swarming with fighters); and Neah Bay is the nearest town in the United States to the Russian islands in the Bering Sea. Out beyond Cape Flattery, constantly veiled by mist, buffeted by winds, and washed by gray seas, there lies a small island. Its buildings cling together among the seas, as if they were trying to keep each other warm, and it bristles with radio masts and installations. There are radar stations far to the north of this, in Alaska and the Canadian Artic; but Tatoosh Island lies there like an outrider, all the same, with its eyes on the northern Pacific.

All this salt-spray activity occurs to the west of Seattle; and the port faces the sea, and feels close to Alaska, to Japan, and the islands of the South Pacific. But not far to the east of the city (if you turn your back on the ocean) you will cross one of the great climatic barriers of America, and soon find yourself in spirit a million miles from Puget Sound, among the airy spaces of the Great Plains. It is a dramatic road to take. It runs out of Seattle staidly enough, leaving the sea behind, and running through the endless dreary suburbs, all petrol stations and car dealers, that have settled like a blight upon the periphery of every American city. The country outside is the wettest in the United States, and the air is misty and moist. There is a genuinely English flavor to these fresh, fertile regions; the fields are green and lush, the produce abundant; at the state fair at Olympia you are likely to meet many shy lean folk with English names, looking very like countrymen attending some sleepy Cotswold market One distinguished Englishman, indeed, finds this combination of worlds, this happy amalgam of English countryside and American living, so appealing that he has settled on a Washington farm, and, as he sits in his library among old prints, first editions, and brandy, hears the scream of the whistle outside as the diesel "streamliner" pounds north to Seattle.

But the Pacific northwestern states are cut down the middle, almost symmetrically, by the line of the Cascade Mountains, which offer their splendid profiles to the observer anywhere from the Canadian border to the northern part of Nevada. It is not long before the traveler encounters this range, and at once the character of his journey alters. The road climbs steadily into the mountains, through forests of Douglas pine, beside the great railway tunnel which pierces these highlands from one side to the other. Behind, the narrow green plain stretches away to the sea, enveloped in a warm and friendly haze, with an atmosphere of damp, and timber, fishing Indians, ships, gentle fields, homely farmers, and oysters. But once over the crest of the Cascades, and you are in another America. It is miraculous. Here all is dry, hot, and sunny; there are huge apple orchards, cornfields of theatrical gold, wide empty plains awaiting irrigation; dams, deserts, and rawboned horsemen. So significant are the Cascade Mountains that their presence makes two countries out of one. To the west of them, you are attuned to the call of the Pacific;

to the east, you are entering the heartland of America; and as you drive across those great expanses of plain and farmland, you find yourself moving imperceptibly, through infinite gradations of mood and appearance, into the home of the new Americanism, the Middle West.

PART FIVE

THE MIDDLE WEST

ᘓ 27. ᘔ

Portals

OBODY KNOWS quite what the Middle West is, for the geographers, the sociologists, and the political economists have never agreed upon a satisfactory definition of it. It is an amorphous region, a slab of eight or nine states deposited in the center of America, surrounded by areas of more decided and homogeneous character—the melancholy South, the vivid expanse of the West, the mellowed East. Hardly anybody wants to be a Midwesterner, for the area does not possess the allure of the West, nor the fragrant nostalgia of the plantations. Within its nebulous frontiers there are shades of every social flavor, from the feudal pride of the Southern states to the backwoods temperament of the territories that lied along the forty-ninth parallel.

The accepted southern border of the Middle West is the Ohio River, which runs placidly through beautiful wooded hills to join the Mississippi at Cairo. Across the river is Kentucky, which is very conscious of its southern connotations (whisky, colonels, gallantry, blue grass, and fine horses, Confederate memories and strong convictions); but on both sides of the stream there are river towns of unmistakable Middle Western atmosphere. There may be racial segregation in Hawesville, Kentucky, for example, while across the Ohio in Indiana the Negro is theoretically emancipated; but the people of Hawesville speak with the rasping and angular speech of the Middle West, not the lilt of the South, and they probably have fewer affinities with their fastidious capital, Frankfort, than with the metallic drive of Indianapolis (where an official pamphlet says of the ugliest of all war memorials that it is "universally admitted to be the grandest achievement of Architectural and Sculptural Art in the World"). These places, standing like bastions along the river, are frontier towns, marking the boundary where one philosophy of life gives way to another; and the most important of them, the splendid old river port of Louisville, was my own southern gateway into the Middle West.

I drove into Louisville on its annual day of greatness—the day of the Kentucky Derby, when the city is thrown into paroxysms of pride, gaiety, and determined excitement. From all over (as the Americans say) the racegoers were thronging into Louisville that morning. Some crowded off the diesel "streamliners" which came throbbing into town, all vista-domes and observation parlors, from Pittsburgh and the East; some came by the huge gaudy buses whose diesel fumes swirl about so disagreeably as they sweep past you on the road; thousands came in their great shiny cars, sweeping into the city across the bridges from the Middle West, or rolling up aristocratically from the deep South; some flew in by private seaplanes, landing dashingly, amid clouds of spray, on the river; and a few even came by stern-wheeler from Cincinnati, to moor alongside the cobbled landing stage and sip their cool drinks on deck, watching the traffic go by with an enviably Olympian detachment.

As always, Louisville opened its hospitable doors to this influx, turning its back gardens into parking lots (two dollars for the day); mixing its mint juleps with an urgent hospitality; stringing its streets with flags; summoning from cold storage all its most romantic traits and associations, so that the air of the place was sticky with the perfume of magnolias, and its pavements seemed almost to be peopled with swaggering southern soldiers, crinolined ladies, faithful darkies, handsome owners, and patriarchal planters; and all the talk was of racing memories, Man o' War, the gambling of steamboat men, the winner in '22, the prices, until, what was the turmoil, and the enthusiasm of it all, and the constant metaphorical blowing of trumpets and thudding of hoofs, by race time one's head was beginning to swim, so packed was it with traditional images. Almost the whole city contributed to this votive offering; only a few residents of long standing and very determined character standing altogether aloof from it.

Then there were the contemporary celebrities to admire. The bosomy film star stepped from her Cadillac with a rustle of silk, a casual adjustment of furs, and a wave to her entranced admirers. The cantankerous television performer, whose ill-temper makes headlines, beamed from his box, rather disconcerting those who loved him best when he was nastiest. The eminent businessman from New Orleans wore his ermine suit studded with pearls and rhinestones. ("His taste is terrible," remarked his tailor to the press, "but it's all in fun.") There was the scholarly linguist, who comes to the Derby each year to enlarge his vocabulary of *Rogue's American,* and whose hotel room is visited by a stream of cooperative criminals, old friends of his by now, happily dropping in to tell him to latest accretions to their argot, and not even pocketing a spoon or a fountain pen as they leave with hoarse protestations of goodwill to pursue their duties elsewhere. There was a retired general, over from Los Angeles for the day, with his wife in powder blue this time, and his son on leave from Fort Knox. There was the oil millionaire in his lizard-skin shoes, deep in his race card. There is always a former President or two to adorn such a gathering as this, and probably a forthcoming Presidential candidate as well, looking spruce, hopeful, and beyond reproach. On Derby Day half of America comes to Louisville.

I forget the name of the horse that won the race—a gray from California, with jaunty jockey and a proud double-breasted owner—but I recall vividly the wave of sentimental tension that surrounded its running. The huge crowd worked itself up gradually to the occasion. The first races had been run, to mild and chiefly mercenary interest; the first fine sheen of toilettes had worn off little, leaving dresses a trifle crinkled and coiffures a trifle wispy; the resolute smiles of the stars were still present, but were looking a little strained at the corners; the Negro waiters had wandered successfully through the crowd selling their mint juleps (simply Bourbons in exotic disguise) with the cry: "Mint juleps, mint juleps, *only* one twenty-five, and keep the souvenir glass!" The innumerable small parties in the bars grew dizzier; the tipsters more vociferous; the elderly ladies peddling ideologies more earnest. It was the moment of the race.

Poor Americans! They have so avid a yearning for pageantry, brought up as they are with only a flag to honor. Their big parades are nearly always spoiled by commercialism, sex, or incompetence, and even their best soldiers, hampered by the slovenliness of their foot drill, lack the true martial inspiration. So when there arises an occasion so imbued with glamour as the Kentucky Derby, they like to make the most of it. As the hands of the big clock ticked around to four o'clock, a solitary outrider in a red coat rode slowly on to the field, and to a perceptible tightening of heartstrings, the band struck up "My Old Kentucky Home," played with such intensity of feeling, to an audience so universally receptive, that Lord North himself, transported to this gathering, could scarcely resist if appeal. As this old melody was vibrantly played (Stephen Collins Foster of Pittsburgh wrote it for a minstrel show) and as the horses came on to the field, one by one, a wave of slightly sticky sentimentality swept over Churchill Downs, uniting pickpocket and President in its glory.

After this heady interval, befuddled both with emotion and mint juleps, the great crowd watched the race itself with a less than avid attention; and very soon after its finish, to some conscientious cheering and the presentation of garlands, and cups, the distinguished assembly began to disperse; with a roar of powerful engines, a last gracious smile, a final quip to the reporters, a swing of mink, and a waft of perfume, the cabbages and the kings went home. Soon Louisville was back to its agreeable normal (on any other day of the year it is a city of most urbane and enlightened tastes) and I was driving through the sunshine across the river into Indiana.

This is one portal of the idle West. To illustrate the range and diversity of the country, let me describe another. Far in the north near the Canadian border, surrounded by forestlands and lonely lakes, lie the iron mines of the Mesabi Range, in Minnesota. For decades these were the ultimate source of American strength; because of the presence of these mines, America was able to feed her greedy steel mills laying the foundations of her power and influence, winning her wars, enriching her magnates. The chief city of the iron country is Duluth on the shores of Lake Superior, a place as far in spirit from the Kentucky Derby or the civilization of the mint julep as Leeds is from Darjeeling (though the name is aristocratic, for the city was called after Daniel de Greysolon Sieur de Lhut). This is a hard northern country, healthy but unenticing of climate; not so moist or endearing as the Pacific Northwest, but similarly Scandinavian in some of its aspects. My first glimpse of Duluth came as I drove over the hills from Minneapolis; when, turning a bend in the road, I suddenly saw below me the cold and forbidding surface of the lake and the docks along its edge. It was a gray scene. The lake was very gray, and the town, lying between the water and the hills, looked clean but colorless. Loading at one of the quaysides far below was an iron ore ship, built in the graceless manner (bulk and brute force) of all the Great Lakes freighters. The air was till and heavy and I could hear the distant clatter of cranes and hatches echoing from the docks. Presently there came heaving up the railway line beside me an enormous steam engine, spitting and hissing, pulling 100 empty wagons, on its way back to the mines to pick up another load of ore. The driver leaned out of his cab to wave to me, and I remember him as my symbol of Duluth: he wore the dungarees of his calling, slightly oily, and decorated with thin blue stripes, like pajamas; but on his head, instead of the engineer's peaked cap, he wore the skin hat of the pioneer and the flatboat man, its round fur top tilted racily over his eyes, its raccoon tail hanging down behind his head and getting tangled in the steamcocks. The northern part of the Middle West contributes lavishly to the wealth and business of the region; but it is enlivened by some few faint memories of younger days, when its forests were the haunts of trappers and unconventional woodsmen.

Even in the cities there is a little of this quality still. "There's a moose on the golf course," a man remarked casually to me as we sat in a bar in Duluth. "Haven't seen one for years. When d'you last see a moose in town, Charlie?" And it is not so long since a large bear wandered into that very bar, and was only driven out (so the story runs) after two or three very stiff Scotch-and-sodas. The country between Duluth and the Canadian frontier is still rugged and unspoiled, dotted with innumerable small lakes, from whose isolated banks (on a Saturday evening) you may hear the sounds of hunters' carousals, the popping of corks or the sudden expectant hush that precedes the *dénouement* of a smoking-room story. "My Old Kentucky Home" would raise no handkerchiefs here; this is a purposeful and unmaudlin place, close to the frontier times. The grayness of its nature affects its inhabitants, and makes them (like Scotsmen) blunt, honest, and resilient.

The mines lie among unprepossessing hills in the heart of this forest country. The woods were mostly destroyed long ago, by merciless exploitation and by disastrous fires (300 people were trapped and killed in one Minnesota blaze), so that most of the trees are young and modest, giving the forests a sparse, anemic air. To reach the mines from Duluth you must drive through fifty or sixty miles of such unspiritual woods (no leagues of protection here, or impassioned lovers of the woodland sprites) until you arrive in the arid wasteland of the iron range, stretching drably away like a tedious argument.

It is, of course, by no means wasteland in the economic sense; but it is less generous than it used to be, for the high-grade ores are running out. I was not surprised to hear this when they showed me the largest of the open cast-iron mines, the Hull-Rust-Mahoning pit at Hibbing, for this is unquestionably the biggest hole on earth, and an astronomical amount of ore—70,000,000 tons, at least—has been removed from it since the first tentative sod was moved. It is a horrible sight. The soil is sandy and unnatural-looking, as if it needs a good wash, and the mine sinks down into the earth in a series of enormous terraces. The hole is three miles long and covers 1,300 acres. It is so big that you can hardly see the end of it, and the trains that work in its recesses are little more than puffs of smoke and dark smudges of trucks. The whole enclave is alive with activity. Trains scurry up and down its terraces; cranes swing their booms jerkily; cars run around the bottom of the pit; hoppers tip, shovels dig; there are even a few men, far down among the dirt, swinging pickaxes. In this single mine there are fifty-five miles of railway track (which would take you, if it were straightened out, from Paddington to Didcot), and outside the pit huge and splendid trains move in almost endless procession down to the docks. Their wagons are weighed to a pound, and carefully sorted according to the grade of their ore; and the trains are so long that the engineer talks to the guard by radio.

In the past all this was a relatively simple operation. The ore was mined; put into trains; processed by fairly easy means; loaded into ships; and sold. But half a century of mining, with wars and booms and extraordinary industrial expansion, has practically emptied the range of high-grade iron ore. I was shown one expanse of dirty ground, loaded with such good ore, which has not been mined but is reserved for a national emergency; but most of the stuff has gone, leaving behind the sort of inferior material that the pioneer miners would have scorned to extract.

Rock bearing this inferior ore is called taconite. People have been trying to use it profitably for thirty years or more, but it is really only since the war (which so disastrously depleted the reserves of ore) that satisfactory ways of processing it have been devised. It is still very expensive to extract good iron from it, but the mining companies seem to have no choice, it being generally agreed that the better Mesabi ore deposits cannot last more than thirty or thirty-five years. Huge and intricate are the mills that have been built to prepare the taconite. First huge lumps of rock from the mine are flung into crushers, like the gold ore at Homestake, and the resulting pebbles are ground in water into an odious muddy substance. The iron is then extracted by magnets, and it comes out (for a reason I have not been able to master) in the form of a thick, black liquid, before being converted by a process of rolling and baking into iron pellets like big cricket balls. The cost is enormous, but on the other hand the reserves of taconite are incalculable. Before long the chief activity of the Minnesota mines will probably be this laborious and costly process.

So, on the frontiers of the Middle West you can meet two such totally disparate societies: the northern iron men, living among their wild lakes and intrusive moose, dealing in big things, iron and ships and great steam trains, a strong and open-air community; and the people of Louisville, at once cultivated and emotional, fond of the comfortable facets of existence, in delicate and lovely countryside of white fences and inviting green fields. Between these extremes (and the other outposts, east and west) lies the expanse of the Middle West, fitting into no convenient category, like the child who finds no school to suit her, or the man who takes size twelve in shoes.

～ 28. ～

Chicago

*I*TS SUMMIT (if one can use the word of a region so uniformly flat), its crown and symbol, the prime product of its energies, the pride of its heart, is the city of Chicago, on the shores of Lake Michigan. I first approached this place by train, and since there is perhaps no city in the world more readily and universally preconceived, I looked out of the windows of my sleeper to glimpse some token of its vigor or catch the distant staccato flashes of its guns. I was prepared for almost anything in Chicago. Was not one nineteenth-century traveler informed, as he rode on *his* train into the city: "Sir, Chicago ain't no sissy town?" Had we not been told by Middle Westerners everywhere of the unsurpassable blast, bustle, and energy of Chicago, its boundless intentions, its sprawling size, its self-confidence, its incomparable resources of brawn and muscle? Did not Carl Sandburg, poet of the Middle West, describe it (with a straight face) as "laughing the stormy, husky, brawling laughter of youth, half-naked, sweating"? Even Bismarck, whom one somehow does to instinctively associate with Illinois, once remarked wistfully to an American visitor: "I wish I could go to America, if only to see that Chicago."

On my first evening in Chicago, I was taken down to the waterfront to see the lights of the city. Behind us the lake was a dark and wonderful void, speckled with the lights of steamers bringing iron ore from Duluth or newsprint from Canada. Until you have been to Chicago—crossing half a continent to reach it—it is difficult to realize that it is virtually a seaside city. It has its sea storms and its rolling waves, its sunny bathing beaches, its docks; you can board a ship for Europe in Chicago, and see the flags of many nations at its quays. So wide is this Lake Michigan and so oceanic in aspect, that more than once I have been compelled to walk down to its edge and reassure myself that it really contains fresh water, not salt. It is not only vast, but also treacherous; the captains who navigate the big Lakes steamers are greatly skilled and highly priced seamen. As for the foreign sailors who arrive in the Middle West by way of the lake, they must surely be approaching a state of lethargy by the time they put into Chicago; for having crossed the dreary Atlantic they have then had to make their slow way through the Gulf of St. Lawrence and into the St. Lawrence River; past Quebec and Montreal into Lake Ontario; past Buffalo, in New York State, into Lake Erie; past Detroit, in Michigan, into Lake Huron; through the Straits of Mackinac into Lake Michigan; until, after days of this intolerable succession, they arrive at the port of Chicago. Soon, it appears, many more unfortunate seamen will be subjected to the ordeal. If the St. Lawrence seaway is ever completed most of the products of the Middle West will be shipped to the sea direct *via* the lakes; more and much larger vessels will be able to make the journey, and Chicago will be one of the great ocean ports of the world.

So we stood with this queer landlocked sea behind us, and looked at the city lights. The lake front is the best façade in America; more regular and uniform than New York's, so that it presents a less jumbled and tangled mass of structures; bigger and grander than Miami's, which shines with a beckoning gaiety across the water of Biscayne Bay; less brassy and frontierlike than the waterside aspect of Seattle. Its glittering row of big buildings extends for miles along the lake, brilliantly lit; some of its skyscrapers are clean and clear-cut, some are surmounted by innumerable pinnacles, turrets, and spires, so that the generally functional effect is tempered by a few touches of the educational. Beside this magnificent row there sweeps a great highway, following the line of the lake, and along it scurries a constant swift stream of lights, with scarcely a pause and scarcely a hesitation, except when some poor unacclimatized woman stalls her engine or loses her way, and is deafened by a blast of protest from behind; then the line of lights wavers for a brief moment, until with a roar of engines and a spinning of wheels the traffic diverts itself and races away, leaving the poor lost soul behind, biting her lower lip, and having a terrible time with the gears.

For Chicago is still a heartless town, in many ways. The incompetent will meet few courtesies in its streets; the flustered will be offered no cooling counsel; it is necessary in life to get places, and to get there fast. Between the buildings that stand like rows of hefty sentinels above the lake, you may see numbers of narrow canyons leading covertly into shadier places behind. The façade of Chicago is supported by no depth of splendor; hidden by its two or three streets of dazzle is a jungle of slums and drab suburbs, a dirty hodge-podge of races and morals.

In the daylight, indeed, the bright glamour even of the business district is not quite so irresistible, if only because of the din and the congestion. This must surely be the noisiest place on earth. The cars roar; the elevated railway rumbles; the policemen blow their strange two-toned whistles, like sea birds lost in a metropolis; the hooters shriek, the horns hoot; the typists, on their way back from coffee, swap their gossip at the tops of their tinny voices. Across the crowded intersections scurry the flocks of shoppers, like showers of sheep, while the policemen wave them irritably on and the cars wait to be unleashed. The tempo of Chicago is terrible, and the overcrowding desperate. Just as each new plan to improve the life of the Egyptian peasant is overtaken and swamped by the inexorable march of the birthrate, so in Chicago every new parking place is obliterated, every new freeway blackened, by the constantly growing flood of motorcars. Each morning the highways into the city are thick with unwearyingly cars, pounding along head to tail, pouring in by every channel, racing and blaring and roaring their way along, until you think it will be impossible to cram one more car in, so bulging and swelling is the place, so thickly cluttered its streets, so strangled the movement of its traffic. It is good business in Chicago to knock down offices and turn them into parking lots. And it is decidedly unwise for the nervous or overconsiderate driver to venture into the turmoil of its streets, for in this respect, as in others, Chicago still ain't no sissy town.

Crime and corruption are still powerful influences here, and the best-laid plans of honest men to clean up the city and rid it of its crooked parasites nearly always seem to go a-gley. I talked to a number of young politicians who had such an ambition, some of them bravely outspoken in their comments on the Syndicate, the shadowy and nebulous body of corruption that still controls so much of Chicago's life. "You may say the old gags about gunmen in Chicago are exaggerated," said Alderman Robert Merriam in one public speech. "but there have been 700 unsolved murders *since* the days of prohibition and Al Capone. Perhaps the crimes of violence have diminished…but they have diminished only because the Syndicate has murdered its way to monopoly. Here in Chicago…segments of both political parties are in cahoots with this monopoly of murder." When I was in Chicago nearly everyone admitted the truth of all this, but few were ready to fight the situation; and when Merriam later stood for Mayor, he was, to nobody's surprise, defeated. People have too much to lose to meddle with such perilous matters. The big men may lose contracts, the little man the dubious cooperation of his local policemen or petty boss. Extortion, on many levels, is still a commonplace in Chicago. A policeman wrote to the *Chicago Tribune* not long ago complaining about the word "cop," which he said was derogatory. The letter brought blistering and revealing reply from a Chicago citizen. "How do you address a you-know-what," he asked in a series of such rhetorical demands, "when he stops you without cause and questions you or searches you or your property? How do you address a you-know-what when you've been looking for one of them a long time and finally find one mooching free drinks in a saloon? *How do you address a you-know-what when one comes around to your place of business soliciting funds you don't dare refuse to give?*" Everyone knows that a five-dollar bill slipped to your examiner will help you pass your driving test. Everyone knows too, if only by reading his papers, that murders occur almost every day in Chicago; but when I talked to a senior Chicago police officer on the subject, he adroitly slipped away to the twin topics (for they seem to go arm in arm) of traffic congestion and prostitution.

All this sordid unhealthiness would be less intrusive if the city itself were spacious and wholesome of appearance. But despite the illusory grandeur of its lakefront, Chicago is a festering place. From the windows of the elevated railway, which clangs its elderly way through the city with rather the detached hauteur of a bath chair, you can look down upon its disagreeable hinterland. The different sectors of slumland each have their national character—Italian, Chinese, Puerto Rican, Lithuanian—but externally they merge and mingle in a desolate expanse of depression. Here is a brown brick building, crumbling at its corners, its windows cracked or shattered, its door crooked on its hinges, with a Negro woman in a frayed and messy blouse leaning from an upstairs window with a comb in her hand. Here an old Italian with long mustache squats on the steps of a rickety wooden tenement, its weatherboards an off-white color, its balcony railings sagging and broken. Slums are slums anywhere in the world, and there are probably areas just as blighted in Glasgow; but here the misery of it all is given added poignancy by the circumstances of so many of its inhabitants, people of a score of races who came to America to be rich, and have stayed on to live like unpampered animals.

In such a climate of existence racial prejudices thrive, and you can often catch a faint menacing rumble of their dangers in a bus or on a street corner—a drunken Negro cursing the white people as he slumps in his seat, a white man arrogantly pushing his way through a group of Negro women. There have been some tragic race riots in Chicago, and there may well be more. During my stay there, hundreds of policemen were on duty each day at a big new housing project erected in an inflammable quarter of the city; for into one of the apartments a young Negro family had moved, and their white neighbors (of many national origins) had sworn to drive them out by force; so that sometimes in the evening, when the policemen were momentarily distracted, the Negroes in their shuttered rooms would hear the thud of a stone on their window, or the murmur of threats and imprecations from the street below.

Such standards of morality have inevitably eaten away like a corrosive at the old blithe and regardless self-confidence of Chicago. Not so long ago Chicagoans were convinced that their city would soon be the greatest and most famous on earth, out-ranking New York, London, and Paris, the center of a new world, the boss city of the universe. During the period of its fabulous nineteenth-century growth, when millionaires seems to be two a penny and the treasures of the continent were being summoned to Chicago, it was not unnatural for such an eager and unsophisticated community to suppose that the center of territorial gravity was fast shifting to the Middle West. In a sense, I suppose it has; the railway tracks, the sprawling stockyards, the factories of Chicago and its sister cities are the sinews of the United States, and so of half the world. But the blindest lover of Chicago would not claim for the place the status of a universal metropolis. So much of the old grand assertiveness has been lost. Nobody pretends that Chicago has overtaken New York; instead there is a provincial acceptance of inferiority, a resignation, coupled with a mild regret for the old days of wild boasts and ambitions. For one reason and another, the stream of events generally passes Chicago by, for the city is so isolated in the center of this enormous heartland, so very far from either Europe or Asia (though you can now fly to Paris direct from Chicago). Even the Chicago theater, once a lively institution, has fallen into dull days, and makes do with the second run of Broadway productions, and a few mildewed and monotonous burlesques. Despite the tumult and the pressure, Chicago sometimes feels like a backwater.

The impression is only partly accurate, for there are many wonderful and exciting things in Chicago. There are magnificent art galleries—one of the best modern French collections in existence—and splendid libraries. There is a plethora of universities, of varying degrees of academic distinction. The symphony orchestra is good, if hampered in the past by the determinedly fashionable character of it audience, which has apparently restricted some of its conductors (so intricate are the channels of snobbery) in their choice of programs.

Nor indeed has the old manly energy entirely evaporated; there is still much virility and enterprise in Chicago life. The city itself is physically expressive of this continued resilience. The huge marshalling yards lie lounging over the countryside, littered with trains. The bridges over the Chicago River open with a fascinating and relentless ease to let the great freighters through. The *Chicago Tribune*, which calls itself the World's Greatest Newspaper, is certainly among the sprightliest and most vigorous. There are brave schemes of expansion and improvement—plans to run a new highway bang through the heart of the place, to build a new suburb on an island in the lake, to erect a huge new office building astride the elevated railway, so that the trains will rattle through its open legs.

But such driving activity no longer represents the spiritual temper of the city. Chicagoans are still pursued by the demon of progress and haunted by the vision of possible failure, so that the pressure of their existence is relentless; but the strain of it all, and the fundamental rottenness of the place, has blunted some of their old intensity and lavishness of purpose. They have accepted their station in life, no longer swaggering through the years with the endearing braggadocio of their tradition, but more resigned, more passive, even (perhaps) a little disillusioned. Chicago is certainly not a has-been; but it could be described as a might-have-been.

༄ 29. ༄

In Suburbia

$\mathcal{C}$ HICAGO has always had, though, a flourishing intellectual and cultivated minority, and it was the center of the great Middle Western literary and artistic movement which had its heyday between the wars. Around its wide perimeters today there are a number of handsome suburbs which, without having pretensions to intellectual distinction, nevertheless represent a comfortably literate way of living, and have not their exact equivalents or equals, perhaps, elsewhere in the world. The world "suburbia" has not acquired those overtones which taint it in England. In the hubbub of American urban life it is long common sense to live in a suburb, though some of the more earnest sociologists profess to be disturbed about the movement away from the centers of towns; and the large stores cater to this trend by opening excellent little minor versions of their enormous emporia, scattered about the more expensive outskirts of the cities. The most attractive residential area I saw in America was the suburb built on the top of Lookout Mountain, in the country of the snake-worshippers; but most of the big cities of the Middle West have their counterparts, well-tended, clean, prosperous, complete with their own rich little shopping centers, teeming with clubs, societies, discussion groups, and other manifestations of the American social appetite. The Middle West is full of intense local patriotisms, but when a small frontier settlement blossoms into a metropolis Americans demand some more intimate loyalty, and are inclined to scuttle some of their fervor for Detroit or Chicago, let us say, in favor of such desirable suburbs as Grosse Pointe, Michigan, or Lake Forest, Illinois.

Lake Forest is characteristic of these well-fed communities. The best way to reach it from Chicago, if you can endure forty minutes of conviviality, is to persuade some friend to take you on the evening "club car." The American railroad can still be surprisingly personal and flexible in its services—as anyone knows who has discussed a transcontinental ticket at Pennsylvania Station in New York. There is none of the monolithic detachment of British Railways about these lively enterprises. What the customer wants, he gets (providing it pays). Accordingly it is not difficult, on many American lines, for a group of commuting businessmen to arrange for a private coach to be hitched each morning to the 8:15 and each evening to the 6:38; and quite a modest subscription is enough to acquire membership in such a mobile club, and to share the services of the calm and adaptable Negro servant who travels with it every day.

So each evening at Lake Forest, when the club train pulls in, a most cheerful and well-acquainted group of businessmen emerges from its cushioned recesses, and parts with fond expressions of fraternity. How comfortable a process this is, compared with that dreary daily grind from Waterloo to Axshott! There they sit in their swivel chairs, a glass of bourbon in the hand, a selection of friends round about, an attentive lackey padding among the seats, a stack of new magazines, a whole coach to wander in, instead of those dark Satanic cabinets that are all too often provided by the Southern Region, with their gray and aging upholstery, their cramped corridors, and the squeezing anxious crowd that presses into them. Moreover, when these fortunate Illinoians reach the little station at Lake Forest, another pleasant circumstance awaits them; for there parked beside the line are the long polished rows of their limousines and shooting-brakes, a well-dressed wife at each wheel, an expectant child or two skipping about the seat, a couple of poodles or a huge lugubrious mastiff peering through the back window. What a world away from the bus queue outside the Surrey station, or the bicycle locked with its padlock in the stationmaster's office, or even the Morris that is beginning to burn oil! There are probably no commuters anywhere in the world who travel home more comfortably than the burghers of Lake Forest.

But there are disadvantages, not always apparent, to so soothing a progression. The wife in her black nylon looked very nice from the station platform, but inside the car there is a dauntingly purposeful air to her ensemble. The Lake Forester will, however, be more depressed than surprised by her air of impending festivity, for dinner with the Rodney Bells, or the Howard J. Spriggses, the Afschleters or the Edmund Browns is something that befalls him frequently. They need only run back and drop the children while he freshens up; it is rarely black tie in America, and he is therefore able to step with scarcely a pause from club car to cocktails.

But the evening is likely to be an agreeable one. The guests will find themselves in one of two kinds of houses: a comfortable and well-preserved little mansion built by some complacent plutocrat in the early years of the century, and having a parklike garden and an atmosphere if not actually horsy, at least distinctly doggy; or a house of uncompromising modernity, with mobiles floating about the drawing room, a hostess who keeps Abyssinian cats, and a host who talks about the G-factor of the roof. Few American households have servants. The wife cooks the meal herself, slipping a crisp and colorful apron over her dress, and inviting her women guests (as the men drink their cocktails) to join her from time to time in the kitchen. If she is unlucky she may be burdened with an epicurean husband, for "knowing about cooking" has become as popular an esoteric exercise among American men as it has among British (though probably no American takes it quite so seriously as the Oxford don who subscribes to *Le Figaro* for its daily recipes). If so, it is the husband who leads the way into the kitchen, placing his Martini on the top of the refrigerator as he demonstrates his techniques. He is sure to have acquired the very best equipment: rows of heatproof dishes, rolls of aluminum foil, and an oven at shoulder height, so that he need not strain his knees bending for the joint. The Americans do not take their eating lightly, and there is no dishing up an old stew or reaching for the sausages when Lake Foresters entertain.

Among many of them, on the other hand, there is a determined rejection of formality, a vestigial relic of frontier times or an inherited reaction (which they would fervently disclaim) against the imperial splendors of Europe. There are many houses in Lake Forest where you can rely upon polished oak tables, monogrammed napkins, and candles; but you should be prepared, when you accept an invitation, to eat your dinner literally on the floor. It is the custom to serve the meal in the manner of a buffet, the guests queueing a little self-consciously while the host and hostess, at the head of the serving table, ladle the soup or give encouragement. Having received your portion, you must then dispose yourself about the house to eat it; and for some reason or other—I am never quite sure whether it is intentional or not—there are not enough chairs to go round, so that the more girlish of the ladies, and the more resigned or flirtatious of the men, must sit on the carpet. I know of few less relaxing exercises than that of eating a plate of curried prawns with one hand, clutching the support of a neighboring chair leg with the other, trying to avoid destroying a priceless china dog with one's feet, and discussing the Meaning of Truth with one's companion.

For the conversation is unlikely to be entirely frivolous. You cannot depend upon an evening of utter escapism, as you can in England; you will meet no girls, however anxiously you search, of an utter emptiness of intellect; and few men whom you can trust implicitly not to talk about the next elections. The Middle Westerner has reached his apogee of creature comfort by a commendable gift for labor and application; and he is still, beneath a veneer of sophisticated congeniality, an earnest and a serious person. So is his wife. I remember all too clearly a conversation I had with one Lake Forest woman, sitting on just such a floor, eating just such a curry, in which she displayed some anxiety to arrange in corresponding order the Kings of England and the Presidents of the United States; and in which, while she rattled through the Georges and the Williams, hesitating only over the details of a year of two, I floundered distressingly among the Presidents. Who was the fifth President of the United States? For that matter, who was the fourth? Was Van Buren a President? Who was Millard Fillmore? Luckily she did not notice my inadequacies, for the conversation spread, and soon the entire company was busy discussing the relationship between Catherine de Medici and Bonnie Prince Charlie. There is always an encyclopedia in such a house as this; and the children, poor things, sometimes seemed to me to be weighed down with reference books and inducements to learning. It is an atmosphere healthily demanding accuracy of mind. Though you can survive the wildest opinions, you should try to avoid errors of fact; unless, that is, you are an expert, for expertise is sacrosanct, the specialist is never doubted, and a few technicalities interlarded with authority will make almost any statement acceptable. (A visiting agent for a firm of English sanitary engineers was once introduced to a group of Middle West women reporters, as a somewhat heavy joke, as "Sir Henry Middleton, leader of the 1949 Everest Reconnaissance." "Oh, Sir Henry," they gushed, "tell us, do, what it was like!"—and when with scarcely a pause for reflection he replied that it really wasn't much fun cutting crampons on the West Col, they wrote it down in their notebooks with awed excitement; for though he was portly, sagging and wildly ignorant, he was indubitably an expert.)

The evening is likely to be dominated by women. This is not surprising, for not only are they generally more intelligent, but they form a closely interwoven society of their own. Miss Freya Stark refers in one of her books, describing some very different society, to "the universal sisterhood of women." In the well-to-do suburbs of the Middle West this nebulous mystery is reinforced by the American women's invincible urge to join things. The impression you take away with you from the dinner party is likely to be that while the male guests had not seen each other for a month or two, the women had spent most of that day together, and the day before too, and would be meeting again tomorrow morning if not for breakfast, at least for morning coffee. The highly integrated social activities of these ladies are naturally not quite so straightforward as those of the ladies of Cranbury, New Jersey. There must be Presbyterians in Lake Forest, but they are a great deal more subdued, and I have heard religious opinions expressed there that would lead to agonizing reappraisals of social standing among the simplicities of Cranbury. The fêtes are smarter and more expensive; the discussion groups more inclined to talk about Kafka and less likely to read *Ivanhoe* aloud in relays; the dance committees much more anxious to secure a foreign title or two for effect. For it cannot be denied that many of the people of Lake Forest, though in theory thorough democrats, have at the back of their minds some slight yearning for a more aristocratic form of society. Many are the obscure English baronets or German princes who are paraded in their drawing rooms or casually introduced to envious neighbors. Subtle indeed are the means by which the arrival of such a worthy is made known to the social columns of the local paper, or one to the gossip pages of the Chicago press. You can meet your thrusting self-made Americans in Lake Forest, proud embodiments of the old legend about office boy to high executive; but you can meet at least as many who will drop a hint about "the old place" in England, or assiduously preserve the faintly European accent they acquired at Harvard, or drive about in an English sports car, or wear clothes of unmistakably Savile Row ancestry. I was once walking down a road in Lake Forrest when I heard from over a garden wall the beguiling wail of bagpipes. Could it be, I wondered, that the Stockyards Pipe Band of Chicago, a well-known Middle West institution, had come out to Lake Forest in charabancs for some fashionable carnival? Or was it the band of some ancient regiment of the line, shipped to the Middle West by the ever-active British Information Services, as they once shipped two London buses complete with drivers and direction plates to Hackney Wick? I looked over the garden gate and there, marching solemnly up an down the lawn, were the pipers, two young men in kilts who happened to be identical twins. They were watched by an elderly lady of distinguished appearance, dressed in tweeds, who sat in a chair at the head of the lawn surrounded by admirers, as if she were ordering the sea to retreat, or was expecting the head of John the Baptist. This was a characteristic Lake Forest occasion. The lady was Dame Flora Macleod, head of the Clan Macleod; the twins were her two grandsons; and they had come to America to meet members of their clan and invite them to visit the ancestral castle in Scotland, a prospect of sublime appeal for those many Lake Foresters to whom the lure of ancient stones and immemorial titles is irresistible.

Lake Forest, indeed, has its own nobility, inhabiting the fine houses that stand along the shore of Lake Michigan. Some of these houses are very grand indeed, beyond the means of all but the most successful Italian marquises, and of a state of preservation and convenience utterly beyond the ambitions of the average English duke. One such house has a splendid staircase leading down to the water, embellished with a series of Grecian figures; and such is the rudeness of the Chicago climate, and such the conscientiousness of the owner, that when these statues are not being used, so to speak, they are enveloped in transparent containers, and stand there modestly and mysteriously muffled, ghosts in shrouds of cellophane. Lake Forest, like a hill station in the evening of an Empire, has its own subtle social tiers, its own barons, landgraves, and caciques. It has its sporting club, too, to which in the long summer evenings the commuters are whisked for parties, just as the Major, home from evening stables, would be conveyed to Gezira for dinner with the Lauries of the 9th. This tight little community, living so comfortably among its trees and shady lawns, no longer feels the magnetic pull of the big city, nor the call of the land, but has evolved its own polished and intricate civilization. It has its failings of pretension, perhaps, but it shares a grace and an easy style that is one of the more attractive American contributions to social progress.

↜ 30. ↝

Ex-Communists

$\mathcal{S}$OME OTHER such contributions have been more extreme or experimental in character. "We tried communism," a man from a refrigerator factory observed to me one day, "but we decided to change over to capitalism, and I guess it's working pretty well, on the whole, like it usually does."

There are very few places in the world where a man of business could make such a remark as this, and not many people, asked to guess where the refrigerator factory was, would plump for the Middle West of America, the prime force of free enterprise and the competitive system. Nevertheless, in the history of the United States there have been many examples of little communistic settlements which were established on American soil, flourished for a few years, and then faded into obscurity and oblivion. In the days of the old American individualism such expressions of ideological belief were regarded as religious heresies rather than subversive activities, and many were the economic cranks and political visionaries who were welcomed to America and permitted to establish their vestigial Utopias as they pleased. Because of the dates of its settlement, the Middle West absorbed many of these experiments (just as Chicago received many of the German liberals who left Europe after the 1848 revolution), and from time to time as you wander through its states you may come across relics of their fervors, crumbling communal halls and dwelling houses, estates of geometrical design, in villages that have long since abandoned such high intentions and cheerfully subscribe to the maxim that business is the business of America.

My refrigerator man, though, lived in a community that has only recently forsaken communism, after an experiment that lasted almost 100 years. The Amana of Iowa are members of a community of German origin which crossed to America in the 1840s and set up a benevolent autocracy in New York State. They prospered there, found themselves outgrowing their land, and moved in 1854 to Iowa, where they built six villages, acquired their own railway station, wove their own cloth, and soon had a flourishing, religio-communist settlement with a distinctly German flavor.

Physically, the Amana villages have changed relatively little since then. Their red-brick houses are plain and handsome, with stout wooden doors, square chimneys, and gardens full of vegetables, grape vines, and fruit trees. Their farms are clean and spacious, their barns gentlemanly. Their inns are famous for good food and beer, and have check tablecloths and genial blonde maids. Their cemeteries are suitably egalitarian, in that the gravestones are of uniform size, and there are no gilded urns, obelisks, or fortified mausoleums. Their drawing rooms are full of solid local furniture, slightly enlivened by embroidered cushions and speckled sofas. Sometimes in the pleasant streets of these villages one sees a lady in a poke bonnet, or a group of women (on their way to church) wearing the traditional dark shawls over their heads. In the shops there are splendid hams and jams; in a few modest workshops craftsmen still make chairs, rugs, and wooden figures by antique methods.

But if in general the Amana externals remain much the same, the basic pattern of life in the villages changed with revolutionary abruptness in April, 1932. The old leaders of the Community of True Inspiration had been good men, but egalitarians of dedicated intensity. Worthy and pious indeed were the tenets of their faith, and no inner caucus of the Cominform holds its adherents under closer rein than did the early Amana Church hold its hapless congregation. The sharing of pleasures and labors was a strictly compulsory blessing; indeed, a divine revelation (not unlike those sacred manifestations which, from time to time, encouraged the Crusaders in their strategy) made it clear that any opponent of the system would be shamed and disgraced, and his unfortunate children would "suffer want and be unblessed in time and eternity." The rule of the thirteen elders was rigid and terribly sensible, and the villagers were led firmly down the paths of communal virtue. Drab were the clothes they wore, and eminently sedate the society they shared. The women did their cooking in big communal kitchens, carrying food home in baskets to the men, who had been busy all day milking the communal cows, working the communal looms, or keeping the communal ledger. Prudence and diligence were the watchword of life. Even the gardens of the houses must grow no flowers, but only nutritional plants, so that edible creepers grew up the cottage walls, and the lovelorn girl at her bedroom window would dreamily finger a bean pod or pluck the blossom of a vegetable marrow. Dutiful Brothers and Sisters went to church eleven times a week.

But to the intense joy (one can only suppose) of the entire community, the system failed miserably. The beginnings of the Iowa settlement were successful enough. The Inspirational Church, taking a spiritual interest in every aspect of Amana life, organized affairs with some efficiency. The Amana Society prospered, its hams and woolen goods selling all over America; and its individual members, sharing the profits with scrupulous integrity, did not do at all badly. But the years passed, the quality of the divine inspiration seemed to be degenerating, and the villagers, basking in fair-shares-for-all, grew lazy. In defiance of the old rules, labor was brought in from outside to do some of the less congenial work, with deplorable economic results. The big woolen mill was destroyed in a fire. Production fell, and the old devotional unity relaxed, leading to petty internal squabbles and rivalries. The Depression of 1929 hit the Community of True

Inspiration much as it hit less enlightened segments of society, and by 1931 the colony was on the brink of bankruptcy.

Then in a characteristically American *volte-face*, the people of Amana decided to switch to a modified form of capitalism. The church withdrew from its position of supreme authority and a stock cooperative was established. Each member of the old society received stock in it, and younger people had a right to acquire their share when they came of age. Almost at once (so the villagers told me) the spirit of capitalism had its usual invigorating, if not supremely altruistic, effect. The villages, which had begun to look a little seedy, were spruced and painted. The housewives, relieved of the intolerable duty of sharing a kitchen with all their neighbors, distributed the kitchen utensils among themselves and pushed them proudly home in wheelbarrows. Churchgoing became a less insistent routing, and the congregations lost a little of their solemnity and earnestness of bearing. Electricity was brought to the villages, people voted in elections, there was a dance in 1933, a young man called Willie "Zum Zum" Zuber became a famous pitcher for the New York Yankees.

At the time of this startling transition Amana common stock was valued at $50; today it is worth more than $3,300. The Amana people have proved to be astonishingly adept free-enterprisers, previous experience apparently being unnecessary, and they have turned their trim villages into a high-powered business operation. The woolen mill, first established by the original Amana settlers of Iowa, is not only selling large quantities of its excellent woolen materials, but is also producing synthetic fibers. The meat markets still cure their hams in the time-honored Westphalia manner, but nowadays the finished hams are packed in cellophane, stamped with sundry trade marks and mystic signs, and generally made to conform with the exigencies of the Kleenex age. Ten thousand of these hams are shipped out of the Amana villages each Christmas; and one of the most agreeable experiences that can befall the traveler in the Middle West is to wander into one of the Amana inns, all brown wood and warm comfort, and to be served at the polished counter with a sandwich, delectably prepared, containing sizable slices of these delicious meats.

The most astonishing result of the Amana's ideological conversion has been the rise of the refrigerator factory. There are now seven Amana villages—West Amana, South Amana, High Amana, Middle Amana, East Amana, Amana, and Homestead (they remind me of the menu chalked outside a Louisiana country restaurant: "Fresh Catfish: Broiled Catfish: Fried Catfish: Ice"). Of these, the most urban is Middle Amana, where there is not only a print shop, a winery, a lily pond, and a cemetery, but also one of the most profitable refrigerator factories in America. It is an extraordinary fact that the Amana community, which has so recently blossomed out of its rigid sectarianism, makes more "home freezers" than any other single producer in the world. Amana Refrigeration Inc. produces about one-fifth of all such freezers made in the United States, and it also makes air-conditioning equipment. This concern has made the name of Amana a household word all over he country. When the Amana people abandoned communism in 1932 two members of the community began making beer coolers, as their modest contribution to the new economy. Their enterprise, transferred first to the ownership of the society, then to the control of a group of outside investors, has developed into this great industry. The factory is surrounded by fields, cottages, gardens, and country living; but the firm spends at least one million dollars a year on advertising, and produces something like one and a half million freezers annually.

I need hardly stress how satisfying it is for Midwesterners to be able to recount this story, proof positive of the superiority of the chosen system over the alien ideologies of Europe. The Amana Society is still not an example of complete American capitalism, for it has something of the flavor of a particularly well-to-do welfare state. The doctors and dentists of the villages, for instance, are paid by the society; and when a member takes a prescription to the chemist he pays only the cost of the materials. This means that the motives of the Amana villagers are still slightly suspect to some of those fervent opponents of creeping Socialism who dominate the medical profession of the Middle West. (If you would have an evening of controversy, or sense something of the latent savagery of this country, or if you enjoy baiting a tied bear or taunting a retreating warrior, try discussing socialized medicine with a Middle West doctor. There is no topic more galling to his soul and no antipathy he can more clearly or more revealingly express.)

Nevertheless the Amana villages are a source of pride among Iowans. Not far away from these pleasant places is the city of Cedar Rapids, a characteristic Middle West manufacturing town, where they make (in particular) breakfast cereals. I was a guest at a business dinner in this thrusting and uncompromisingly materialistic town, and was tackless enough to remark that in some ways the few years of Socialist Government in Britain had been of miraculous benefit. There was, for a moment, a hush around the table, only a faint thud of mastication penetrating the silence. "Well, we tried communism in Amana," said the man from the refrigerator factory, as a logical progression of thought, "and I guess we find capitalism suits us better, yes sir, though that may not go for you British…"

ᖉ 31. ᖉ

Two Men

*I*T IS astonishing how accurately the provincial American
sometimes reflects the general character of his region. You
may be able to tell a Manchester man by his accent, but
deposit the chairman of that Cedar Rapids dinner in the heart of the
Antarctic, and you would know him for a Midwesterner by the jib of
his chin and the merest whiff of his climate of thought. I met two
men in the Middle West whom I remember as especially representative of its livelier and more independent elements, and whom an enlightened selection committee might well choose to symbolize it
(dressed in dungarees and rimless spectacles) in some patriotic
holiday carnival.

I encountered the first of them fortuitously. One pleasant autumn morning I was driving through the countryside of southern
Wisconsin, not far from the lovely little state capital of Madison.
This is a gentle and unspoiled country for the most part, with
German, Swiss, and Scandinavian overtones, its fields wide and well
tended, its farmhouses clean and prosperous, its cattle fat, its milk
appropriately creamy. If there is one state in the American interior
that fulfills the requirements of a Promised Land it is Wisconsin; for

here there are no deserts, no harsh mountains, and no hideous sprawling wens, but only lakes, woods, green fields, and the attractive lakeside city of Milwaukee. The farming people of Wisconsin are not, however, always expressive of their good fortune. They are a taciturn and unyielding lot, so that if you are rash enough to engage one in conversation over a glass of beer you may well extract only grunts and heavy breathing by your inquiries. With their caps and overalls, their countless tractors and machines, they sometimes seem less like farmers than engine drivers on some remote and uneconomic branch line; though occasionally at a country market, where the women wear their head scarves, the ducks have their legs tied up in sacking, and old men wander creakingly about poking cows with walking sticks, you might well be back in an antique and unprogressive Europe.

Many of the farms are notable for the magnificence of their barns, unique in America and apparently having both Swiss and Scandinavian architectural origins. They have huge solid walls, peaked roofs, and attendant aluminum silos, and they often look much grander and more luxurious than their parent farmhouses. Often and again, as you travel along the country roads, one of these bulky structures rears itself over a distant horizon, apparently alone among the pastures; and as you drive by you can look through its open door and see, in the steamy comfort of its interior, cows idling in the hay and the long rows of metal mechanisms with which they are soon to be milked.

On this particular October day one of these barns caught my eye as a splash of color in the fields (there are relatively few trees in southern Wisconsin, and a vivid roof or a bed of crimson flowers can often be seen from miles away). When I reached the structure I found it was remarkable even among Wisconsin barns; for across the whole of its side, painted in the boldest of colors and the finest of lines, was an enormous mural. It showed a conventional country scene, with hills, clumps of trees, cows, and a little stream, and so gay and guileless was it, and of such an infectious *joie de vivre*, that it dominated the countryside with its cheerfulness. I asked a passerby who had painted this picture, and he said a Mr. Engebretson did it, or some such name, lived over Brodhead way, a real nice guy, the same as did the picture on the Schmidt farm in Lafayette County.

So I drove to Brodhead to meet the artist. It is a village near the Illinois border, the very epitome of those small Midwestern towns so often portrayed in the movies, where the beautiful girl arrives off the "streamliner" with her bag, and is welcomed by the lovable old philosopher in the straw hat. Like most such villages, it is a place of white frame houses and unfenced gardens, shaded by groves of big and rather gloomy trees. The houses (or the "homes," as one must call them in the Middle West) are dotted haphazardly about the place, so that back doors open into front yards and there is plethora of odd outhouses, potting sheds, and carpentry huts.

I would be able to recognize the Engebretson house, a man told me at the store, because outside it there stood one such shed totally covered in one of his murals; and this was the kind of thing, he added reasonably, that one could not easily miss. Sure enough there it stood among the trees, blazing with color, and I very soon found myself sitting in Mr. Engebretson's parlor eating cheese. The atmosphere was agreeably Scandinavian. Engebretson and his wife are both of Norwegian stock, and their house is full of wooden things and the savor of plain cooking. Mr. Engebretson is an elderly man with a wrinkled outdoor face, spectacles, and a lively and engaging air, and for fifty years or more his passion in life has been painting. The walls of his rooms are hung thickly with his oils; though his style is simple rather than fashionably primitive, these pictures are vivid and arresting. But it is as a painter of outdoor murals that he has achieved his local celebrity ("and they wrote me up in *Life* magazine too, here's the clippings").

He is a house painter by trade, and his first barn mural was an advertisement showing a group of Holstein cows; it was so much admired that soon, when farmers wanted their barns painted, they would simply ask him to do one of his murals, covering the whole of the barn wall and thus combining aesthetic stimulation with practical economy. These huge murals, sometimes ninety feet long, are as near to a folk art as you can find in the modern Middle West; and luckily Wisconsin is one of the few states in America where Mr. Engebretson would find a ready recognition. The state university at Madison is enlightened enough to employ a resident artist, supplying him with a studio, a salary, and materials, and helping him with liberal encouragement. John Steuart Curry was one holder of this happy office, and during his tenure he fostered a vigorous rural art movement in Wisconsin. Many are the farmers and housewives who now contribute every year to a rural art exhibition in Madison, and many are the amateur artist who (like Mr. Engebretson) have been helped and advised. There are many places in the Middle West where an artist-farmer would still be decidedly suspect: Curry himself, at his home in Kansas, used to be followed through the village streets by the cry of derision: "Sissy-pants Curry paints pictures! Sissy-pants Curry paints pictures!" Mr. Engebretson certainly suffers from no such stigma. Not only are his murals in constant local demand, but he is to Brodhead rather as Mr. Sinclair Lewis was to Sauk Center, to the north, or even as Mr. Faulkner is to aromatic Oxford, Mississippi. Every visitor to the town is taken to see Mr. Engebretson's murals, and they have been described or pictured in many publications, from *The Times* of London to the *Prairie Farmer*. The artist is understandably pleased by this modest accumulation of fame, and readily shows you his cuttings, and discusses the value of his work. "Mind you, they won't last," he says cheerfully. "Some of them's fading already. If you paint a house you don't expect it to last forever, do you? You've got to keep repainting it. Same with my murals. If they don't get repainted, they'll fade. Paint on a wall—that's all they are!" What with painting the originals, making requested alterations, and repainting those whose owners are farsighted enough to commission him, Mr. Engebretson estimates he has executed two miles of murals—which is, as an admiring neighbor remarked to me, "a powerful lot of art." I hope his big pictures are not allowed to fade, for they are the product of a true country craftsman, and bring the unsuspecting traveler close to those great days of the Middle West, when it was still a country of pioneer individualists.

If Mr. Engebretson is well known in Brodhead, Mr. Harry Truman is scarcely less prominent in Kansas City, Missouri, for he has grown up with its brashness, matured with its brazen politics, and formed an essential part of its fabric since the turn of the century. It is true that he has gone off to Washington now and again, has decided the fate of nations once or twice, and for a time (with the vast fleets and armies under his direct command) bestrode this narrow world as an unlikely Colossus; but he is still unmistakably and unashamedly a Missouri boy. There is, of course, quite a pervasive homespun, party-headquarters flavor to Washington itself. It is a city of conscious grace, dotted with monuments and political shrines, fragrant with cherry blossoms, graced with ornamental ponds and waterways and scenic wonders; but behind its symbolisms one can perceive, as in a haze, a vision of distant country conventions and the beer-stained green of billiards tables. In the Hall of Fame in the Capitol there is a statue of Huey Long, the most detestable of these dictators; and on the lawn of the Supreme Court there is a notice prohibiting roller-skating. Mr. Truman must have fitted easily enough into the Washington scene, during his decades of activity there; but he slips even more smoothly and satisfyingly into the milieu of Kansas City, a highly political stockyards town.

Most people think of Kansas City politics in terms of "Boss" Pendergast (with whom, as the more virulent Republicans like to recall, Mr. Truman had some professional association). There is a place in the city where you may see a small stream, meandering pleasantly through the public garden. This is Brush Creek, a stream of little consequence except for one strange circumstance; Mr. Pendergast had interests in a cement factory, and when he gained political control of the city he caused the city authorities to pave the whole of Bush Creek with cement; so you can see it now, looking rather foolish with its immaculate bottom, a memorial to an era in American politics. Pendergast was a representative of his times, and for sordid and corrupt politics Kansas City in the 1930 must have been unsurpassable. Nowadays its atmosphere is robust without being generally criminal, and it is a handsome city. A network of great parkways surrounds it and connects its wealthy suburbs; its principal hill, high above the Missouri river, is crowned with a complex of stout skyscrapers; at the entrance to the stockyards, stands a mammoth figure of a Hereford bull, perched on the top to a column, the Nelson of Kansas City. "K.C.," as it is known in the Middle West, still has a quality of excitement, for it is an energetic railway and market town, a hub of communications. From the very center of the city you can look down upon its busy airport; by some vagary of real estate, the municipality from the city center, so that there is probably not a city in the world with an airport more conveniently situated. Kansas City is no haven of rest; but if you can bear for a time with the tiresome push and brawn of the Middle West, you will find it pleasant enough to visit.

Mr. Truman's home is in Independence, a large suburb which is of sacred significance to many Mormons, because they believe it will one day be the capital of a Sacred Kingdom. He has an office, however, in one of the main thoroughfares of Kansas City, in a block which was once the scene of a spectacular bank robbery. "Shall I need security clearance?" I asked when I was invited to visit him there. "And how shall I identify myself to the policeman on duty?" "Lord bless you, Harry doesn't have any policeman," I was told indulgently. "Does Maisie's drugstore have a policeman? Harry just walks into his office like anyone else. Take the elevator up, his secretary will show you in." I was welcomed without great ceremony at the building. "Mr. Truman? Sure, this elevator," said the smart young woman who presided over the lifts. "Mr. Truman? Certainly, he's expecting you," said the pleasant secretary upstairs; and in a moment there was his familiar figure, sitting at a big polished desk and silhouetted against a widow. Mr. Truman was busy preparing his memoirs and collating his papers for deposition in a Truman Memorial Library at Independence. The anteroom of his office was therefore filled with rows of huge filing cabinets, securely fastened; and this obscure building in a provincial Middle Western city consequently contained material of incalculable historical value. "It's a lot of work," says Mr. Truman in his flat Missouri voice, "but I regard it as my duty, as former President of the United States."

Nobody could accuse this misleading man of an apathetic approach to greatness, for he is clearly sharply conscious of his place in the history books and of the extraordinary nature of his career ("The Accidental President," they are calling him already). Beside his desk there stands a large and splendid globe, in a frame stand, and from time to time during our conversation Mr. Truman would spin it idly or point to parts of it in a manner that I can only describe as proprietorial. Sometimes he would casually toss off some such revealing phrase as "When I altered the foreign policy of the United States, in…."; and sometimes he would talk with a most agreeable enthusiasm and interest of the other potentates of his time, the Churchills and the Stalins who shared the stage with him. "There now," he said, handing me a menu from a banquet at the Yalta Conference, which had been signed by all the distinguished Allied leaders present. "There now," said he, rather in the manner of a nanny asking why the chicken crossed the road, "see if you can find Stalin's signature in *that* lot!" Alas, I knew exactly where to find it, scrawled in diagonal arrogance across the card, for I had seen a reproduction of the thing in a magazine; but I played my part as best I could, if only to see Mr. Truman's evident delight at having to point it out.

One often feels of English politicians, as they parry the election meetings or summon their transitory charm at garden gates, that they are riding serenely over the surface of local life. They may be locally bred, but have long ago discarded parochial loyalties and affinities, and come back to their own country smoothened and aloof. Or they may, indeed, have no local associations at all, and find themselves chosen because it is a safe seat, or a resistant constituency, or because they need experience, confidence or a good lesson. The American politician, on the other hand, even at the Congressional level, usually seems positively symbolic of his region, like the State Flag, or the State Bird, or the State Anthem, or the State Motto, or the State Crest, which so belabor the patriotism of American schoolchildren, and so befuddle the efforts of ill-informed heralds. The recognized nickname of Missouri is "The 'Show Me'

State," implying a certain inquiring distrust and suspicion, such as is common among crusty country shopkeepers. I can well imagine Mr. Truman using this very phrase, when confronted with some high-sounding international commitment, or asked to swap a sphere of influence. His roots are still deep in the Missouri soil. His standards are still Missouri standards. He has a fine stock of regional jokes and regional allusions, and his experience of high diplomacy has never blunted his appetite for local politics.

What is more, I suspect most Midwesterners admire a man more for his local attainments than for any reputation he may achieve in a wider world. Everyone in Kansas City knows Harry Truman, and sees him walk into his office each day, and has visited his home at Independence. His neighbors are naturally pleased that he became President; but they do not seem to be inordinately interested in the part he has played in world affairs, nor even to realize fully that his responsibilities extended far beyond the forty-eight states of the Union. "You are leaving the house of a master," said an old man to me as I walked away from Mr. Engebretson's home in Brodhead. But when I spoke to a group of Kansas City businessmen about my interview with ex-President Truman, "Harry?" said they, "a great little politician!"

‿ 32. ‿

Newspapers

HIS SORT of unquestioning parochialism is often fostered by the powerful press of the Middle West. There are, of course, no national newspapers in the United States in quite the British sense of the phrase; the nearest equivalents are perhaps the *Wall Street Journal*, which is printed in several American cities, and the *Christian Science Monitor*. As a result, the local daily newspaper enjoys great influence and prestige, especially in the Middle West where the distances between cities are considerable but the populations are large. Sometimes the local pride of these newspapers allows them to color the news to a comic degree. In Des Moines I was shown the front page of the issue of the local paper that recorded the sinking of the *Titanic*. A big black streamer headline announced the loss of the ship across the top of the page; but directly beneath it there was a second headline, almost as big, almost as black, announcing with satisfaction: "No Des Moines Passengers aboard."

Oddly enough, though, the Middle West supports most of the best newspapers in America and two or three of the best in the world. The region is swamped and cluttered with television transmitters. There is scarcely a city where you have not a choice of two or three channels, and the great television stars of New York or Hollywood are as familiar as those local notables who offer their news bulletins or weather forecasts day by day with the same forceful mannerisms and indomitable interest. Almost every week, it seemed to me, the quality of these programs improved. There is much less blatancy and vulgarity on American television than there is on sound radio, and less objectionable matter than you can extract any Saturday evening from one of the B.B.C.'s smuttier and sweatier variety programs. It has a bit and sparkle arising partly from the newness and excitement of the medium, and partly (like the stimulation of Manhattan) from the selfish but exhilarating drive of American free enterprise. Nor is it all aimed at the moronic. While I was in America I watched on television a hitherto unperformed Respighi opera of such unparalleled tedium and worthiness that the Third Programne itself might well have rejected it.

But despite this lively competition (plus the threat of color television, the advent of the wide-screen cinema, and the huge circulations of the magazines) the newspapers of the Middle West seem to fare prosperously, on the whole, and have maintained their position as presidents of the public conscience. To see their impact most clearly, you must visit a newspaper office in some very small town, so obscure that no big-city paper will take any notice of it, so remote that it is still a close and family-like community. Many are the offices I visited on my journey for a chat with the editor (who is also, as likely as not, the reporter, compositor, printer, and photographer); for the Middle West journalist is often not only the most liberal and intelligent member of his society, but also much the best informed. In the popular mind he is an elderly rustic philosopher, a chaw of tobacco in his mouth, an eyeshade on his forehead, his chin a trifle prickly, his drawl slow and pithy; in fact he is often a young ex-serviceman who has taken a course at the state university and prefers the independence of his own small newspaper to the excitements of metropolitan journalism. As you sit there talking over a cup of coffee a constant stream of visitors walks unheralded into his room: a farmer with news of a prize bull (to whom you can conveniently tell the story of that prudish English newspaper magnate who unsexed a picture of such a beast, for decency's sake); a lady with a list of wedding guests, and an interminable and repellent description of her daughter's dress; a hearty young clergyman with his weekly spiritual contribution, in which he insists upon referring to the divinity as "The Man Upstairs"; the sheriff, who has some baffling political complaint to make; a man selling carbon paper; the owner of the local store, who sinks heavily into a leather chair for a long talk about economic conditions. There is no aristocracy, to arrive in tweeds with news of the coming garden party; this is a classless society, and if it has a fulcrum or a figurehead, it is the newspaper.

Such little country sheets are generally quiet and conservative, but sometimes you find one of pronounced vigor. The most famous in this genre was the *Emporia Gazette*, which became world-famous because of the writings of its remarkable editor, William Allen White. Nowadays, they are more often notable for commercial enterprise than for literary ability. In Iowa I crossed the tracks of one little paper that had deftly taken note of the methods of the giant magazines. A funny little country café, thirty miles out of Council Bluffs, announced its identity with a placard; and underneath its name, in the approved *Life* manner, appeared the phrase: "As Advertised in the *Oakland Acorn*."

Sometimes in the larger country towns, big enough to support a daily newspaper, one comes across relics of the true American crusading journalism, a product of brave nineteenth-century days and the old American liberalism. I spent a couple of nights in Madison at the height of the McCarthy controversy, when the name of the unpleasing freak was on everyone's lips, and when the mere threat of a McCarthy hearing was enough to set the Middle West intellectual aquivering (whether with fear or with *saeva indignatio* it was difficult to tell). As Samuel "Hudibras" Butler put it:

For men will tremble and turn paler
With too much or too little valour.

McCarthy is a native of Madison, or thereabouts, and I asked if there was no one in that delectable city who was then opposing him loudly enough to be heard. Certainly there was, everybody told me. Mr. William Evjue of the *Capital Times*. I bought some copies of his paper before I called on him, and found that the anti-McCarthy campaign it was fighting was as full-blooded as any Victorian newspaper war, full of rumbustious phrases and startling evidence, pulling no punches and fearing no consequences. Long before the tide turned against McCarthy the *Capital Times* was exposing those flaws of character that later became his downfall, and was beginning to demolish, with no trace of timidity, his political structure of half-truths, bluffs, and innuendoes. Mr. Evjue fitted precisely my idea of a bold reforming editor. He was graying, gay, and easygoing, but with a formidable wallop to his conversation; and when he strolled around the square for a coffee everyone knew him and said "Good morning," from the street sweeper to the passing Senator.

They say his is a dying breed, but I doubt it. Everywhere in America I was impressed by the personal quality of the newspapermen, of an undeniably higher caliber and more enviable status than their colleagues in Europe. If you want agreeable conversation, anywhere in the Middle West, look for the local journalist. If you admire the astringent in American humor, you will find it most easily in the newsrooms or in those many bars where the newspapermen forgather. There is a story told of an American journalist who was posted by his newspaper to Egypt, but who found the aridity of Cairo so distasteful that whenever possible he made a trip to Beirut and sunned the days away on the terrace of a seaside hotel. Alas, he always chose the wrong time to take these unofficial vacations; and there he sat in the sun as one crucial event after another occurred in Cairo. Riots, revolutions, and sundry convulsions occurred, and always he was away on his terrace; until finally he missed the abdication of King Farouk. The next day a cable arrived from his head office in America, and was handed to him in his chaise longue. "King Farouk has abdicated," it said, and added simply: "What are *your* plans?"

So it is always agreeable to sample this temper of thought by visiting one of the important newspapers of the Middle West. Some of them are produced in conditions of great splendor. The *Chicago Tribune*, for example (which grows its own trees, turns them into paper, and ships them to Chicago in its own ships), lives in a pretentious skyscraper which was the winning design in an international architectural competition. This newspaper, despite the high quality of many of its employees, suffers from delusions of grandeur, and inserted in the fabric of its office are fragments from the other great buildings of the world—the Houses of Parliament, for example, and the Great Pyramid. Outside its front door there is a figure of some well-known personage of American history whose part in the Revolution (either as a spy for the British or as a shining hero for the Americans) is still a little obscure to me. Many people assume this classic figure to be a semblance of the late Colonel McCormick, who made the paper what it is; others believe that a colossal statue of the Colonel stands on the very summit of the building, so high as to be out of mortal vision. In fact, though the spirit of the Colonel haunts the place, the *Chicago Tribune* itself is sufficient memorial to him. Not only is it the most inanely prejudiced in America; it is also undeniably one of the best produced, and it has a devoted and skillful company of workers who are evidently able to reconcile themselves, by some premature process of "double speak," to the pervasive malice of the paper. It is easy for anyone to see these people at work, for the newsroom of the *Chicago Tribune* has a public gallery, for all the world like Congress or the Church Assembly. Instructed by a guide, you may stand there behind its plate-glass windows and look down on the enormous floor below you, a mass of desks, clocks, copyboys, trays, and papers, with the ladies of the social department tidying their hair in the left-hand corner.

Other Middle West newspapers, too, admirably suit their premises to their personalities. The *St. Louis Post-Dispatch*, perhaps the most distinguished of them all, has a dignified old-fashioned place in the heart of that mature old river city. The lifts are elderly, but highly polished and greased. The corridors are lined with dark wood, and suitably evocative of scholarly thought and liberal opinion. The editorial rooms are gracefully modest. Another great liberal organ, the *Milwaukee Journal*, has on the other hand premises of sumptuous modernity. This paper is partly owned by its employees, and there is thus a feeling of intense corporate pride and enthusiasm. Everybody seems to have had a say in the design of the building, and it is all laborsaving, convenient and clean. These offices are more than the headquarters of a newspaper. They are focal points of civic activity, centers of advice and general information, where you may just as easily pickup a town plan or some statistical information as place an advertisement in the personal column. But to my mind the queen of Middle Western journalism (if she will forgive my relegating her to that generally unromantic region) is the *Louisville Courier-Journal*, almost a paragon of honest opinion, good writing, and healthy local influence. I wrote a lighthearted report for this newspaper on the Kentucky Derby; and having written my piece, a little hastily, I handed it to the newsroom and went off to attend one of the myriad parties with which Louisville celebrates its day of fame. During the evening there was a telephone call for me. It was the duty editor of the *Courier-Journal*. He thanked me warmly for my report, which was (he said) just what they wanted of me. There was, however, just one small thing. The horse I had named, with a flurry of high writing, as having won the race in fact finished seventh. He had been reluctant to bother me, said the editor, but he just wondered, would I like him to correct it, or should he leave it as it stood?

This is a gentlemanly approach to newspaper work (though I need hardly add that the capable subeditors of the paper had corrected it hours before) and the whole flavor of the *Courier-Journal* is witty and urbane. Its principal stockholder and editor-in-chief, Mr. Barry Bingham, is different from most American newspaper proprietors in that he has a deep personal knowledge of Europe; and his newspaper always actively supported the European cause in the days when the stoppage of a check from Washington could send proud capitals headlong into oblivion. Mr. Bingham's circumstances are, to be sure, more Southern than Midwestern. He lives in a splendid mansion on a wooded hill, from which (during the hot summer evenings) you can watch the towboats passing on the Ohio River, and even hear the insistent pulse of their engines. Nevertheless the instrument he has helped to mold speaks for the enlightened Midwesterner rather than the citizen of the New South. Its temper is that of the liberal intellectuals who fostered the Middle West renaissance in the 1920s and who still (if you can find them) give some of its conversations a maturity and inherent cynicism that is as refreshing as anything in America. The *Milwaukee Journal* sometimes has a slight feeling of slickness about it. The *St. Louis Post-Dispatch* has been a reforming virtuoso for so long that its progressive virtue has acquired a slightly sticky and self-conscious manner, like a blistering evangelist who has long ago mellowed, written his bestsellers, and become a party lion. But the *Courier-Journal* is at once vigorous and dignified, and even sometimes funny; and I know of no more stimulating American group than the editorial conference which assembles each morning in its pale-paneled board room, to discuss the news with a combination of fun and erudition.

Such a big paper as this probably has its own radio and television stations too, and there are many instances in the Middle West of companies which have a near monopoly on all media of information. Sometimes such a joint operation has disadvantages for its employees. Colonel McCormick, for example, used to deliver a weekly lecture on his broadcasting station, Station WGN (for "World's Greatest Newspaper"), in which he meandered for half an hour or more through devious and obscure pathways of history. The next day the *Chicago Tribune* was statutorily obliged to print a verbatim report of this turgid delivery, to the constant chagrin of the technicians responsible for producing the paper. Sometimes the logic of the lectures was so confused as to be hypnotic, and I have seen men in trains puzzling over their sentences for minutes at a time, determined, if only for the personal satisfaction of it, to make some kind of sense out of them.

On the other hand sometimes, if the control is wise and kindly, a paper which is master of several channels of information can make its presence powerfully felt to the good of the community. Mr. Henry Wallace, often smeared as a communist or a "fellow-traveler" by the fascist elements of America, lives in the medium-sized city of Des Moines, where he is a prominent citizen and businessman. In most cities of the Middle West, I am sure, he would be the target of perpetual waspish criticisms and annoyances. The fact that in Des Moines one rarely hears him reproached is partly due to the generally restraining influence of the *Des Moines Register* and its associated radio and television stations, whose strong Liberal Republican influences have made Des Moines an oasis of good sense and moderation.

Nevertheless, in general the mental climate of the Middle West is something less than enlightened, and for this the press of the region must carry a share of the blame. The individual newspapermen of the central states are amusing and agreeable to meet; its best newspapers are almost unsurpassed; but it remains true that many of the papers educate the ignorant with ignorance, and guide the prejudiced with prejudice. In the whole of America there is no spectacle quite like that of the British Sunday press; for though the celebrated American horror comics pander to the same kind of tastes, they do it with much less insidious skill. But frequently the Midwestern newspaper is marked by a deadness of outlook and narrowness of aspiration that is exactly matched by the character of its readership. The dull jingoism of the Standard American is reflected in these columns, the complacency and self-righteousness, the patronizing contempt for older and grander societies, the materialism and poverty of thought. Such journalism is playing its potent part in the slow transformation of America.

ꝏ 33. ꝏ

The Cooling Crucible

THEY used to say that the Middle West was the supreme American crucible, where the temperature of the racial melting pot was at its highest; and it is still a kaleidoscope of elements, where the scattered peoples of Europe find themselves living as neighbors—not only in the cities, where a town dweller from any country is likely to feel at home, but also in the countryside, in which the lingering rural traditions of one ancient society may find themselves disconcertingly cheek-by-jowl with the folksy customs of another.

So to the American idealist there are few more agreeable experiences than a journey through Wisconsin, for example, where you can see such a bucolic potpourri precariously preserved, and (if your eye is kindly enough, and well-disposed toward the consciously picturesque) you may catch some touching glimpses of antique heritages. There is a cheese-making village in this state where scarcely a corner eludes some reminder of Switzerland—a gable here, a peasant costume there, coffee shops with Swiss names, picture postcards of yodelers, Alpine hornists and pinkly snow-capped peaks. In the center of the town there is a spick-and-span new cheese factory, all white coats and scientific packaging. "This is the best Swiss cheese in the world," says the proprietor with decision, handing you a very small piece of it on a wooden knife. "Much better than the stuff they make in Switzerland. The pasture's better. The cows are better. The methods are better. Look at this hydromatic semisonic electrically operated cheese-swirler. That cost me $8,000. It's the only one of its kind in Wisconsin. That machine"—and here he paused with his hand on a switch for a moment of dramatic effect—"can swirl 18,000 gallons of cream in twenty-four hours, that means nine quarts of cream per kilowatt-hour, which is cheap, boy, cheap. Taste it! Isn't that *real* good?" This same man, so totally immersed in the machine philosophy, likes to decorate his house and his factory with simple and pastoral Swiss designs, and above the door there are paintings of Alpine hornists, pinkly snow-capped mountains, yodelers, and the rest. "I can remember very clearly," he says, a suspicion of the maudlin entering his eyes, "sitting in my dad's log house in the mountains, churning the cream by hand. Beautiful memories! Long, long ago! There I would sit beside the fire, turning the handle of the old wooden churner, as my fathers had done before me! I was only a boy! Happy boyhood hours, but it was all *very* unscientific."

Or not so very far away, in another small town, you may see in the window of a confectioner: "Pasties today!" This was once a mining town, and many men from Cornwall came to work here. They built their rugged stone cottages higgledy-piggledy up the side of a small hill, just as they would on the Cornish moors, and they ate their Cornish pasties faithfully. A few of their descendants still live in the town, and at the pastry cook's pasties are still made twice a week, Tuesdays and Saturdays. Not many of their cottages are left, but at the foot of the hill there are two which have been carefully restored and which are guarded and inhabited by two young men of antiquarian tendencies. There is the open fire in the parlor, and there are the copper kettles, and the warming pans, the china figures and the big teapots, gathered if need be from Old England herself, and now deposited with an institutional air for the Middle West trippers to admire. "It's been a truly wonderful experience," said one lady to me as we passed on the threshold of these cottages. "This, to me, is truly educational—to know how the English really live, in these truly quaint old houses, and to think that they once lived like that right here in Wisconsin. Oh, but the world's a wonderful place!"

Farther north in this same state you may find communities of Finns scattered and hidden away among the forests. This is no longer a great lumber country, for its resources were whittled away by the nineteenth-century adventurers; but there was a time when the only people who would work in some of its dark, remote fastnesses were Scandinavians from the extreme north—Norwegians, Swedes, many Finns. To this day, if you motor through the woodlands, among the young second-growth trees, you will from time to time come across a lonely wooden house in a clearing, and hear from its recesses snatches of an obscure Scandinavian tongue, and see a genuine European peasant woman emerge from its door, her head covered in a scarf, her dress longer than is fashionable, in her hand a tray of food for the dog. I spent a night at a small community in Minnesota, southwest of Duluth, and had occasion to examine the local telephone directory. It was issued by a local company, affiliated to one of the great combines, to be sure, but still with its own board of directors and its own intensely regional flavor. The list of names was overpoweringly Scandinavian. There were eighty-one subscribers in all; I chose the letter P to test the racial homogeneity of the place, and found that every subscriber claiming that initial shared, in one form of spelling or another, the good old Nordic name of Peterson. In the twenty years before 1900, one-fifth of the entire population of Norway and Sweden emigrated to America.

In the cities of the Middle West, of course, the races are more intimately jumbled; but there are still whole quarters, or even whole towns, forming recognizable national enclaves. Thus Milwaukee has people of many nationalities, Poles, Italians, and Bohemians, but the Germans have been predominant for so long, and play so leading and enlightened a part in civic affairs, that the place has a distinctive beer-and-sound-sense flavor. This had led, *inter alia*, to a particularly sensible approach to the problems of race relations, which (in a region so racially crisscross and mangled) are often a worry in the Middle West. The police department publishes a booklet on the subject for the benefit of officers under training. Milwaukee, it says, contains people of many racial origins who intermingle daily but who are divided "by the fact that our grandparents, or even we, have emerged from different and alien cultural backgrounds, so that we do not dress, eat, and live alike, and, most important, do not look alike." The booklet's moral is that such racial and national groups can provoke dangerous and unjustifiable generalizations. "Until we realize that there are just as many different kinds of Negroes as there are different kinds of policemen, we shan't be able to make intelligent and creditable decisions."

Certainly in the past the sudden unreasoning flare of racial prejudice has been a constantly latent menace. Each "unAmerican" group had its sobriquet—you were a wop, a chink, a polack, a hunky, a kike, a cholo, a chili-picker, a jig, a nigger, a hillbilly, a cracker, a redneck: just as in the Middle West today you may well be a pinko, a commie, or an internationalist. Indeed, this substitution of epithets well illustrates the metamorphosis that is overcoming the Middle West. The melting pot has done its work, and is cooling. The flow of immigration has almost stopped. Generations of Americanization and intermarriage have smoothed the more awkward racial bumps, the wops and chili-pickers are being absorbed, and there emerges the familiar figure of our Standard American. He is *par excellence* a Middle Westerner, the result of that enforced and feverish patriotism that was necessary to produce a united people out of a gallimaufry of immigrants, ventures and miscellaneous pioneers. Once established, the process of transformation is inexorable. Along comes the succession of little Midwesterners, no longer subject to loyalties of Europe or the individualities of the frontier, but instead material for a molding machine that is rigid and outdated; in the old days it made Americans out of wanderers, now it makes bores and chauvinists out of Americans.

It is startling how quickly and completely the stamp of the breed can be place upon a generation. Mom and Pop may be as uncompromisingly Czech as Santa Claus, talking with a thick accent, reading the Czech papers from Chicago, speaking nostalgically of Prague in the spring, wearing their Central European clothes in a distinctly Central European manner. But Junior and Sis, we may be sure, will be as totally American as Coney Island or Miss Marilyn Monroe; he with his crew cut and gay shirt, she in jeans and sandals, her hair tied with a ribbon, her make-up impeccable, her bosom startling in its definition. It is not merely that their vocabulary has changed; or their way of thought; or their clothes; or their aspirations; their physique has been altered, no less, the very shape of their heads and bodies, by the insidious force of the American mutation. "Assimilation in *excelsis!*" as Lord Fisher once exclaimed. "The boa constrictor swallowing a bull isn't in it!"

So if the islands of Europeanism linger on much longer in this American sea, it will be as curiosities; perhaps even, since they have their didactic worth, as minor moneymakers. Today there have still sufficient survivors of an older generation to give them some degree of spontaneity; and the monastery of Holy Hill (for example), high on its eminence near Milwaukee, still finds many simple pilgrims to wonder at its relics and miracles of healing. But the old European-Americans are disappearing, and even the religions of the Middle West are acquiring the all-American patina. There is a social as well as a spiritual purpose nowadays in attending the spotless white Lutheran churches that adorn the Middle West landscape; on a Sunday morning their courtyards are thronged with the expensive cars of the farmers, and inside the wives are dressed in their most competitive fineries. Everywhere the American Way is winning. Within sight of some sweet and sleepy farmhouse, standing among its rich furrows like a homestead in a Grant Wood painting, you may find a ghastly jazz-ridden, neon-lit roadhouse, and be served by a girl with that standard synthetic smile, while the truck drivers in their peaked caps eat hamburgers, tinned baked beans, or two fried eggs ("up and over").

Passionate though you may be in your hunt for antique survivals, in the Middle West you cannot escape the signs of this metamorphosis. First among them is that unwearying drive for success, position, esteem, wealth, that is so overpowering in Chicago and which one can related to the violence of American climate and history. The Middle West family is insatiable in its thirst for success—success material and social, financial and personal. To be a high executive at the office, and a popular member of the community—these are the twin ambitions into which, by the alchemy of Americanism, have been translated the hungry and ill-defined desires of the pioneers. To achieve them, the real American must be unrelaxing, casting off relentlessly those old lazy predilections of his European forebears. "If you don't wanta get ahead, move over, bud."

Then there is the complacent chauvinism (no longer isolationism) that has presumably arisen from incessant doses, over the generations, of compulsory patriotism. The intellectuals of the Middle West are exceptionally catholic and enlightened in their tastes; and there are many other Middle Westerners, especially of the middle classes, whose zest for experience and knowledge is delightful; but the ignorance of the majority of these people is matched only by their self-satisfaction, and their hardly hidden contempt for foreigners is unshakable. This is, I suspect, no longer the symptom of an inferiority complex. Such have been the somersaults of history that the standard American really believes in his own pretensions now, and is no longer battling suppressed envy and self-doubt (unless it be envy of those who are even more American than he is).

Colonel McCormick, in his patriarchal management of the *Chicago Tribune*, reflected these Middle West traits admirably; and the blatant bigotry of his newspaper's columns probably expresses the true viewpoint of the Middle West more accurately than the visiting European likes to suppose. "It's all very well for you British to talk," the Colonel remarked to me one day in his office at the top of Tribune Tower, "but you don't have our responsibilities. Our armies, thanks to the criminal foolishness of successive administrations in Washington (I see where President Eisenhower is playing golf again today)—our armies are flung all over the world, because of all this mad internationalism and appeasement. You, on the other hand, have all your forces concentrated in England, paid for entirely by the American taxpayer, ready to deal with any attack."

"On the contrary," I ventured to remark, "practically none of our forces are in England, and it often worries us. They are more scattered than they have ever been."

"Where are they, then?"

"Well, there are some in Germany, some in the Middle East, some in Hong Kong, some in Malaya, some in—"

"Ah, yes," said the Colonel, putting an end to the exchange, "but in Chicagoland *we don't believe in colonies!*"

The genuine Midwesterner does not believe in colonies; he does not really believe in Europe; he does not believe, so persuasive have been his mentors, so vivid his inherited memories of an older world, in monarchies. The very word "Empire" is repugnant to him, perhaps because to the nineteenth-century immigrant it denoted the oppressions of Europe rather than the gay if regrettable battles of the Fuzzy-wuzzy wars. An Englishman who came to learn his business in a Chicago store told me that his departmental manger once remarked to him: "Say, do those Lords push you about much over there?" When I was in America a chief cause of Middle West complaint was the cost of the Royal yacht *Britannia*; the price of which, the press had often intimated, had been covered entirely by American grants in aid. How often and how tediously, in response to such rancorous murmurings, I have tried to explain the principles of constitutional monarchy, beginning with the unacceptable thesis that the Queen is no longer entitled to cut people's heads off, ending (as often as not) by assuring my listeners that we even have television in England nowadays: "Yeah, and plenty of time to look at it!" one man in Indiana remarked darkly.

Queen Elizabeth's Coronation in 1953 touched off the extremes both of this kind of sentiment, and of the fervent Anglophile royalism which is naturally fostered, among a resolute and slightly snobbish minority, by so determinedly egalitarian an attitude. It was long after the event when I arrived in the Middle West, but I was shown with pride the program of a mammoth commemorative banquet organized by the Anglophile societies of Chicago. Scores of English and Scottish names appeared on it, but the usherettes included Mrs. Michael Krezevitch, Mrs. Theodore Markstahler, and Mrs. Edward Schmidt. Among the contributing organizations were the International War Brides Travel Club, the British Honduran-American Association, the Chicago Manx Society, the Orkney and Shetland Literary Social and Benevolent Society, the Daughters of Scotia, the Daughters of the British Empire in Illinois, and the Welsh Women's Club. A verse printed at the end of the program included the pleasant stanzas:

> The lavishness, the splendor,
> The jewels she must wear,
> Are but traditional symbols
> Of burdens she must bear.
>
> Her dreams...her thoughts are hidden...
> To her...What does it mean
> As millions join in singing
> "God bless the gracious Queen"?

But do not be misled by the lavish enthusiasm of all this. For every member of the Orkney and Shetland Literary Social and Benevolent Society, for every Chicago Manxman who enjoyed his Edinburgh Broth and Commonwealth Salad, a thousand Middle Westerners agreed with the newspaper which greeted the Coronation with the headline: "Wake Up, Fairyland!"

In the old days, I am sure, this dislike of alien systems stemmed largely from feelings of inadequacy. Now it is immensely bolstered by America's position of world supremacy, and her status as creditor to the earth. To the Middle Westerners, work is sacred; and all the splendid forms and manners of Europe are but symptoms of laziness, of a readiness to sit back and let others provide the cash. There is no virtue in leisure, as you will find at the end of your lunch engagement in Detroit, when at the first stroke of two your companions gulp the last dregs of their coffee, grab their hats, and bolt for the office. If France is not producing enough, is not earning money, is not "making friends and influencing people," it must be because she is lazy, and also degenerate. If Germany is selling her cars all over the world, is rich and energetic, is "delivering," she must be "smart" and hard-working and therefore in every way a desirable ally for the American democracy. "Smart" is the ultimate commendation of this philosophy, and, indeed, the watchword of the new Americanism. "He's a real smart boy, he's making loads of money." Or: "You gotta be smart if you wanta stay on top." What a depth of arrogance, egotism and shady dealing is instinct in this horrible use of the word!

And, as we all know, anyone who looks askance at these criteria is necessarily suspect. You simply must not be singular, long at lunch or agnostic. It is not only in politics that conformity is the rule. If you are wise, you do not differ often with your managing director, or your Dean, the president of your women's club, the editor of your paper, the most popular member of your set, the head of your fraternity. The Yankee watchman of Gloucester would not fit easily into many Middle West societies, nor would multitudes of lounging careless Westerners, bitter and brilliant Southerners, or gentlemen of San Francisco, who are decidedly not amenable to having their opinions shuffled for them.

The Middle West is not all like this, as we have seen; but these wealthy central states are the stronghold of the standard Americanism. From here our wandering character sets out, to travel the world in his superior ignorance, to bore the Kiwanians with his lantern slides, to shove his way (with a book of checks, a pot of pills, and his familiar version of thou) through a world whose nuances he fails to detect, and whose immemorial values he fails to understand. Alas! If old Crèvecoeur wants a truly contemporary answer to his question, he must go to the Middle West for his new man, and see what the years of struggle and prosperity have produced.

Envoi

E LEFT America classically, sailing out of New York harbor on an American clipper, the steamship *United States*, whose log often recorded thirty-five knots as she swept us home across the Atlantic.

It is always sad to leave a country you love and admire, and sadder still if you suspect that it will never be quite the same again. Americans can be variable people, shifting their opinions unpredictably, swayed sometimes by a wisp of wind or a stray paragraph in a newspaper. It may be that the Standard American has reached his zenith, to be displaced by those countless hopeful and eager citizens who understand his menace and dread the intolerable tedium of his zeal.

There is always the possibility, though, so dreadfully foreseen by the eggheads, that he is now advancing into total supremacy, and that his is the dominant national character emerging from the subsiding mélange of immigrant peoples. Who can tell? Perhaps you will indeed contemplate his presence as often in Chimayo as in Cedar Rapids; perhaps the South will really be tainted with his heavy complacency, and the lumbermen think only of the money, and the old individualist beside the lake at Cranbury fade away like the good old soldier he is. Perhaps before long that ponderous voice in the European hotel lobby, declaiming the unlikelihood of the same kind of discomfort ever being encountered back home, will truthfully speak for the American people.

I do not pretend to know: but I caught some glimpses of the other America, and the Americans will always be half-brothers of mine.

WELSH JOURNALIST, historian, biographer, and novelist Jan Morris is the author of more than forty books, many about travel, but others on subjects as diverse as the history of the British Empire and her own sex change at a time when such procedures were rare and scandalous. She burst onto the literary scene as a young reporter for the *London Times* when, as James Morris, she accompanied the 1953 British expedition that made the first successful ascent of Mount Everest and scooped the world with a report that hit the papers the very day of Queen Elizabeth II's coronation. This experience would later be recounted in *Coronation Everest*. Twenty years after the climb, Morris would go through the surgery that made her Jan Morris, a journey recounted in the book, *Conundrum*.

She is considered Britain's foremost travel essayist and historian, and her trilogy on the British Empire, *Pax Britannica*, was hugely popular when released and remains an enduring work of literary history. She led the way for an entire generation of travel writers who rely on evocation, atmosphere, and cultural curiosity to draw a portrait of a place and experience. She is an Honorary Fellow of the University College of Wales and has received numerous nominations for the Booker Prize.

She has been dubbed "the Flaubert of the jet age" and has achieved that rare stature of larger-than-life character for her intelligence, wit, good-heartedness, and prodigious literary output. Without a doubt she will be remembered long after she is gone as one of the literary pillars of this age, an author of timeless appeal and unmatched erudition. Her final book, *Trieste and the Meaning of Nowhere*, was published in 2001 to great acclaim, and her first book, *Coast to Coast*, reveals the talents of this young author who would go on to produce book after book of engaging social, and world, commentary.

TRAVELERS' TALES
THE SOUL OF TRAVEL

Footsteps Series

THE FIRE NEVER DIES
**One Man's Raucous Romp
Down the Road of Food,
Passion, and Adventure**
By Richard Sterling
ISBN 1-885-211-70-8
$14.95

"Sterling's writing is like spit-
fire, foursquare and jazzy with crackle...."
—*Kirkus Reviews*

LAST TROUT
IN VENICE
**The Far-Flung Escapades
of an Accidental
Adventurer**
By Doug Lansky
ISBN 1-885-211-63-5
$14.95

"Traveling with Doug Lansky might result in
a considerably shortened life expectancy...but
what a way to go."　　　　—Tony Wheeler,
Lonely Planet Publications

ONE YEAR OFF
**Leaving It All Behind for a
Round-the-World Journey
with Our Children**
By David Elliot Cohen
ISBN 1-885-211-65-1
$14.95

A once-in-a-lifetime
adventure generously shared.

THE WAY OF
THE WANDERER
**Discover Your True Self
Through Travel**
By David Yeadon
ISBN 1-885-211-60-0
$14.95

Experience transformation through travel
with this delightful, illustrated collection by
award-winning author David Yeadon.

TAKE ME
WITH YOU
**A Round-the-World
Journey to Invite a
Stranger Home**
By Brad Newsham
ISBN 1-885-211-51-1
$24.00 (cloth)

"Newsham is an ideal guide. His journey, at
heart, is into humanity." —Pico Iyer, author
of *Video Night in Kathmandu*

KITE STRINGS OF
THE SOUTHERN
CROSS
**A Woman's
Travel Odyssey**
By Laurie Gough
ISBN 1-885-211-54-6
$14.95　—★★★—

*ForeWord Silver Medal Winner
—Travel Book of the Year*

THE SWORD
OF HEAVEN
**A Five Continent Odyssey
to Save the World**
By Mikkel Aaland
ISBN 1-885-211-44-9
$24.00 (cloth)

"Few books capture the soul
of the road like *The Sword of Heaven*,
a sharp-edged, beautifully rendered memoir
that will inspire anyone." —Phil Cousineau,
author of *The Art of Pilgrimage*

STORM
**A Motorcycle Journey
of Love, Endurance,
and Transformation**
By Allen Noren
ISBN 1-885-211-45-7
$24.00 (cloth)
—★★★—

*ForeWord Gold Medal Winner
—Travel Book of the Year*

Travelers' Tales Classics

COAST TO COAST
A Journey Across 1950s America
By Jan Morris
ISBN 1-885-211-79-1
$16.95

After reporting on the first Everest ascent in 1953, Morris spent a year journeying by car, train, ship, and aircraft across the United States. In her brilliant prose, Morris records with exuberance and curiosity a time of innocence in the U.S.

TRADER HORN
A Young Man's Astounding Adventures in 19th Century Equatorial Africa
By Alfred Aloysius Horn
ISBN 1-885-211-81-3
$16.95

Here is the stuff of legends —tale of thrills and danger, wild beasts, serpents, and savages. An unforgettable and vivid portrait of a vanished late-19th century Africa.

THE ROYAL ROAD TO ROMANCE
By Richard Halliburton
ISBN 1-885-211-53-8
$14.95

"Laughing at hardships, dreaming of beauty, ardent for adventure, Halliburton has managed to sing into the pages of this glorious book his own exultant spirit of youth and freedom."
— *Chicago Post*

UNBEATEN TRACKS IN JAPAN
By Isabella L. Bird
ISBN 1-885-211-57-0
$14.95

Isabella Bird was one of the most adventurous women travelers of the 19th century with journeys to Tibet, Canada, Korea, Turkey, Hawaii, and Japan. A fascinating read for anyone interested in women's travel, spirituality, and Asian culture.

THE RIVERS RAN EAST
By Leonard Clark
ISBN 1-885-211-66-X
$16.95

Clark is the original Indiana Jones, relaying a breathtaking account of his search for the legendary El Dorado gold in the Amazon.

Travel Humor

NOT SO FUNNY WHEN IT HAPPENED
The Best of Travel Humor and Misadventure
Edited by Tim Cahill
ISBN 1-885-211-55-4
$12.95

Laugh with Bill Bryson, Dave Barry, Anne Lamott, Adair Lara, and many more.

THERE'S NO TOILET PAPER...ON THE ROAD LESS TRAVELED
The Best of Travel Humor and Misadventure
Edited by Doug Lansky
ISBN 1-885-211-27-9
$12.95

★ ★ ★   ★ ★ ★

Humor Book of the Year —Independent Publisher's Book Award   *ForeWord Gold Medal Winner— Humor Book of the Year*

LAST TROUT IN VENICE
The Far-Flung Escapades of an Accidental Adventurer
By Doug Lansky
ISBN 1-885-211-63-5
$14.95

"Traveling with Doug Lansky might result in a considerably shortened life expectancy...but what a way to go."
—Tony Wheeler, Lonely Planet Publications

Women's Travel

A WOMAN'S PASSION FOR TRAVEL
More True Stories from A Woman's World
Edited by Marybeth Bond & Pamela Michael
ISBN 1-885-211-36-8
$17.95
"A diverse and gripping series of stories!" —Arlene Blum, author of *Annapurna: A Woman's Place*

A WOMAN'S WORLD
True Stories of Life on the Road
Edited by Marybeth Bond
Introduction by Dervla Murphy
ISBN 1-885-211-06-6
$17.95

—★ ★ ★—

Winner of the Lowell Thomas Award for Best Travel Book— Society of American Travel Writers

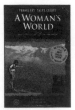

WOMEN IN THE WILD
True Stories of Adventure and Connection
Edited by Lucy McCauley
ISBN 1-885-211-21-X
$17.95
"A spiritual, moving, and totally female book to take you around the world and back." —*Mademoiselle*

A MOTHER'S WORLD
Journeys of the Heart
Edited by Marybeth Bond & Pamela Michael
ISBN 1-885-211-26-0
$14.95
"These stories remind us that motherhood is one of the great unifying forces in the world" —*San Francisco Examiner*

Food

ADVENTURES IN WINE
True Stories of Vineyards and Vintages around the World
Edited by Thom Elkjer
ISBN 1-885-211-80-5
$17.95
Humanity, community, and brotherhood comprise the marvelous virtues of the wine world. This collection toasts the warmth and wonders of this large, extended family in stories by travelers who are wine novices and experts alike.

FOOD (Updated)
A Taste of the Road
Edited by Richard Sterling
Introduction by Margo True
ISBN 1-885-211-77-5
$18.95

—★ ★ ★—

Silver Medal Winner of the Lowell Thomas Award for Best Travel Book— Society of American Travel Writers

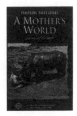

HER FORK IN THE ROAD
Women Celebrate Food and Travel
Edited by Lisa Bach
ISBN 1-885-211-71-6
$16.95
A savory sampling of stories by some of the best writers in and out of the food and travel fields.

THE ADVENTURE OF FOOD
True Stories of Eating Everything
Edited by Richard Sterling
ISBN 1-885-211-37-6
$17.95
"These stories are bound to whet appetites for more than food."

—*Publishers Weekly*

Spiritual Travel

THE SPIRITUAL GIFTS OF TRAVEL
The Best of Travelers' Tales
Edited by James O'Reilly and Sean O'Reilly
ISBN 1-885-211-69-4
$16.95

A collection of favorite stories of transformation on the road from our award-winning Travelers' Tales series that shows the myriad ways travel indelibly alters our inner landscapes.

THE WAY OF THE WANDERER
Discover Your True Self Through Travel
By David Yeadon
ISBN 1-885-211-60-0
$14.95

Experience transformation through travel with this delightful, illustrated collection by award-winning author David Yeadon.

PILGRIMAGE
Adventures of the Spirit
Edited by Sean O'Reilly & James O'Reilly
Introduction by Phil Cousineau
ISBN 1-885-211-56-2
$16.95

———★*★———

ForeWord Silver Medal Winner
—Travel Book of the Year

A WOMAN'S PATH
Women's Best Spiritual Travel Writing
Edited by Lucy McCauley, Amy G. Carlson & Jennifer Leo
ISBN 1-885-211-48-1
$16.95

"A sensitive exploration of women's lives that have been unexpectedly and spiritually touched by travel experiences.... Highly recommended."
—Library Journal

THE ROAD WITHIN
True Stories of Transformation and the Soul
Edited by Sean O'Reilly, James O'Reilly & Tim O'Reilly
ISBN 1-885-211-19-8
$17.95

———★*★———

Best Spiritual Book—Independent Publisher's Book Award

THE ULTIMATE JOURNEY
Inspiring Stories of Living and Dying
James O'Reilly, Sean O'Reilly & Richard Sterling
ISBN 1-885-211-38-4
$17.95

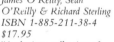

"A glorious collection of writings about the ultimate adventure. A book to keep by one's bedside—and close to one's heart." —Philip Zaleski, editor, *The Best Spiritual Writing series*

Adventure

TESTOSTERONE PLANET
True Stories from a Man's World
Edited by Sean O'Reilly, Larry Habegger & James O'Reilly
ISBN 1-885-211-43-0
$17.95

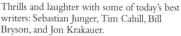

Thrills and laughter with some of today's best writers: Sebastian Junger, Tim Cahill, Bill Bryson, and Jon Krakauer.

DANGER!
True Stories of Trouble and Survival
Edited by James O'Reilly, Larry Habegger & Sean O'Reilly
ISBN 1-885-211-32-5
$17.95

"Exciting...for those who enjoy living on the edge or prefer to read the survival stories of others, this is a good pick."
—Library Journal

Special Interest

365 TRAVEL
**A Daily Book of
Journeys, Meditations,
and Adventures**
Edited by Lisa Bach
ISBN 1-885-211-67-8
$14.95
An illuminating collection
of travel wisdom and
adventures that reminds us
all of the lessons we learn while on the road.

THE GIFT
OF RIVERS
**True Stories of
Life on the Water**
Edited by Pamela Michael
Introduction by Robert Hass
ISBN 1-885-211-42-2
$14.95
"*The Gift of Rivers* is a
soulful compendium of wonderful stories that
illuminate, educate, inspire, and delight."
—David Brower, Chairman of
Earth Island Institute

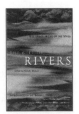

FAMILY TRAVEL
**The Farther You Go,
the Closer You Get**
Edited by Laura Manske
ISBN 1-885-211-33-3
$17.95
"This is family travel at its
finest." —*Working Mother*

LOVE & ROMANCE
**True Stories of
Passion on the Road**
*Edited by Judith Babcock
Wylie*
ISBN 1-885-211-18-X
$17.95
"A wonderful book to
read by a crackling fire."
—*Romantic Traveling*

THE GIFT
OF BIRDS
**True Encounters
with Avian Spirits**
*Edited by Larry Habegger
& Amy G. Carlson*
ISBN 1-885-211-41-4
$17.95
"These are all wonderful,
entertaining stories offering
a *bird's-eye view!* of our avian friends."
—*Booklist*

A DOG'S WORLD
**True Stories of
Man's Best Friend
on the Road**
*Edited by Christine
Hunsicker*
ISBN 1-885-211-23-6
$12.95
This extraordinary
collection includes stories
by John Steinbeck, Helen Thayer, James
Herriot, Pico Iyer, and many others.

THE GIFT OF TRAVEL
The Best of Travelers' Tales
*Edited by Larry Habegger, James O'Reilly
& Sean O'Reilly*
ISBN 1-885-211-25-2
$14.95
"Like gourmet chefs in a French market, the
editors of Travelers' Tales pick, sift, and prod
their way through the weighty shelves of con-
temporary travel writing, creaming off the
very best."
—William Dalrymple, author of *City of Djinns*

Travel Advice

SHITTING PRETTY
How to Stay Clean and Healthy While Traveling
By Dr. Jane Wilson-Howarth
ISBN 1-885-211-47-3
$12.95

A light-hearted book about a serious subject for millions of travelers—staying healthy on the road—written by international health expert, Dr. Jane Wilson-Howarth.

THE FEARLESS SHOPPER
How to Get the Best Deals on the Planet
By Kathy Borrus
ISBN 1-885-211-39-2
$14.95

"Anyone who reads *The Fearless Shopper* will come away a smarter, more responsible shopper and a more curious, culturally attuned traveler."
—Jo Mancuso, *The Shopologist*

GUTSY WOMEN
More Travel Tips and Wisdom for the Road
By Marybeth Bond
ISBN 1-885-211-61-9
$12.95

Second Edition—Packed with funny, instructive, and inspiring advice for women heading out to see the world.

SAFETY AND SECURITY FOR WOMEN WHO TRAVEL
By Sheila Swan & Peter Laufer
ISBN 1-885-211-29-5
$12.95

A must for every woman traveler!

THE FEARLESS DINER
Travel Tips and Wisdom for Eating around the World
By Richard Sterling
ISBN 1-885-211-22-8
$7.95

Combines practical advice on foodstuffs, habits, and etiquette, with hilarious accounts of others' eating adventures.

THE PENNY PINCHER'S PASSPORT TO LUXURY TRAVEL
The Art of Cultivating Preferred Customer Status
By Joel L. Widzer
ISBN 1-885-211-31-7
$12.95

Proven techniques on how to travel first class at discount prices, even if you're not a frequent flyer.

GUTSY MAMAS
Travel Tips and Wisdom for Mothers on the Road
By Marybeth Bond
ISBN 1-885-211-20-1
$7.95

A delightful guide for mothers traveling with their children— or without them!

Destination Titles:
True Stories of Life on the Road

AMERICA
Edited by Fred Setterberg
ISBN 1-885-211-28-7
$19.95

FRANCE (Updated)
Edited by James O'Reilly,
Larry Habegger &
Sean O'Reilly
ISBN 1-885-211-73-2
$18.95

AMERICAN SOUTHWEST
Edited by Sean O'Reilly
& James O'Reilly
ISBN 1-885-211-58-9
$17.95

GRAND CANYON
Edited by Sean O'Reilly,
James O'Reilly &
Larry Habegger
ISBN 1-885-211-34-1
$17.95

AUSTRALIA
Edited by Larry Habegger
ISBN 1-885-211-40-6
$17.95

GREECE
Edited by Larry Habegger,
Sean O'Reilly &
Brian Alexander
ISBN 1-885-211-52-X
$17.95

BRAZIL
Edited by Annette Haddad
& Scott Doggett
Introduction by Alex
Shoumatoff
ISBN 1-885-211-11-2
$17.95

HAWAI'I
Edited by Rick &
Marcie Carroll
ISBN 1-885-211-35-X
$17.95

CENTRAL AMERICA
Edited by Larry Habegger
& Natanya Pearlman
ISBN 1-885-211-74-0
$17.95

HONG KONG
Edited by James O'Reilly,
Larry Habegger &
Sean O'Reilly
ISBN 1-885-211-03-1
$17.95

CUBA
Edited by Tom Miller
ISBN 1-885-211-62-7
$17.95

INDIA
Edited by James O'Reilly
& Larry Habegger
ISBN 1-885-211-01-5
$17.95